Foreign Relations of the GCC Countries

This book examines the foreign policies of the Gulf Cooperation Council (GCC) countries six years after the Arab uprisings, in terms of drivers, narratives, actions and outcomes, paying particular attention to Middle Eastern countries, Iran and Western international powers. The assessment focuses on current affairs, but also contributes to establishing a productive link between empirical studies and the existing theoretical frameworks that help explain the increasing foreign policy activism of the GCC countries. All in all, the articles collected in this book shed light on and provide a more solid and fine-grained understanding of how regional powers such as Saudi Arabia, as well as the other smaller GCC countries, act and pursue their interests in an environment full of uncertainty, in the context of changing regional and global dynamics and power distribution.

The book brings together the articles published in a special issue of *The International Spectator*.

Eman Ragab is Senior Researcher in Regional Security in the Middle East, Al-Ahram Center for Political and Strategic Studies, Cairo, Egypt. She is also an Adjunct Professor of political science at the American University in Cairo, Egypt.

Silvia Colombo is Senior Fellow at Istituto Affari Internazionali (IAI), Italy.

Foreign Relations of the GCC Countries

Shifting Global and Regional Dynamics

Edited by
Eman Ragab and Silvia Colombo

LONDON AND NEW YORK

First published 2018 by Routledge

2 Park Square, Milton Park, Abingdon, Oxfordshire OX14 4RN
52 Vanderbilt Avenue, New York, NY 10017

Routledge is an imprint of the Taylor & Francis Group, an informa business

First issued in paperback 2019

British Library Cataloguing in Publication Data
A catalogue record for this book is available from the British Library

ISBN 13: 978-1-138-57404-5 (hbk)
ISBN 13: 978-0-367-89256-2 (pbk)

Typeset in Minion Pro
by diacriTech, Chennai

Publisher's Note
The publisher accepts responsibility for any inconsistencies that may have arisen during the conversion of this book from journal articles to book chapters, namely the possible inclusion of journal terminology.

Disclaimer
Every effort has been made to contact copyright holders for their permission to reprint material in this book. The publishers would be grateful to hear from any copyright holder who is not here acknowledged and will undertake to rectify any errors or omissions in future editions of this book.

Contents

CONTENTS

Citation Information

The chapters in this book were originally published in *The International Spectator*, volume 52, issue 2 (June 2017). When citing this material, please use the original page numbering for each article, as follows:

Editorial Note
Foreign Relations of the GCC Countries amid Shifting Global and Regional Dynamics
Silvia Colombo and Eman Ragab
The International Spectator, volume 52, issue 2 (June 2017) pp. 1–2

Chapter 1
Between Accommodation and Opportunism: Explaining the Growing Influence of Small Gulf States in the Middle East
Máté Szalai
The International Spectator, volume 52, issue 2 (June 2017) pp. 3–18

Chapter 2
Status and Foreign Policy Change in Small States: Qatar's Emergence in Perspective
Babak Mohammadzadeh
The International Spectator, volume 52, issue 2 (June 2017) pp. 19–36

Chapter 3
Beyond Money and Diplomacy: Regional Policies of Saudi Arabia and UAE after the Arab Spring
Eman Ragab
The International Spectator, volume 52, issue 2 (June 2017) pp. 37–53

Chapter 4
Foreign Policy Activism in Saudi Arabia and Oman. Diverging Narratives and Stances towards the Syrian and Yemeni Conflicts
Silvia Colombo
The International Spectator, volume 52, issue 2 (June 2017) pp. 54–70

Chapter 5

The Evolution of Saudi Foreign Policy and the Role of Decision-making Processes and Actors
Umer Karim
The International Spectator, volume 52, issue 2 (June 2017) pp. 71–88

Chapter 6

Iran, the GCC and the Implications of the Nuclear Deal: Rivalry versus Engagement
Riham Bahi
The International Spectator, volume 52, issue 2 (June 2017) pp. 89–101

Chapter 7

US-Arab Gulf Relations amidst Regional and Global Changes
Dania Koleilat Khatib
The International Spectator, volume 52, issue 2 (June 2017) pp. 102–114

Chapter 8

Russia as a Gravity Pole of the GCC's New Foreign Policy Pragmatism
Alexander Shumilin and Inna Shumilina
The International Spectator, volume 52, issue 2 (June 2017) pp. 115–129

For any permission-related enquiries please visit:
http://www.tandfonline.com/page/help/permissions

Notes on Contributors

Riham Bahi is an Associate Professor of International Relations at the Faculty of Economics and Political Science, Cairo University, Egypt. She is also Visiting Professor at the American University in Cairo, Egypt.

Silvia Colombo is Senior Fellow at the Mediterranean and Middle East Programme, Istituto Affari Internazionali (IAI), Rome, Italy. She is an expert on Middle Eastern politics and in this capacity she is working on Euro-Mediterranean cooperation, transatlantic relations in the Mediterranean and domestic and regional politics in the Arab World.

Umer Karim is a Doctoral Researcher at the University of Birmingham, UK. He is researching Saudi foreign policy, decision-making and its implications for the politics and security of the Middle East.

Dania Koleilat Khatib is Executive Director of the Al Istishari Al Strategy Center for Future and Economic Studies, Abu Dhabi, United Arab Emirates.

Babak Mohammadzadeh is a PhD candidate at the Department of Politics and International Studies, University of Cambridge, UK. His research interests include historical sociology of the state, statebuilding and state society relations and the political economy of hydrocarbon exports.

Eman Ragab is Senior Researcher in Regional Security in the Middle East, Al-Ahram Center for Political and Strategic Studies, Cairo, Egypt. She is also an Adjunct Professor of political science at the American University in Cairo, Egypt.

Alexander Shumilin is Head of the Center for Middle East Conflicts at the Institute for USA and Canada Studies of the Russian Academy of Sciences, Moscow, Russia.

Inna Shumilina is Senior Fellow at the Institute for USA and Canada Studies of the Russian Academy of Sciences, Moscow, Russia.

Máté Szalai is an Assistant Lecturer at the Corvinus University of Budapest, Hungary, and coordinator of the Middle East program at the Institute for Foreign Affairs and Trade, Budapest, Hungary.

EDITORIAL NOTE

Foreign Relations of the GCC Countries amid Shifting Global and Regional Dynamics

Six years after the Arab uprisings, the Gulf Cooperation Council (GCC) countries have developed an increasingly active posture in their foreign policies towards the Middle East. Alongside the strategic shifts caused by the wave of popular unrest that swept the region from the end of 2010, the GCC countries' foreign policies are increasingly influencing the changes taking place in a number of countries, such as Syria, as well as redefining or restructuring the matrix of regional roles and alliances among the international powers interested in the region, such as the United States, Russia and some European countries.

These developments have prompted many academics and policymakers to argue that the centre of gravity in the Middle East North Africa (MENA) region is shifting towards the Gulf region, namely towards Saudi Arabia and Iran, the old regional contenders, and new players (the UAE, Qatar and Oman). During the second half of the twentieth century, the main actors in the region were Egypt, Saudi Arabia, Syria and Iraq, constituting a regional order that was deeply influenced by the Cold War. The military intervention in Iraq in 2003, the ongoing armed conflict in Syria, the unravelling of the transition in Egypt after the fall of the Mubarak regime, and the civil war in Libya, coupled with the changing priorities in the region of the Obama administration, have left a power vacuum that the GCC countries have aspired and contributed to filling. This trend is likely to continue in the next years, given the uncertainties that characterise the Trump administration and the increasingly passive role of the European Union (EU) in its neighbouring region.

Two main aspects connected to the increasing activism of the GCC countries in the Middle East stand out. The first concerns the domestic and regional dimensions: the increasing activism of small countries, namely Qatar, the UAE and Oman, seems to be a direct consequence of the shifts caused by the Arab uprisings, as well as of these countries' willingness to capitalise on the wealth they have accumulated and the broad network of relations they have developed with Western policy, business and academic circles. Notwithstanding crucial differences in the three countries' attitudes, their increased regional clout limits the opportunities left for Saudi Arabia to play the role of regional hegemon. Saudi Arabia was traditionally considered the main pillar of the Gulf security architecture, as well as the most powerful factor legitimising US policies in the region aimed at fostering stability. But now, Saudi Arabia itself is witnessing a shift in its foreign policy, in terms of becoming increasingly interventionist and favouring the use of military means to influence political change in neighbouring countries. This was evident in the case of the direct Saudi intervention in Bahrain in February 2011 and in Yemen in 2015, as well as in the support it continues to lend to local opposition groups in Syria. These shifts in the domestic and regional contexts raise the question of whether Saudi Arabia will continue to pursue a strategy of 'omnibalancing' by engaging in a form of power balancing at both the domestic and international levels. Finally, the emergence of the smaller countries on the regional chessboard opens up space for competition and rivalry within the GCC, which may ultimately impinge on the integration prospects of the regional organisation.

The second aspect relates to the international relations of the GCC countries. Indeed, it is possible to speak of an increased 'pragmatism' of the GCC countries' foreign policies with regard to other regional and global powers. This pragmatic attitude is driven by their domestic interests and security requirements (for example *vis-à-vis* Iran), as well as by the need to diversify their foreign relations to include other players, such as Russia, European countries and Turkey. Historically, the United States was the main international player in the Gulf region and the GCC countries were loyal allies, despite tensions that arose from time to time. It can be argued that the shifts caused by the Arab uprisings are defining new rules of the game for the relationship between the United States and the GCC countries. These are reflected, on the one hand, in the US' shifting priorities regarding its policies towards the Gulf and the Middle East in general, and on the other, the changing security perceptions of the GCC countries themselves.

This Special Issue examines the foreign policies of the GCC countries six years after the Arab uprisings in terms of drivers, narratives, actions and outcomes, paying particular attention to Middle Eastern countries, Iran and Western international powers. The assessment focuses on current affairs, but also contributes to establishing a productive link between empirical studies and the existing theoretical frameworks that help explain the increasing foreign policy activism of the GCC countries. All in all, the articles collected in this Special Issue shed light on and provide a more solid and fine-grained understanding of how regional powers like Saudi Arabia, as well as the other smaller GCC countries, act and pursue their interests in an environment full of uncertainty, in the context of changing regional and global dynamics and power distribution.

The Special Issue brings together a selection of articles originally presented and discussed at the Seventh Gulf Research Meeting (GRM) organised by the Gulf Research Centre Cambridge at the University of Cambridge on 16-19 August 2016. We thank the organisers of the meeting as well as all participants in the workshop for engaging in a stimulating debate on one of the most topical issues concerning the future of the Gulf region and the Middle East in general. Furthermore, we wish to thank the anonymous reviewers and the editor of *The International Spectator*, respectively, for their constructive comments and meticulous editing of the various drafts of the articles.

Guest editors
Silvia Colombo
Eman Ragab
Rome-Cairo, March 2017

Between Accommodation and Opportunism: Explaining the Growing Influence of Small Gulf States in the Middle East

Máté Szalai

ABSTRACT

Smaller members of the Gulf Cooperation Council defied theoretical and practical expectations as they were able to enlarge their international influence during the years of the Arab Spring. They adopted markedly different foreign policy strategies, which can be seen as stances lying between accommodation and opportunism, depending on the extent to which they respected the security concerns of their geopolitical patron, Saudi Arabia. The mainstream schools of IR theory – neorealism, neoliberalism and constructivism – offer different explanations for these phenomena. Although none of the three schools can provide a completely exhaustive explanation, neoliberalism seems to offer the most comprehensive framework for analysis.

During the 'Arab Spring,'[1] two interrelated processes took place along the shores of the Persian Gulf, both interesting from theoretical and practical points of view. First, the small states of the region – Bahrain, Kuwait, Oman, Qatar and the United Arab Emirates (UAE), namely all the members of the GCC except Saudi Arabia – defied expectations and surprised regional powers by exercising unprecedented influence far beyond their borders. Second, they implemented markedly different foreign policies vis-á-vis each other and the two closest 'giants', Saudi Arabia and Iran. Neither development is easily explained by conventional international relations (IR) theory and small state studies,[2] which expect relatively small entities to implement similar and minimalist foreign policies.

In the following pages, we seek to explain these two phenomena from a theoretical perspective. After a short description of the main foreign policy strategies adopted by the small Gulf states, we try to discover the reasons behind 1) their enhanced role and 2) the discrepancies in their behaviour. We will use three different traditions of small state theory,[3] namely structural realism (focusing on the regional balances of power and geopolitics), neoliberal institutionalism (emphasizing the role of domestic and international institutions, as well as complex interdependencies) and social constructivism (stressing the importance of identity and norms).

---

[1]The timeframe considered is 2011-15.
[2]"Small states" are conceptualised here in terms of their territory, population, economic and military capacities.
[3]See the three methodological views in small state studies listed by Neumann and Gstöhl, "Introduction", 16-22.

The comparison of the applicability of IR theories is relevant for many reasons. First, the majority of articles focus either on an empirical description[4] or simply use a 'mixture' of theories, thus disregarding the boundaries of the different methodologies.[5] Despite their success in interpreting individual cases, these attempts fail to provide a thorough analysis of *why* and *how*. Second, in practice, distinguishing between theoretical schools means differentiating between diverse types of causes (systemic, domestic, institutional, etc.), which helps identify whether these processes are pre-determined or rather are the result of voluntary decisions. Third (and consequently), the use of different models can shape our expectations about the durability of the phenomena, whether they are long-lasting or temporary. The conclusions at the end of the article provide a reflection on these questions.

Between accommodation and opportunism – the strategy of small Gulf states

After 2011, all the small Gulf states enhanced their international activities and tried to realise their interests in the region. Generally, the aims of the six members of the Gulf Cooperation Council (GCC) were similar – preventing the spread of anti-establishment movements at home while trying to capitalise politically on the unfolding events.[6] To achieve these goals, the six states used a wide range of tools including soft power (especially through the media), financial support and direct military intervention.

Nonetheless, the actions taken by the different regimes were alike in terms of coordination and self-determination. Traditionally, the small Gulf states had followed the lead of Saudi Arabia and, despite their existing bilateral tensions, had not gone directly against the interests of Riyadh. This notion changed significantly during the last years of the Arab Spring as the neighbours' perception of Saudi dominance varied significantly: some tolerated it, some questioned it and seemingly only Bahrain supported it.[7]

The attitudes of the small Gulf states towards Saudi Arabia are of strategic importance from both an empirical and a theoretical perspective: alliance-making in the international arena is considered the most important decision of a small state as it can guarantee security. Therefore, disavowing the Saudi lead reflects strategic shifts under the surface. Naturally, the choice is not a binary one, it is more realistic to picture foreign policy strategies on a scale between *accommodation* (total acceptance of Saudi leadership) and *opportunism* (going 'rogue' – challenging or neglecting Saudi security interests).[8]

On the left side of the line are those states which continued to respect the general strategic framework of Saudi foreign and security policy. Although they increased their activity in the last years, they remained in line with Saudi Arabia (especially with respect to Iran and Yemen).[9] Thus Bahrain, Kuwait and the UAE (from left to right) can be classified as accommodative states with different levels of involvement. Among them, the Emirates played the biggest role regionally, contributing independently to the Libyan intervention

---

[4]E.g. Kausch, "Promise of Middle Eastern Swing States"; Neubauer, *Oman*.
[5]E.g. Young, "Foreign Policy Analysis" or Ehteshami, "GCC Foreign Policy".
[6]Kostadinova, *The Gulf Arab Countries*.
[7]Al-Rasheed, "Saudi Arabia's Foreign Policy", 35-9.
[8]Especially in terms of the perception of the threat posed by Iran and/or the Muslim Brotherhood.
[9]Guzansky, "The Arab Gulf States"; Ulrichsen, *Small States with a Big Role*; Kausch, "The Promise of Middle Eastern Swing States"; Matthiesen, *Sectarian Gulf* and Neubauer, *Oman*.

Table 1. The foreign policy of small Gulf states portrayed on a scale between accommodation and opportunism.

Strategic turning point

(The acceptance of Saudi security interests and leadership)

and the fight against the Islamic State. Nonetheless, all of these actions were in line with and did not harm Saudi interests.

On the other side of the scale, the two remaining states (namely Qatar and Oman, "the opportunists") used their enhanced leverage to widen their autonomy vis-á-vis Saudi Arabia and at times put Saudi policies in danger. Throughout the region, Qatar funded and supported the Muslim Brotherhood (MB), Saudi Arabia's fiercest ideological competitor.[10] Alongside Abu Dhabi, Doha also intervened in Libya, albeit with different aims and supporting MB-related groups in the country.[11] In Egypt, Qatar sided with the Islamist President Mohammad Morsi against the Saudi-backed military, turning the situation in the North African country into a proxy cold war.[12] In Syria, Doha followed a similar path, supporting its own networks (such as *Ahrar as-Sham*) with the ultimate aim of setting up a friendly Brotherhood-led government. Therefore, since Saudi goals involve combatting Iranian and the Brotherhood's influence, the two Gulf countries confronted each other many times.[13] Qatar was also less enthusiastic about supporting Saudi initiatives on the Arabian Peninsula.

Oman, as the other opportunist state, defied Riyadh's foreign policy several times. Muscat upheld relations with the Assad government in Damascus and also communicated with Moscow.[14] It mediated between the Western governments and Iran, most notably on the nuclear question,[15] and was the only GCC country that did not support the Saudi-led intervention in Yemen,[16] maintaining ties with the Houthi rebels of Yemen, some of whom still reside in the Omani capital.[17]

Altogether, the opportunist stance resulted in an intensive diplomatic and political debate between Saudi Arabia and Qatar during 2014.[18] Although the problem was seemingly solved by the end of the year, reportedly following a Saudi threat to isolate the tiny country,[19] it is rather questionable whether Doha renounced its ambitions. In parallel, Omani-Saudi relations seem stable but could easily deteriorate in the coming years.

The choice between accommodation and opportunism is not self-explanatory. There is no single factor that explains the behaviour of the five small GCC countries. In the following,

---

[10]Al-Rasheed, "Saudi Arabia's Foreign Policy".
[11]Gaub, "From Doha with Love", 52-5.
[12]Szalai, *Turmoil in Egypt*.
[13]Phillips, "Gulf Actors and the Syria Crisis", 42-9.
[14]Kausch, "Promise of Middle Eastern Swing States"; Neubauer, *Oman*.
[15]Al-Rasheed, "Saudi Arabia's Foreign Policy".
[16]Kausch, "Promise of Middle Eastern Swing States".
[17]Neubauer, *Oman*.
[18]Roberts, "Qatar's Strained Gulf Relationships", 27-8.
[19]"Saudi Threatens to Isolate Qatar for its Support of Muslim Brotherhood", *Middle East Monitor*, 9 April 2014, https://www.middleeastmonitor.com/20140409-saudi-threatens-to-isolate-qatar-for-its-support-of-muslim-brotherhood/.

we seek to explain both the growing influence and the differences between the behaviours adopted by the Gulf states from three different theoretical perspectives.

Theoretical explanations of small state behaviour in the Gulf

Balance of power, geopolitics and capabilities – the neorealist narrative

Although there have been theoretical advances, neorealism remains the most frequently used IR theory, in terms not just of general world politics but also of Middle Eastern affairs. In dealing with the region, the majority of researchers focus on the role of geopolitics, the balance of power and the "traditional concern for power and regime survival".[20] Scholars of the Middle East define "complex realism" as a descriptive framework of foreign policy, according to which survival and the balancing effort between material and ideological challenges are the two primary drivers of state behaviour in the region.

In this framework, since small Middle Eastern states have relatively limited resources and usually lack the capacities needed to defend themselves and alter their environment, "self-reliance in defence and security matters is a difficult, if not unachievable"[21] goal. Therefore, they must form alliances with external actors who can protect them, even at the expense of narrower practical sovereignty[22] – a notion generally called bandwagoning (or *cliency*).[23]

From this point of view, the enhanced participation of the small Gulf states and the independence of their foreign policy is neither self-explanatory nor anticipated[24] and should be the result of systemic or external changes.[25] From a neorealist point of view, there can be three possible causes for these developments:

- changes in the regional balance of power;
- power accumulation by small states vis-á-vis their neighbours;
- shifting geopolitical circumstances.

Changes in the balance of power. The Gulf region has traditionally been a three-pillar security system made up of Iran, Iraq and Saudi Arabia, with the influence of the United States as an external actor.[26] The Iranian revolution of 1979 and the Gulf crises in the 1980s and 1990s incremented the threat Tehran posed for the Arabian Peninsula.[27] Due to their geopolitical exposure, the small Gulf states considered Saudi Arabia and the United States as their main allies and protectors in this constellation.[28] This was a clear example of the neorealist notion of bandwagoning; even though they had their reservations about both alliances, especially with Riyadh, the imperatives of regime security and survival were paramount.

The events of 2003 urged the small Gulf states to change their bandwagoning strategy. As a consequence of the fall of Baathist Iraq, Iran's regional influence was strengthened

[20]Young, "Foreign Policy Analysis", 6-7.
[21]Baabood, "Dynamics and Determinants", 156.
[22]*Ibid.*
[23]Tetreault, "Autonomy, Necessity", 567-70.
[24]East, "Size and Foreign Policy Behavior", 563-4.
[25]Elman, "The Foreign Policy of Small States", 149.
[26]Ulrichsen, *Insecure Gulf*, 3.
[27]Ehteshami, "GCC Foreign Policy", 16-7.
[28]Wright, "Foreign Policy in the GCC", 88.

while that of Saudi Arabia started to weaken.[29] This transformation of the status quo and the uprisings of the "Arab Spring" drove Tehran and Riyadh to engage in regional rivalry.[30] Moreover, the distribution of power became more diffuse than ever. These processes resulted in a "long-term instability and power vacuum" in the region,[31] a framework of "competitive multipolarity", in which "a range of regional and external players of different sizes and weights are likely to compete in shifting, overlapping alliances", and in which "alliances are likely to take more passing, functional forms".[32]

Rapid changes in the distribution of power makes it imperative for small states to be flexible in terms of alliances. According to the small state literature, such changes can be beneficial for them. Rothstein distinguishes three kinds of balances of power – the conservative frozen, the competitive and fluid and, thirdly, the bipolar. While the first kind, characterised by established and inflexible alliances, provides the highest level of individual security, the second, which fits the empirical description of competitive multipolarity, enables the widest leverage.[33] The Middle East today seems to be moving from the first to the second kind of balance of power, stimulating small states to be more active in the international sphere.

In such circumstances, the small Gulf states can capitalise on the emerging multipolarity, as their relative weakness is reduced. This phenomenon is nothing new in IR literature: in 1967, David Vital anticipated that after the erosion of hegemonic power, small states could become more active.[34] This notion gave rise to the emergence of the concept of "swing states", namely "ambitious small and midsize powers" that would like to alter their environment.[35] In this regard, the emergence of the leverage of small Gulf states is a result of the systemic changes taking place in the Middle East.

Accumulation of power.[36] When it comes to material sources of power, the small Gulf states have considerably improved their regional stance in the 21st century. In 1990, the five countries jointly produced only the 11.7 percent of regional GDP. By 2000, this had grown to 16.3 percent and by 2014 to 22.98 percent. More importantly, the group aggregately surpassed the economic output of Iran in 1993 and that of Saudi Arabia in 2011. Individually, the UAE have the highest nominal GDP among the five small states, producing more than 150 percent of the regional average. The second place is occupied by Qatar (which surpassed Kuwait in 2010), registering the biggest relative growth in the Gulf.

The economic growth has partly manifested itself in military terms, as the Gulf states are now among the most militarised countries in the world. The UAE were the fourth biggest arms importers between 2010 and 2014, surpassing Saudi Arabia and China. The small GCC members' military expenditure amounted to the 3.8-6.3 percent of their GDP in the same years, constantly surpassing the Iranian ratio, meaning that aggregately, they spent more money on defence than Iran. In spite of these developments, they remain relatively weak, especially vis-á-vis Saudi capacities, as the Kingdom remains the strongest force on the peninsula.

---

[29]Kausch, *Competitive Multipolarity*.
[30]Matthiesen, *Sectarian Gulf*, 19-20.
[31]Lorenz, *How Should the NATO*.
[32]Kausch, *Competitive Multipolarity*, 11.
[33]All considerations in this paragraph found in Keohane, "Lilliputians' Dilemmas", 63.
[34]Vital, *The Inequality of States*, 133.
[35]Kausch, "Promise of Middle Eastern Swing States".
[36]All data in this section are from *The World Bank Database*, http://data.worldbank.org/.

All in all, accumulation of power can only partly explain the growing role of small Gulf states. In the last fifteen years, all, especially the UAE and Qatar, have been able to realise substantive economic gains. Yet, while their enhanced activity is a manifestation of their desire to reshuffle regional roles and have the voice they deserve at the table, this narrative fails to explain the choices between opportunism and accommodation.

Geopolitics. Geopolitical circumstances have a huge effect on small states' foreign policy. In the Gulf region, it is clear that all smaller GCC members are vulnerable to Saudi Arabia, while Bahrain is the most exposed to Iran (and Kuwait to Iraq). In addition, specific geopolitical factors can explain many of the differences in their foreign policy strategies. These include:

- the special considerations of Qatar and Oman (the common natural gas field with Iran and the Strait of Hormuz, respectively) which create a need to cooperate with the Islamic Republic. This makes them less interested in an intensification of rivalry between Tehran and Riyadh;
- the UAE's decades-long disputes with Iran concerning the islands of Abu Musa and the Tunbs;[37]
- Qatar's withdrawal in 2014 from an implicit rivalry with Saudi Arabia after alleged threats from Riyadh based on its geopolitical vulnerability;[38]
- Kuwait's ambition to build stronger ties with Iraq's Shia-dominated governments due to the emirate's geopolitical exposure to its neighbour (despite Saudi Arabia's reluctance to do so);[39]
- Bahrain's constant loyalty to Saudi Arabia due to its highly vulnerable position with respect to Iran;
- Oman's independent policy towards Yemen due to its geopolitical exposure to its neighbour (see the Dhofar region).

In the neorealist view, the growing leverage of small Gulf states is mainly due to the emergence of competitive multipolarity in the Middle East and to some extent to the accumulation of power taking place in the 21st century, especially in the UAE and Qatar. However, the choice between accommodation and opportunism can mostly be attributed to geopolitical considerations, such as relations to Iran and Yemen which are, for example, the primary motivators of Qatar's and Oman's relative independence.

Nonetheless, despite its popularity, the neorealist narrative fails to explain key developments. From a structural perspective, Qatar's support for the Muslim Brotherhood seems highly random, while the disinterest of the UAE (as the strongest small Gulf state) in becoming more independent is also left unexplained. That is why other factors have to be brought into the analysis.

Interdependencies and domestic politics – the neoliberal school of thought

Neoliberal institutionalism is somewhat more optimistic about the possibilities of small states in the international system. Since the representatives of this school consider world politics as less conflictual, they do not see material capacities as paramount. Small entities

---

[37]Sadjadpour, *The Battle of Dubai*, 10-1.
[38]Cole, "A New Arab Cold War".
[39]Ehteshami, "GCC Foreign Policy", 16.

can theoretically affect their neighbourhood on the basis of their position in the regional or global network of interdependencies, making them less vulnerable to their external environment.[40]

From the institutional perspective, several researchers also focus on the domestic institutional and political characteristics that affect international behaviour. Nonneman lists "the nature of the state" and decision-making systems as vital determinants,[41] whereas Ehteshami considers the creation of states and unique domestic government structures as the main drivers of foreign policy.[42]

The inclusion of internal aspects is particularly important given the particularity of the Middle Eastern Arab state. Brichs and Lampridi-Kemou found the emergence of regimes and circular power struggles to be the main features of these structures, where the state is considered purely as a resource in the hands of the ruling elite.[43] In this regard, foreign policy is not separable from domestic policies and should be interpreted as part of regime survival strategies.

Position in the network of interdependencies. Complex interdependence is a key notion in investigating Gulf states – especially since the very term surfaced when the 'oil weapon' was used in 1973.[44] Therefore it is a viable hypothesis that the growing activity of the five small GCC members was enabled by their enhanced position in the network of interdependencies, both regional and global.

In the region, there has always been a clear dependency between oil producers and other states, manifested primarily in the form of unilateral financial transfers. "The regional balance in the Arab region", argues Luciani, "has been moving relentlessly (…) towards the oil-rich 'parvenus'. (…) The traditional centres of Arab politics are in decline while oil exporters enjoy all opportunities."[45] Although this one-sided dependency has existed since at least the 1970s, it has intensified in the last decades. The rise in energy prices between 2003 and 2014 created huge surpluses in the Gulf – estimated at more than 900 billion dollars[46] –which were used consciously to amplify existing power relations. Using a well-planned investment policy,[47] the GCC states expanded their financial aid portfolios, seized business opportunities abroad and manipulated oil and gas prices.[48]

The Gulf states enlarged their influence not only regionally, but also globally, especially on energy markets and, after the 2008 crisis, on financial markets.[49] Pouring unprecedented amounts of capital into their governmental-controlled sovereign wealth funds, the six GCC countries were able to manage 46-60 percent of world investment capital, which they allocated mostly in Western and East Asian markets.

Apart from the realisation of profit, these Gulf investments in global markets had two strategic aims. First, (by enlarging their overall share and influence over governments and companies) they gave GCC members more influence in the international economic system, especially in terms of the global financial architecture, energy governance and climate

---

[40]Keohane and Nye, *Power and Interdependence*, 109.
[41]Nonneman, "Analyzing the Foreign Policy", 12.
[42]Ehteshami, "GCC Foreign Policy", 13-5.
[43]Brichs and Lampridi-Kemou, "Sociology of Power".
[44]Keohane and Nye, *Power and Interdependence*, 10.
[45]Luciani, "Oil and Political Economy", 98-9.
[46]Ulrichsen, *Small States with a Big Role*, 3.
[47]Ehteshami, "GCC Foreign Policy", 17-21.
[48]Young, "The New Politics".
[49]Bahgat, "Sovereign Wealth Funds".

change regimes.[50] Second, by strengthening interdependencies with extra-regional powers through investments in their key economic sectors, the GCC countries gained greater leverage over them. One can assume that this strategy contributed to the overall silence of Western countries regarding the Gulf states' activities in the Middle East (i.e. intervention in Bahrain, Libya, Egypt and Yemen).

Moreover, the interdependencies between each small Gulf state, on the one hand, and Saudi Arabia or Iran, on the other, also help to explain their foreign policy choices. The fact that the Qatari economy relies more on exporting natural gas than on oil explains a certain level of independence from Saudi Arabia. Simultaneously, Oman has been moving closer to Iran in the past years economically. Since the signing of the Ashgabat Agreement in 2011, Oman and Iran are cooperating with Turkmenistan, Uzbekistan and more recently India and Kazakhstan on an "international transport and transit corridor".[51]

On the other hand, the more accommodative states, especially Bahrain and the UAE, tend to be more dependent on the Saudi economy or lack significant connections to the Iranian one. First of all, since Saudi Arabia has an unquestionable role in energy pricing, reliance on oil incomes means an asymmetric interdependence with Riyadh for both countries. Secondly, Bahrain's dependence on Riyadh[52] is also strengthened due to the strong bilateral trade ties, the direct aid flowing from Saudi Arabia and further cooperation in several sectors,[53] making it difficult for Manama to break ties with the Saudi government.

In the case of the UAE, domestic interdependencies play an important role. [54] There are economic connections between the federal state and Iran, but they are mostly with Dubai and the smaller Emirates which have a more open trade-based financial system than the oil exporter Abu Dhabi. Consequently, the Emirates have different perceptions of Iran – Abu Dhabi opposes its growing influence, while Dubai has strong economic ties with the Islamic Republic and is, therefore, more open to dialogue and discussion.

On the federal level, the Emirates' foreign policy towards Iran is constrained by the power relations between the member states. Abu Dhabi's prominent role has been strengthened since 2008, when Dubai's economy was hit severely by the economic crisis; the Zayed regime of Abu Dhabi basically bailed out the Dubai economy, putting it into a subordinate position. As a result, there is no question about foreign policy at the federal level being dominated by the former rather than the latter, strengthening its anti-Iranian stance.

Economic dependencies can provide very useful explanations, but do not give a complete picture. To help combat the ongoing protests in 2011, Oman allegedly agreed to receive USD 10 billion from Saudi Arabia in the following ten years,[55] making Muscat interested in stronger ties. The loyalty of Abu Dhabi to Riyadh also remains an open question, as the lack of deep economic ties with Iran is, by itself, not enough to explain the Emirate's behaviour. Kuwait is only partly dependent on Saudi Arabia despite their coordination in oil price policy, shared oil field in the Neutral Zone and relatively strong trade ties. Based on these data, neither Abu Dhabi nor Kuwait has strict limitations towards Riyadh or Tehran.

---

[50]Ulrichsen, *Small States with a Big Role*, 4-6.
[51]Cafiero, "Oman and Iran". Moreover, an agreement was reportedly reached by Iran and Oman in 2015 to facilitate the construction of an LNG-pipeline connecting the two countries, expected to be completed in 2018. Studies suggest that Oman is going to buy 60 billion USD worth of natural gas from Iran in 25 years. On a yearly basis, that would mean 2.4 billion USD, which is two and a half times more than the current Saudi exports to Oman (Shah, *Where does Oman*, 6).
[52]Matthiesen, *Sectarian Gulf*, 30.
[53]Cordesman, *Saudi Arabia Enters*, 79-80.
[54]Sadjadpour, *The Battle of Dubai*.
[55]Bank *et al*. "Durable, yet Different", 171.

The domestic political environment. In the first years of the Arab Spring, the comparison of republics and monarchies in the Middle East was frequently used to distinguish between stable and unstable regimes. There is a clear (but not exclusive) correlation between forms of governments and the strength of the protests that occurred in 2011.[56] Therefore, one might assume that the enhanced role of the small Gulf states is related to the stability provided by their monarchic structure.

However, several aspects need to be included in the investigation to avoid over-simplification. First of all, the monarchy did not secure the positions of all rulers. The Bahraini 'Spring' is a case in point. Second, as Bank *et al.* point out, the regimes reacted differently to the ongoing events due to their diverse institutional evolution and attributes.[57] On the basis of various factors, they distinguish between three categories of monarchies – five rentier and dynastic Gulf states, the "linchpin" monarchies of Jordan and Morocco, and the mixed case of Oman. The tools available to the regimes did not derive solely from their monarchic structure, but more from their domestic institutional environment.

Another approach considers the different domestic power groups that challenged the power of the rulers. It assumes that those Gulf states that tended to cooperate in foreign policy have the same threats (i.e. the Muslim Brotherhood) in their domestic arena while the more opportunistic states might have different considerations. As many researchers point out, the presence of the Muslim Brotherhood in Gulf states is a good indicator of their foreign policy. Both Saudi Arabia and Abu Dhabi consider the movement a threat because of its domestic support inside their borders.[58] In the case of the UAE, relations with the Brotherhood also play a key role in the rivalry between the member states, given that the smaller Emirates have a much less negative connection with the movement than Abu Dhabi. In Qatar and Oman, the role of the MB is not perceived as a substantial threat to the regimes – Doha has practically established a political alliance with it, since its reach in Qatari society is limited and lacks anti-establishment sentiments. In the Ibadi-majority Oman, the dominantly Sunni MB has never managed to evolve.[59] On the other hand, the regimes' perceptions of the Brotherhood are quite mixed in Bahrain and Kuwait: the Sunni regime of Manama, ruling over a Shia majority, does not oppose the MB;[60] whereas in Kuwait, where the moderate Islamists are part of the opposition, they are considered more nationalists who do not express revolutionary goals, but seek to "make incremental changes through the existing system and with the ruling family".[61] The MB in Kuwait has actually broken away from the international movement due to its lack of support during the 1991 Kuwaiti crisis.[62]

In the domestic sphere, the sectarian narrative is also a frequently used one. [63] The basis of this argument is that the Sunni regimes with large Shia minorities will have a more aggressive anti-Shia stance than others, and will therefore have a greater incentive to follow the Saudi lead against Iran. Qatar and Oman, on the other hand, lacking a large anti-establishment Shia minority, are able to implement a more opportunist foreign policy.

---

[56]Lucas, "Monarchies and Protests", 197.
[57]Bank *et al.* "Durable, yet Different".
[58]Diwan, "Future of the Muslim Brotherhood".
[59]Boghardt, *The Muslim Brotherhood.*
[60]*Ibid.*
[61]Freer, *Rentier Islamism*, 8.
[62]*Ibid.*
[63]Wright, "Foreign Policy in the GCC", 76; Guzansky, "The Arab Gulf States"; Colombo, *The GCC Countries.*

Even if the sectarian narrative works well in the case of Bahrain, it has severe limitations. First, it is doubtful whether Shia minorities are capable of posing a vital threat to the regimes in the Sunni-majority countries (with the exception of Bahrain). In fact, the presence of Shias, in itself, does not pose a security threat to most Gulf states. Even among the more accommodative small states, Shia communities often play a constructive role in domestic politics (for example in Kuwait).[64] In the UAE as well, there is no imminent pressure on Abu Dhabi to take a leading role in the anti-Iranian and anti-Shia camp. It is true that the Shia communities in the federation are more concentrated in Dubai and the smaller Emirates, yet they have not constituted an instrument or basis for domestic rivalry. Second, as Matthiesen argues, the sectarian policies adopted by some of the Gulf regimes in both the domestic and foreign spheres are more a political tool than an actual cause of tensions.[65]

To sum up, the theory of neoliberal institutionalism can explain quite a lot about the behaviour of small Gulf states. Their enhanced position in the network of complex interdependencies has increased their leverage in the 21st century, especially vis-á-vis global actors. Moreover, intra-GCC economic connections and the domestic political landscapes can help explain the choices between accommodation and opportunism. The only exception is Kuwait, which is not dependent on Riyadh economically and does not share its interpretation of the Muslim Brotherhood and Shias as existential threats to the regime.

The most important conclusion of the neoliberal institutional inquiry is that the states adopting a strategy of accommodation accept Saudi leadership for different reasons. Neither economic ties, nor the perception of the MB or other Shia movements can, in and of themselves, explain Gulf foreign policies. Therefore, from this point of view, the alliance between accommodative states and Saudi Arabia is quite fragile, with only Bahrain closely aligned with Saudi foreign policy. Kuwait is not systematically dependent on Riyadh and, if the Muslim Brotherhood were to be defeated in the UAE, its inclination to respect Riyadh's security considerations could weaken.

Identity and the nature of power – social constructivism

Constructivist approaches are becoming more and more popular among scholars of the Middle East. One of the fiercest debates in this academic field is "between those who advocate the primacy of material structures and those that champion ideational factors". While, neorealism deduces international relations from geopolitics and capabilities, the constructivist approach considers the system "at least partly constituted by normative inter-subjective understandings which state elites construct through their disclosure and interactions with their populations and each other".[66] State formation, elite structures and competitive identities shape perceptions and self-perceptions which affect foreign policy to a great extent.

In investigating the growing role of small Gulf states, many researchers seek to interpret the events relying partly or entirely on constructivist approaches. Most of them focus on two distinct points – the transformation of power in the regional and global international system, and the changes and differences in regime identity.

---

[64]Matthiesen, *Sectarian Gulf*, 99.
[65]Ibid.
[66]Both quotations are from Hinnebusch, "Explaining International Relations", 243.

Transformation of power. The changing nature of power has been one of the most important notions of international relations in the 21st century. According to Ulrichsen, the re-evaluation of power in the academic discourse terminated the strong correlation between size and power, enabling small states to enlarge their international presence.[67] Qatar and the UAE have been able to capitalise on the situation to the greatest extent, using media outlets, mediation and strategic investments to change perceptions and realise their interests abroad. Kostadinova describes how the transformation of power has enabled regional actors to influence developments with soft power measures like mass communication, financial support, tribal and personal relations, development and aid policies.[68] Analysing such trends with respect to the foreign policy of Doha, Kamrava introduces the concept of subtle power, "the ability to exert influence from behind the scenes".[69] Chong calls such strategies conducted by small states "virtual enlargement",[70] which includes, for example, image-building or mediation, a standard tool of the foreign policy of Qatar and Oman.[71]

While one can hardly disagree with these observations, they have two important limitations. Firstly, the transformation of power should affect small states alike and should thus have changed the foreign policy of Jordan, Qatar, Morocco to the same extent. Differentiation between specific small states needs further elaboration. Secondly, transformation of power has been a constant development at least since the Second World War. Therefore we have come no closer to explaining why the members of the GCC exert unprecedented influence *now* and did not years or decades ago.

Regime identities. Some researchers have tried to explain the foreign policy of small Gulf states during the Arab Spring by looking at regime or state identities, both in terms of their growing influence and the differences between their foreign policies, especially in the case of the opportunists. Young considers leadership shifts as a primary reason for the growing influence of the smaller GCC states:[72] Hamad bin Khalifa Al Thani changed Qatar after 1995; while Khalifa bin Zayed Al Nahyan (alongside Mohamed bin Rashid Al Maktoum) has transformed the Emirates since the mid-2000s, preparing them to take on a more substantive role in the Middle East. Matthiesen attributes the strong cooperation between Riyadh and Manama to some extent to the Bahraini national identity, which includes strong ties with some Saudi tribes (and family connections between the ruling dynasties).[73] Many ascribe the independence of Omani foreign policy to the distinct evolution of the Omani state identity as a maritime empire, as well as Sultan Qaboos bin Said Al Said's positive personal sentiments towards Iran.[74] According to Ehteshami, the events of 2003 made the small GCC members "come out of their shell" to become more active in the Middle East, so they had to define themselves in the international order. "We have", argues Ehteshami, "therefore seen an increasing diversity in GCC foreign policies and the member-states' role conception".[75] The Qatari "black sheep identity" was also strengthened by the change of emirs in 2013,

---

[67]Ulrichsen, "Small States with a Big Role", 9-12.
[68]Kostadinova, *The Gulf Arab Countries*, 21-3.
[69]Kamrava, *Qatar*, 59-60.
[70]Chong, "Small State Soft Power Strategies".
[71]Respectively, Kamrava, "Mediation and Qatari Foreign Policy"; Neubauer, *Oman*.
[72]Young, "Foreign Policy Analysis", 4.
[73]Matthiesen, *Sectarian Gulf*, 30-1.
[74]Neubauer, *Oman*; Al-Khalili, *Oman's Foreign Policy*; Rabi, "The Sultanate of Oman".
[75]Both quotations from Ehteshami, "GCC Foreign Policy", 21-2.

which enabled the small state "to break easily from its GCC partners"[76] – especially since, historically, the Thani family has always had problematic relations with the other tribes of the Arabian Peninsula.[77]

The investigation of regime identity and the ruler's personal perceptions is of importance in the case of the GCC, given the highly centralised and personalised nature of decision-making processes. Changes in leadership can have a strong effect on policy outcomes, especially vis-á-vis other regions with a tradition of more formalised state structures (like Europe).[78] Moreover, foreign policy can also be used as a tool for national identity-building, which is an explicit goal of the GCC regimes, especially with their large migrant worker communities. [79]

Concerning identity, the idea of smallness in the self-perception of the regimes also has to be discussed. If a state does not consider itself small, it will not act like a small state. Therefore it may be a valid hypothesis that smallness and weakness play a bigger role in the self-perception of the more accommodative states than in the that of the opportunists, which is why they did not break with their traditional security partner. One can argue that there is a higher chance of such an atypical identity developing in the Gulf where, historically, the ruling tribes were not necessarily the wealthiest or the strongest, and power was not necessarily based on material resources, but was rather the product of a mixture of tangible and intangible assets.[80]

However, the problematic aspects involved in researching regime identity cannot be overlooked. While making fruitful contributions, most related research lacks a solid methodological basis. As Abdelal *et al.* state, social sciences are still unable to define or measure identities properly.[81] Without consistent operationalisation, using identity as an explanatory factor can become highly arbitrary. Consequently, even if the self-perception of the rulers and members of the regimes undeniably play an important role in foreign policymaking, references to identity have to be taken into account more carefully.

All in all, the social constructivist approach highlights important aspects of the analysis. The transformation of power clearly helps to explain why small states have been able to be more active in the last years, while 'black sheep' regime identities can also be 'blamed' for the atypical foreign policies of the opportunists. Nonetheless, the biggest shortcoming of the constructivist approach lies in its methodology – it is very hard to prove that it was identity that brought about the opportunistists' break with the Saudi leadership.

Conclusion

In the article, we presented the main narratives that claim to explain the role of small GCC states. The main results of the comparison are summarized in Table 2.

Four aspects have been taken into consideration:

- reasons for their growing influence;
- explanations regarding the differences in their behaviour;
- durability of the trends;
- questions left unanswered by the theory.

---

76 Young, "Foreign Policy Analysis", 5.
77 Roberts, "Qatar's Strained Gulf Relationships", 23.
78 Wright, "Foreign Policy in the GCC", 78-81.
79 Chalcraft, "Migration Politics", 76-7.
80 Commins, *The Gulf States*, 10-1.
81 Abdelal *et al.* "Identity as a Variable".

Table 2. Comparison of the three theories.

School of thought	Causes of growing role of the small Gulf states	Causes of the different behaviour of the small Gulf states	How stable are the current trends?	Questions left unexplained
Neorealism	1. Evolution of "competing multipolarity" 2. Absolute power accumulation	1. Absolute power accumulation (UAE, Qatar) 2. Geopolitics (Qatar, Oman, Bahrain)	The most stable.	1. Qatar's support for the Muslim Brotherhood 2. The UAE's "follower" approach
Neoliberal institutionalism	Improving positions in regional and global interdependences	1. Domestic power struggles (Qatar, UAE, Bahrain) 2. Economic dependencies inside the GCC (Bahrain, Qatar, UAE)	Somewhat stable.	1. The Kuwaiti loyalty to Saudi Arabia. 2. Some aspects of Omani foreign policy
Constructivism	Transformation of power	"Black ship" identities in the case of Qatar and Oman	Less stable.	Methodological obstacles

None of the schools of thought answer all the questions. Yet, in our opinion, neoliberal institutionalism is the most efficacious theory. Neorealism was able to interpret many phenomena, but it nevertheless falls short in the cases of Qatar and the Emirates, the two most influential Gulf states. Constructivism, on the other hand, raises crucial questions, but does not have a rigorous methodology and, as such, cannot be used as a general framework for inquiry.

As stated earlier, the most important conclusion that can be drawn from the comparison of the different IR schools is a prediction of the durability of the investigated tendencies. All narratives share the idea that the growing role of small Gulf states is not a temporary phenomenon, although they differ slightly when it comes to the durability of the trends. Neorealism seems to predict the most stable trends, since neither systemic features nor geopolitics can be altered easily. Aspects highlighted by neoliberalism are also solid, but slightly more exposed to changes, as interdependencies and the domestic political environment can be altered by government policies. Constructivism looks at the least predictable developments: while the transformation of power globally is unquestionable, regime identities can be altered after successions, internal struggles or family disputes.

All in all, it is undeniably useful to see the developments of the Middle East from multiple perspectives, but one should take care not to mix them arbitrarily. When we introduce identity, for example, every independent variable loses its 'objective' nature. Methodological consistency is required when analysing international relations – even in the Middle East – in order to be able to shed light on otherwise confusing and multi-layered events.

References

Abdelal, R., Y.M. Herrera, A.I. Johnston, and R. McDemott. "Identity as a Variable". *Perspectives on Politics* 4, no. 4 (December 2006): 695–711.

Al-Khalili, M. *Oman's Foreign Policy*. London: Praeger, 2009.

Al-Rasheed, M. "Saudi Arabia's Foreign Policy: Loss without Gain?" In *The New Politics of Intervention of Gulf Arab States*, Collected Papers 1: 32-40. London: LSE Middle East Centre, 2015. http://eprints.lse.ac.uk/61772/1/The%20new%20politics%20of%20intervention%20of%20Gulf%20Arab%20states.pdf.

Baabood, A. "Dynamics and Determinants of GCC States' Foreign Policy, with Special Reference to the EU". In *Analyzing Middle East Foreign Policies and the Relationship with Europe*, edited by G. Nonneman: 145–74. London: Routledge, 2005.

Bahgat, G. "Sovereign Wealth Funds in the Gulf – An Assessment". In *The Transformation of the Gulf. Politics, Economics and the Global Order*, edited by D. Held and K. C. Ulrichsen: 218–36. London: Routledge, 2012.

Bank, A., T. Richter, and A. Sunik. "Durable, Yet Different: Monarchies in the Arab Spring". *Journal of Arabian Studies* 4, no. 2 (December 2014): 163–80.

Boghardt, L.P. *The Muslim Brotherhood in the Gulf: Prospects for Agitation*, Policy watch no. 2087. Washington: The Washington Institute, June 2013. http://www.washingtoninstitute.org/policy-analysis/view/the-muslim-brotherhood-in-the-gulf-prospects-for-agitation.

Brichs, F.I., and A. Lampridi-Kemou. "Sociology of power in today's Arab world". In *Political Regimes in the Arab World*, edited by F.I. Brichs: 6–35. New York: Routledge, 2013.

Cafiero, G. "Oman and Iran: Friends with Many Benefits". *Al-Monitor*, 29 April 2016. http://www.al-monitor.com/pulse/originals/2016/04/oman-iran-friends-ties-gcc-disapproval-saudi.html.

Chalcraft, J. "Migration Politics in the Arabian Peninsula". In *The Transformation of the Gulf. Politics, Economics and the Global Order*, edited by D. Held and K. C. Ulrichsen: 55-86. London: Routledge, 2012.

Chong, A. "Small State Soft Power Strategies: Virtual Enlargement in the Cases of the Vatican City State and Singapore". *Cambridge Review of International Affairs* 23, no. 3 (September 2010): 383–405.

Cole, J. "A New Arab Cold War: Saudi Arabia Pressures Qatar on Muslim Brotherhood, Amercian Think Tanks". *Informed Comment*, 10 March 2014, http://www.juancole.com/2014/03/pressures-brotherhood-american.html.

Colombo, S. *The GCC Countries and the Arab Spring. Between Outreach, Patronage and Repression*. IAI Working Paper 12/19. Rome: IAI, March 2012. http://www.iai.it/sites/default/files/iaiwp1209.pdf.

Commins, D. *The Gulf States. A Modern History*. London: I. B. Tauris, 2014.

Cordesman, A. H. *Saudi Arabia Enters the Twenty-First Century. The Political, Foreign Policy, Economic and Energy Dimension*. Santa Barbara: Praeger, 2013.

Diwan, K.S. "The future of the Muslim Brotherhood in the Gulf". *The Washington Post*, 10 February 2015. https://www.washingtonpost.com/blogs/monkey-cage/wp/2015/02/10/the-future-of-the-muslim-brotherhood-in-the-gulf/.

East, M.A. "Size and Foreign Policy Behavior: A Test of Two Models". *World Politics* 25, no. 4 (December 1973): 556–76.

Ehteshami, A. "GCC Foreign Policy: From the Iran-Iraq War to the Arab Awakening". In *The New Politics of Intervention of Gulf Arab States*, Collected Papers 1: 12-23. London: LSE Middle East Centre, 2015. http://eprints.lse.ac.uk/61772/1/The%20new%20politics%20of%20intervention%20of%20Gulf%20Arab%20states.pdf.

Elman, M.F. "The Foreign Policy of Small States: Challenging Neorealism in its Own Backyard". *British Journal of Foreign Affairs* 25, no. 2 (April 1995): 171–217.

Freer, C. *Rentier Islamism: The Role of the Muslim Brotherhood in the Gulf*. LSE Paper Series no. 9. London: LSE Middle East Centre, November 2015. http://eprints.lse.ac.uk/64446/1/RentierIslamism.pdf.

Gaub, F. "From Doha with Love: Gulf Foreign Policy in Libya". In *The New Politics of Intervention of Gulf Arab States*, Collected Papers 1: 52-58. London: LSE Middle East Centre, 2015. http://eprints.lse.ac.uk/61772/1/The%20new%20politics%20of%20intervention%20of%20Gulf%20Arab%20states.pdf.

Guzansky, Y. "The Arab Gulf States and the Iranian Nuclear Challenge: in the Line of Fire". *Gloria Center*, December 2010. http://www.gloria-center.org/2010/12/guzansky-2010-12-01/.

Hinnebusch, R. "Explaining International Relations in the Middle East: The Struggle of Regional Identity and Systemic Structure". In *Analyzing Middle East Foreign Policies and the Relationship with Europe*, edited by G. Nonneman: 243–57. London: Routledge, 2005.

Kamrava, M. *Qatar. Small State, Big Politics*. Ithaca, London: Cornell University Press, 2013.

Kamrava, M. "Mediation and Qatari Foreign Policy". *Middle East Journal* 65, no. 3 (Autumn 2011): 539-56.

Kausch, K. "The Promise of Middle Eastern Swing States". *Carnegie Europe*, 12 May 2016. carnegieeurope.eu/2016/05/12/promise-of-middle-eastern-swing-states/iy77open_in_new

Kausch, K. *Competitive Multipolarity in the Middle East*, IAI Working Papers 14/10. Rome: IAI, September 2014. https://www.ciaonet.org/attachments/26875/uploads.

Keohane, R.O. "Lilliputians' Dilemmas: Small States in International Politics". In *Small States in International Relations*, edited by C. Igebritsen, I.B. Neumann, S. Gstöhl, and J. Beyer: 55–77. Reykjavik: University of Iceland Press, 2006.

Keohane, R., and J. Nye. *Power and Interdependence*, 4th ed. London: Longman, 2012.

Kostadinova, V. *The Gulf Arab Countries' Foreign and Security Policies Post-Arab Uprisings: Toward Greater Regional Independence of the Middle East*, GRM Papers. Cambridge: Gulf Research Centre, August 2015. http://grc.net/index.php?frm_module=contents&frm_action=detail_book&pub_type=12&sec=Contents&frm_title=&book_id=86976&op_lang=en.

Lorenz, W. *How Should the NATO Shore up its Southern Flank*, PISM Bulletin no. 103. Warsaw: PISM, November 2015. https://www.pism.pl/files/?id_plik=20895.

Lucas, R.E. "Monarchies and Protests in the Arab Uprisings". *Journal of Arabian Studies* 4, no. 2 (December 2014): 195–214.

Luciani, G. "Oil and Political Economy in the International Relations of the Middle East". In *International Relations of the Middle East*, edited by L. Fawcett: 81–104. Oxford: Oxford University Press, 2009.

Matthiesen, T. *Sectarian Gulf. Bahrain, Saudi Arabia, and the Arab Spring that wasn't*. Stanford: Stanford University Press, 2013.

Neubauer, S. *Oman: The Gulf's Go-Between*, Issue Series no. 1. Washington: The Arab Gulf States Institute, February 2016. http://www.agsiw.org/wp-content/uploads/2016/02/Neubauer_OmanMediator.pdf.

Neumann, I.B., and S. Gstöhl. "Introduction. Lilliputians in Gulliver's World?" In *Small States in International Relations*, edited by C. Igebritsen, I.B. Neumann, S. Gstöhl and J. Beyer: 3–39. Reykjavik: University of Iceland Press, 2006.

Nonneman, G. "Analyzing the Foreign Policy of the Middle East and North Africa: A Conceptual Framework". In *Analyzing Middle East Foreign Policies and the Relationship with Europe*, edited by G. Nonneman: 6–19. London: Routledge, 2005.

Phillips, C. "Gulf Actors and the Syria Crisis". In *The New Politics of Intervention of Gulf Arab States*, Collected Papers 1: 41–52. London: LSE Middle East Centre, 2015. http://eprints.lse.ac.uk/61772/1/The%20new%20politics%20of%20intervention%20of%20Gulf%20Arab%20states.pdf.

Rabi, U. "The Sultanate of Oman: Between Tribalism and National Unity". In *Tribes and States in the Changing Middle East*, edited by U. Rabi: 76–95. London: Hurst &, 2016.

Roberts, D. B. "Qatar's Strained Gulf Relationships". In *The New Politics of Intervention of Gulf Arab States*, Collected Papers 1: 23–32. London: LSE Middle East Centre, 2015. http://eprints.lse.ac.uk/61772/1/The%20new%20politics%20of%20intervention%20of%20Gulf%20Arab%20states.pdf.

Sadjadpour, K. *The Battle of Dubai. The United Arab Emirates and the U.S.-Iran Cold War*, Carnegie Papers. July 2011. http://carnegieendowment.org/files/dubai_iran.pdf.

Shah, A. "Where does Oman and Iran's Pipeline Leave Saudi Arabia?", Gulf State Analytics Report. *Gulf State Analytics*, August 2015. https://gallery.mailchimp.com/02451f1ec2ddbb874bf5daee0/files/GSA_Report_August_2015_.pdf.

Szalai, M. *Turmoil in Egypt: A Proxy Cold War among the Gulf States?* Policy Papers. Prague: Institute for International Relations, June 2014. http://www.iir.cz/en/article/turmoil-in-egypt-a-proxy-cold-war-among-the-gulf-states.

Tetreault, M.A. "Autonomy, Necessity, and the Small State: Ruling Kuwait in the Twentieth Century". *International Organization* 45, no. 4 (December 1991): 565–91.

Ulrichsen, K.C. *Small States with a Big Role: Qatar and the United Arab Emirates in the Wake of the Arab Spring*. HH Sheikh Nasser Al-Mohammad Al-Sabah Publication no. 3. Durham: University of Durham, October 2015. https://www.dur.ac.uk/resources/alsabah/al-SabahPaperUlrichsenno3.pdf.

Ulrichsen, K.C. *Insecure Gulf. The End of Certainty and the Transition to the Post-Oil Era*. New York: Columbia University Press, 2011.

Vital, D. *The Inequality of States: A Study of the Small Power in International Relations*. Oxford: Oxford University Press, 1967.

Wright, S. "Foreign Policy in the GCC States". In *International Politics of the Persian Gulf*, edited by M. Kamrava: 72–94. New York: Syracuse University Press, 2011.

Young, K.E. "Foreign Policy Analysis of the Gulf Cooperation Council: Breaking Black Boxes and Explaining New Interventions". In *The New Politics of Intervention of Gulf Arab States,* Collected Papers 1: 4-13. London: LSE Middle East Centre, 2015. http://eprints.lse.ac.uk/61772/1/The%20 new%20politics%20of%20intervention%20of%20Gulf%20Arab%20states.pdf.

Young, K.E. "The New Politics of Gulf Arab State Foreign Aid and Investment", *Middle East Centre Blog*, 25 November 2015. http://blogs.lse.ac.uk/mec/2015/11/25/the-new-politics-of-gulf-arab-state-foreign-aid-and-investment/.

Status and Foreign Policy Change in Small States: Qatar's Emergence in Perspective

Babak Mohammadzadeh

ABSTRACT

Small states are just as easily seduced by status and glory as other states. When conceived as situated in a stratified international society, small states acquire an inherent tendency to overcome their disadvantage in conventional power terms through the pursuit of status. Hence, it is precisely because of their position in the international hierarchy, not in spite of it, that strategic ideas based on state size stimulate foreign policy change in small states. This mechanism provides an explanation to the question why the small state of Qatar has pursued such a high-profile diplomatic strategy since its emergence in the late 1990s.

Small states are increasingly becoming important and influential actors in international politics. Although the scale of their operations markedly differs from what larger states bring to the table, small states are not easily neglected in a world of disparate power relations. A close look at the diplomatic activity of small states nowadays reveals that their impact on international politics may in fact outstrip their theorised potential. Across the globe, small states form a significant part of the political and economic mosaic and are increasingly gaining greater visibility within global institutions. Small states perform meaningful, and at times highly consequential, functions in global affairs, from occupying key positions in international organisations to playing mediating roles in complex disputes. Small states are thus instrumental to the reproduction of international rules and norms; they do not necessarily take what they get, nor do they simply conform to the established way of doing things.

The Gulf state of Qatar presents a fascinating case for studying the increasingly assertive role of small states and their growing importance in shaping international patterns of change. As a result of a highly beneficial combination of a small indigenous population and massive hydrocarbon wealth, Qatar has transformed its peninsula from an impoverished backwater to a sophisticated metropolis, boasting the world's highest per capita income and immense growth figures. Qatar's fast-paced economic development has facilitated its emergence as an important diplomatic power broker. Amid a precarious regional context, Qatar has pushed forward with an activist international agenda defined by high-profile mediation initiatives and aggressive state branding in the quest for achieving a position of international significance. The diplomacy pursued by Qatar since the late 1990s challenges those International Relations theories that predict that small states are trapped by dint of their material circumstances, either because of their capabilities or because they cannot overcome their dependence in global economic relations. As many observers note, Qatar consistently punches above its weight.[1]

That small states such as Qatar should pursue an activist and energetic foreign policy is not as self-evident as it may seem. Pressed between two regional hegemons, Iran in the north and Saudi Arabia to the south, Qatar has successfully avoided assimilation in either power's orbit. Careful maintenance of its international alignments has allowed Qatar to enjoy cordial relations with staunchly revisionist actors in the region, including Iran, Hamas and Hezbollah, whilst simultaneously providing the United States with a military base for operations in the Persian Gulf, from which the US could theoretically strike at exactly those revisionist actors.

Qatar's contradictory international relations cannot be understood merely in terms of a perennial quest for security and independence. Instead of adjusting to shifting political alignments and keeping out of perilous diplomatic entanglements, Qatar is often itself involved in initiating and shaping political change. At the outbreak of the uprisings in the Arab world in 2011 and 2012, Qatar enthusiastically supported the revolutions in Tunisia, Egypt and Libya, supplied Islamists in Syria with money and arms and gave the green light for the UN Security Resolution that secured a no-fly zone over Qadhafi's Libya, only to change course in mid-2013 under intense pressure from the more status-quo minded members of the Gulf Cooperation Council.[2] The maverick streak in Qatar's approach to foreign policy is clearly riddled with risk and opportunity. It raises important questions about the systematic incentives that drive the push for international visibility among small states.

How should we understand the consistent tendency among small states to pursue an impactful and visible foreign policy, at times even to the neglect of their security concerns? This article argues that status-driven behaviour stimulates foreign policy change in small states. An understanding of the external environment as a realm in which material and ideational rewards are unevenly distributed allows us to see why policy elites in small states are strongly attuned toward improving their place in the international hierarchy through the pursuit of status. The structural incentive for status achieves its full causal potential when conceptions about the role and function of small statehood lead to shifts in the dominant ideas held by foreign policy actors. Small states seek status not only when their material capabilities are low, but especially when they frame their strategic ideas on the basis of their size.

In making this argument, this article draws attention to the mechanism through which status-driven behaviour in small states is generated, and illustrates this mechanism by discussing the emergence of Qatar as an influential diplomatic actor in the Middle East. Given its vulnerable positioning in the Persian Gulf, Qatar serves as a 'hard' – that is, unlikely – case for the argument presented here.[3] After all, the Gulf, has acquired a considerable reputation ever since the 1980s as a conflict-prone region in which excessive posturing of wealth and status can easily lead to foreign intrigue or invasion. With negligible military capabilities of its own, Qatar's defence is almost wholly dependent on the United States' security umbrella

[1]Cooper and Momani, "Qatar and Small State Diplomacy".
[2]Ulrichsen, Qatar and the Arab Spring.
[3]Bennett and Elman, "Case Study Methods", 505.

and may appear to make the pursuit of status little more than a marginal incentive. Thus, if status can be identified as a major foreign policy concern among Qatar's ruling elites, sometimes more important than Qatar's physical security, then we will have found strong support for the main claim of this article, beyond the specific case presented here. Put differently, Qatar's changing foreign policy presents a critical test for the role of ideas in small states, even when small states are located in relatively less mature international societies.

This article is divided in three sections. The first section provides a cursory overview of the literature on small states through a discussion of the vulnerability and resilience of small states. The second section conceptualises the interface between elite policy views and the external environment in generating specific status-driven tendencies in small states and explains why this analytical entry point matters strongly for this particular state type. The third provides a case study of foreign policy change in Qatar and is followed by conclusions.

Small state foreign policy

The literature on small states is primarily divided between those emphasising constraints and vulnerabilities, on the one hand, and more recent perspectives that stress the impressive resilience of small states, on the other.[4] The idea that the major players in international affairs are more deserving of attention by virtue of their more apparent ability to project power and influence across state boundaries is strongly rooted in international thought. English School writers characteristically argue that disparities in power create different responsibilities in international society, as "the management of order and the leadership of the diplomatic dialogue have been entrusted by general consensus to great powers".[5] The corollary assumption is that small states are disproportionally influenced by security calculations, because they face an overarching need for protection against the larger and potentially hostile states. When states confront restrictive strategic environments, it is expected that material concerns largely override the role of ideas in determining states' foreign and security policies.[6] In such accounts, the vulnerability, but notably also the resilience, displayed by small states depends on external circumstances.

Notwithstanding their increasing involvement in international politics, the dominant thinking about small states predicts that the foremost dilemma faced by these actors is their inability to protect themselves either militarily or economically against encroachment by stronger powers. Since small states operate in a setting where, as Thucydides famously observed, "the strong do what they will, while the weak suffer what they must", the challenge of the external environment is seen to leave a permanent mark on small state manoeuvrability. The widespread tendency to derive behavioural expectations from these environmental pressures and constraints originates from the traditional schools of thought in International Relations that emphasise the systemic vulnerability and lack of autonomy of small states. Realist logic, for example, dictates that small states face a narrow set of foreign policy choices, balancing or bandwagoning, to ensure their continued survival, while

---

[4]The theme of small state vulnerability is discussed thoroughly in Vital, *The Inequality of States*, but it also features in the neorealist writings of Waltz, *Theory of International Politics*, and Walt, *The Origins of Alliances*. Recent works putting emphasis on resilience are Ingebritsen, "Norm Entrepreneurs", Steinmetz and Wivel, *Small States in Europe*, and Kamrava, *Qatar: Small State, Big Politics* in the context of Qatar.
[5]Watson, *Diplomacy: The Dialogue Between States*, 190.
[6]Handel, *Weak States in the International System*, 36.

critical and Marxist perspectives are pessimistic about the ability of small states to transcend a stage of economic dependency.

The emphasis on vulnerabilities in the political, military and economic sphere generate expectations for the kind of foreign policy that we might expect from small states. Small states are generally taken to be defensively minded, interested in keeping a low profile and positivity tilted towards global institutions and international law to achieve objectives.[7] In addition, in a globalised economy, small states are perhaps to a greater extent susceptible to exogenous shocks from international markets and developments in the global trade regime over which they have little influence. Thus, external factors restrict the menu of choices for small states. Such determinisms are however less useful in a world where small states have begun to enjoy more international visibility and legitimacy than at any other time in history. More recent perspectives on small states increasingly recognise that small states are not always at the mercy of the stronger and more powerful actors and may actually achieve considerable agency to direct their own fate. The following section highlights the way in which two influential concepts in the small state literature, vulnerability and resilience, relate to Qatar.

The vulnerability of small states

How external factors constrain the units that operate within any given environment depends on the immanent capabilities of the units and their structural autonomy from those forces.[8] Realists traditionally understand capabilities in the most narrow sense, that is in terms of hard power possessions, such as the size of a country's territory and population, economic resources and its military potential, which together determine a state's relative standing in the international system.[9] Scholarship in this tradition agrees that small states are more "exposed to the vagaries of international security and economic competition" than their larger and stronger counterparts. Jack Snyder captures the prevailing realist consensus by arguing that since small states do not "enjoy a substantial buffer from the pressures of international competition", explanations that draw on domestic politics are comparatively less useful for small states.[10]

Critical and Marxist perspectives equally stress the constraining causality of external factors in limiting the autonomy of small states, but they do so by approaching the international environment as a hierarchical rather than an anarchical system. Based on the hypothesis that world hierarchy is determined by capitalist relations of production and control of world economic surplus, they point to dependence as an impediment for substantial autonomy in weak states outside the capitalist core.[11] Best articulated by scholars such as Immanuel Wallerstein, this hierarchy consists of an unevenly globalised state system, the units of which perform specialised functions in economic production and exchange.[12] Relations

---

[7]Hey, *Small States in World Politics*, 5.
[8]Harknett and Yalcin, "The Struggle for Autonomy".
[9]Waltz, *Theory of International Politics*.
[10]Snyder, *Myths of Empire*, 62.
[11]Dependency theorists generally talk about weak states, rather than small states, a term which conveys that states are at an initial stage of development and are therefore prone to great power penetration. It is appropriate to use 'weak' and 'small' interchangeably in this context, because both terms ascribe a similar sort of deficiency to the unit in question.
[12]Wallerstein, *The Capitalist World-Economy*, 6.

between the capitalist core and the periphery are marked by a global division of labour, with capital-intensive and technologically advanced production taking place in the core while the periphery provides surplus unskilled labour and raw materials.[13] In such a setup, dependent states are likely to function as transmission belts for the core, exporting surplus from the periphery to the core and importing capitalist social relations from the core to the periphery.[14] State elites in dependent states facilitate this process by acquiring a class identity that is materially and ideologically tied to the hegemon in the capitalist core, under whose coercive umbrella state elites maintain their local authority. In short, dependency theorists claim that small states are not isolated units with an endogenous pattern of development, but rather globalised units with economic relations that are integral to the overall world market.

A focus on material vulnerability is certainly relevant in discussing Qatar. Qatar's accelerating enmeshment in global networks is primarily the result of the enormous crude oil and natural gas reserves that are located in the soil and waters of its peninsula and the sustained global energy demand that puts it in a favourable position to leverage these resources. The capitalisation of its natural resources has, however, come at a price.

First of all, reliance on rentier income exposes state budgets to shifting oil prices, which can be extremely volatile and may lead to significant shortfalls, putting strains on the maintenance of a redistributive political economy that lies at the heart of the political order in the Gulf monarchies. Extreme reliance on natural resources and imported labour exposes the country to a host of demographic and environmental pressures, including rapid population growth, the emergence of a youth bulge, unequal resource distribution, food and water scarcity, and the implications of long-term climate change.[15] Some Gulf experts argue that the rentier state concept fails to capture the increasingly complex commercialisation and financialisation of the Gulf monarchies, as these countries enter a stage of "late rentierism".[16] Khaleeji capital has certainly become more central to regional finance in recent years as local investment vehicles like Sovereign Wealth Funds and GCC-based private equity firms, banks and stock exchanges have invaded capital markets in the Arab world and beyond. However, the non-hydrocarbon private sector growth in recent decades has not led to a fundamental diversification of the economy. There is a lingering dependence on the vicissitudes of global markets that ensure Qatar a steady supply of rents and labour.[17]

Second, new globalising patterns involving the crossborder flow of people, ideas and capital increasingly "bypass state structures and controls and constitute both an ideational and material threat to their polities".[18] Adherents of the 'omnibalancing theory' explain that the calculations of the ruling elite in the Gulf countries are strongly shaped by the desire to counter security threats that arise across state boundaries, forcing regimes to respond to the overall balance of political forces with which they have to contend, including internal threats which are often more important than the threats emanating from interstate competition.[19] Qatar's ruling elite has perhaps more to fear from a restive migrant labour community and internal Islamists than from its neighbouring states. GCC officials routinely

---

[13]Galtung, "A Structural Theory of Imperialism".
[14]Cox, "Global Perestroika (1992)".
[15]Ulrichsen, *Insecure Gulf*.
[16]Gray, *Qatar*.
[17]Hanieh, *Capitalism and Class in the Gulf*.
[18]Ulrichsen, *Insecure Gulf*, 2.
[19]Nonneman, "Determinants of Saudi Foreign Policy".

castigate migrant workers as "a strategic threat" and consider labour a "national security issue", making it easier to justify repressive laws against them.[20]

For Qatar's royal family, the appearance of ideological and religious purity remains just as important as its ability to provide continuing economic growth to its domestic clients. In this sense, state security is best perceived through the particular ideational and cultural context in which Qatar is embedded, and as such, balancing can be aimed at overcoming ideological threats and subversion from a variety of actors, rather than flowing from an epiphenomenal response to shifts in the distribution of power in the international system.[21] Omnibalancing is a crucial corrective in making shifting alliances intelligible in places such as Qatar, where a long history of nationhood is missing and where sub-state and supra-state loyalties cut across state boundaries.[22]

Lastly, that Qatar's vulnerabilities are increasingly non-military in nature is significantly augmented by the physical and symbolic presence of the United States in the region. While there has been a gradual attenuation of interstate threats facing the Gulf monarchies since the end of the Cold War, the potential for state autonomy is clearly tied to a permissive international context and cannot be seen separately from the rise of US prominence in the Persian Gulf following the second Gulf War. In the wake of Operation Desert Storm in 1991, Qatar concluded a beneficial Defence Cooperation Agreement with Washington, giving the US a considerable stake in domestic stability. Renewed in April 2003, the agreement facilitated the redeployment of US forces, previously stationed at the Prince Sultan airbase in Saudi Arabia, to the southwest of Doha, including basing hubs for the US Central Command (CENTCOM).[23] The primary lesson drawn from Saddam Hussein's failed annexation of Kuwait was that the possession of a standing army and sophisticated weaponry is in itself insufficient to guarantee survival. Instead, small states with "tangible interdependencies and powerful international partners" could count on international support during times of crises.[24] The security umbrella of the United States relieves Qatar from investing in military capabilities, an area in which it could not really compete anyway, allowing it instead to divert vulnerability mitigation efforts into other areas.

The resilience of small states

The notion of resilience has been a part of the literature on small states from the outset. Even as early scholars of small states laboured under the assumption that small states were inescapably constrained by systemic pressures, they acknowledged that the vulnerability of small states could be mitigated by intrinsic (permanent) and contingent (ephemeral) conditions, such as the level of economic development, internal stability, support of the population and geographical proximity to areas of strategic interest. Already in 1967, David Vital conceded that there was not necessarily a relationship between smallness and low state capacity and autonomy, as long as small states deployed skilful statecraft to offset their unfavourable positon "by reducing an unfavourable discrepancy in strength, broadening

---

[20]Quoted in Hanieh, *Capitalism and Class in the Gulf*, 65.
[21]David, *Choosing Sides*.
[22]Hinnebusch, *International Politics of Middle East*, 54–72.
[23]Wright, "Foreign Policies with International Reach".
[24]Ulrichsen, *Qatar and the Arab Spring*, 27.

the field of manoeuvre and choice, and increasing the total resources on which the state can count in times of stress".[25] Small states often possess certain assets in abundance, giving rise to "issue-specific power" through which they may levy their influence.[26] When small states concentrate their resources and effectively utilise their comparative edge, their leverage increases; examples are Switzerland's and Luxembourg's position in international banking, Singapore's mastery of regional shipping and Qatar's role in the global energy industry.

The logic of small state resilience and vulnerability mitigation extends equally to the economic realm. Just as small states have the inner potential to escape the clutches of security competition, small economies ensnared in global markets can change the conditions of their participation. Katzenstein argues that small states, particularly those too dependent on world trade to impose protection, and lacking the resources to transform their domestic industries, may resort to a strategy of complex bargaining and democratic corporatism in order to adapt to exogenous shocks and capitalise on market opportunities.[27] Institutional resilience and policy flexibility at home are thus revealed to be crucial coping mechanisms in dealing with pressures from abroad. In the Gulf, the extreme flexibility of the labour market provides rulers with one such coping strategy. When Qatar was hit by the financial crisis of 2007/08, it cleverly managed to displace the worst effects of market contraction on the expatriate community through massive lay-offs and forcible deportation of South Asian workers.[28] Indeed, smallness does not necessarily have to be treated at the level of interstate relations, where it has usually been studied; it can be treated at the intersection of the domestic and the international, where opportunities and relative advantages emerge.

A significant body of small state research challenges the view that the characteristics of the external environment have a powerful bearing on small state foreign policy. Writing from the perspective of historical institutionalism, Elman argues that domestic institutional arrangements are likely to have lasting policy implications, long outliving the conditions and circumstances responsible for their formation.[29] As a certain path dependence takes hold of the domestic decision-making context, established routines and practices favour certain choices rather than others in a given situation, whilst rendering international determinants less important. For example, Doeser explains how the strategies of government actors and opposition parties in the Danish parliament coalesced to facilitate a structural shift away from the Danish footnote policy within NATO.[30] In these and other accounts, domestic institutional structures significantly complicate a reading of small states based only on their position in the international and regional balance of power.

The idea that small states can engage in a strategy of vulnerability mitigation on the basis of their niche capabilities and their institutional make-up has also been examined in the context of the small monarchies in the Persian Gulf. Qatar's management of its potentially vulnerable position is usually understood by country experts as a function of its adroit and calculated leadership. Mehran Kamrava, for example, discusses this quality in terms of three inter-related forces. First, at the international level, the rising importance of the Persian Gulf

---

[25]Vital, *The Inequality of States*, 134.
[26]Keohane and Nye, *Power and Interdependence*.
[27]Katzenstein, *Small States in World Markets*.
[28]Hanieh, *Capitalism and Class in the Gulf*, 179.
[29]Elman, "The Foreign Policies of Small States".
[30]Doeser, "Domestic Politics in Small States".

as a strategic region and the relative decline of the Middle East's traditional power houses provides small states in the Arabian Peninsula with unprecedented opportunities for an over-sized international presence.[31] Second, the nature of decision-making and centralised leadership in the small Gulf monarchies gives political leaders the necessary responsiveness to capitalise on emerging opportunities as they develop regionally and globally.[32] Thirdly, the ability of political elites to circumvent the wishes of their own population through a mixture of repression and co-optation increases a form of elite autonomy that is ultimately very conducive to swift and agile decision-making.[33] Policy organisation is made much more simple and effective when there are no complicated influences of interest groups that may desire a seat at the table. For example, since ultimate decisions are concentrated in the hands of a relatively small number of individuals in Doha, new policies are formulated, transmitted and received through much smoother channels than elsewhere.[34] The highly personalised style of leadership and the flexible nature of Qatari state institutions make the conduct of foreign policy less institutionally determined and more prone to twists and turns. All of this leads to an understanding of the particular way in which Qatar deploys its small state capabilities, which Kamrava dubs "subtle power".

Thus, instead of assuming an insuperable deficiency in terms of capability and autonomy, scholars of small states increasingly recognise the impressive resilience of some small states against exactly those global pressures that they can scarcely control. Discussions about the choices open to small states have drawn inspiration from liberal and constructivist approaches regarding the position of small states in complex interdependence and institutions, and the active framing of cultural constructs and ideas. The influence of small states can reach deeply into international organisations, drawing on international law, international trade and even on symbolic conceptions of power. While great powers are usually, in the first instance, responsible for the creation and management of international institutions and for creating the ground rules for international regimes, such systems are left open to the active participation of all states, even as the supremacy of the erstwhile great powers declines. In fact, once degrees of institutionalisation are set by the stronger and more powerful states, small states acquire "a legal and political language in which to speak about interstate relations, as a medium and a new resource for small states to manipulate".[35]

Small states may find themselves in a position to manipulate existing rules and organisations extensively to suit their ambitions. The use of what Nye would describe as "soft power" offers great possibilities for small states for whom the exercise of military coercion is not possible and whose immanent power capabilities are relationally construed.[36] Constructivists take the argument about the manipulation of ideas further and point at the alternative means through which small states project their influence, for example, by acting as norm entrepreneurs and norm advocates.[37] As an extensive body of research on decision-making within the European Union shows, hierarchical divisions between its member states are mediated in densely institutionalised policy areas, allowing small states

---

[31]Kamrava, *Qatar: Small State, Big Politics,* 17.
[32]*Ibid.,* 66.
[33]*Ibid.,* 42.
[34]Ulrichsen, *Qatar and the Arab Spring,* 34.
[35]Neumann and Gstöhl, "Lilliputians in Gulliver's World?", 17.
[36]Nye, *Soft Power.*
[37]Ingebritsen, "Norm Entrepreneurs".

to overcome their hierarchical marginalisation and operate at a privileged level similar to great powers.[38] Thus, small states' predisposition towards institutionalised rules and norms in international fora should not be understood merely as a necessary condition of their immanent qualities, but also as a result of their place within a social whole.

Qatar's extensive participation in international fora from which it was previously completely absent attests to the possibility of small states developing and exercising their resilience through membership of international organisations and active manipulation of their cultural and ideational resources. Having achieved election to most United Nations committees and forums, including the Security Council in 2006/07, and working through a diverse array of multilateral bodies ranging from the Gulf Cooperation Council (GCC) and the Arab League to the Fédération Internationale de Football Association (FIFA), Qatar's internationalisation strategy is wide-ranging and not consigned to satisfying a purely status-quo agenda or nourishing the desires of its strategic partners. Beginning with the establishment of Al Jazeera in 1996, Qatar has sought to increase its international visibility, moving beyond the traditional display of diplomacy in international political institutions towards an active presence in the commercial and public realm as well. Broadly speaking, these initiatives appear in five areas: "the development of the Al Jazeera brand, education and culture, sport, international travel and tourism, and cutting-edge global research and development in new and cleaner forms of energy".[39]

Qatar's active foreign policy is usually understood as an outgrowth of its aggressive campaign for state branding. In this view, marketing the country as an international hub for educational, cultural and sporting events delivers substantial international recognition at little cost. State branding pursued in this way attracts business and international investors. However, Qatar seems to be willing to go above and beyond its commercial thrift. Lavish spending on projects which have no immediate commercial gain all contribute to building and propagating "a positive, populist and enlightened" perception of a country that is modern, savvy, and distinctive from other states in the region.[40] By transcending anonymity, state branding through the strategic leveraging of soft power has the potential to create long-term mutual interdependencies which can ultimately enhance security and stability and give other countries a powerful stake in pursuing strong relations with Qatar.[41]

Many scholars on Qatar's foreign policy converge on the viewpoint that there is something instrumental about such a deliberate state branding strategy. John Peterson, for example, argues that small states "must be able to reach a modus vivendi with their neighbours, even at the cost of surrendering territory or other aspects of sovereignty" and generally must attract a security guarantee from a powerful external protector. However, using a carefully calibrated strategy, "they should [also] exploit a unique niche whereby the small state provides a service or commodity that benefits neighbours, the region, or the broader world".[42] State branding gets increased depth when other countries regard Qatar as an impartial and independent broker, interested in providing mediation and conflict resolution to warring parties with no Machiavellian interests of its own. Rigorous neutrality reinforces the idea of Qatar as a committed global citizen doggedly pursuing peace in international relations.

---

[38]Steinmetz and Wivel, *Small States in Europe*.
[39]Ulrichsen, *Qatar and the Arab Spring*, 38.
[40]Roberts, "Understanding Qatar's Foreign Policy Objectives", 236.
[41]Ulrichsen, *Qatar and the Arab Spring*, 71.
[42]Peterson, "Qatar and the World", 741.

The discussion of vulnerability and resilience in the context of small states is useful in order to get a better grasp on the way in which small states apply more complex versions of power. It does not help us understand, however, why small states are driven to pursue international visibility more than other states. While it is undeniable that the pursuit of security and wealth may feed into small states' calculations to pursue an active international agenda, this tendency cannot always be attributed to "collective resilience", a supposed "counter-point to vulnerability" or a strategic move designed to overcome the security dilemma.[43] Instrumentality in foreign policy is not always a given. Some aspects of Qatar's foreign policy may lie outside the control and manipulation of Qatar's ruling elite. Incessant state branding is not just an "ethereal notion" based on selfless motivations, but it cannot always be subsumed under the "rubric of realpolitik" either.[44]

Our thinking about small states is significantly constrained because we operate on major assumptions about what they want. Sometimes, we simply assume that they want the same things as other states – security, wealth and protection – making the small state category less useful as a tool for analysis.[45] And yet, "the social construction of state identities ought to precede, and may even explain, the genesis of state interests".[46] If identity is not seen as an analytically autonomous factor in foreign policy, then explanations regarding Qatar's external conduct may misrepresent, distort or conceal significant motives of social action. It is to this ideational dimension of foreign policy that we now turn.

Ideas of smallness in foreign policy

Why some states behave in ways that are not in accordance with their material interests is a matter about which constructivist scholarship has much to say.[47] In the context of small and weak states, Bukovansky's seminal account of the neutral rights policy of the United States of America[48] from US independence to the War of 1812 stands out. Even small states may sometimes privilege their ideals above their own physical security, leading to foreign policies that are fundamentally at odds with what a purely rationalist framework would describe.[49] Bukovansky provides a convincing explanation of why the United States held on to a neutral rights regime grounded in the American tradition of republicanism instead of submitting itself to the maritime law interpretations of the big naval powers in Europe. However, she is less clear about the way in which the relational weakness of the United States in its dealings with European powers at that time interacted with its self-conception. It may be true that this aspect had no role to play in the construction of early US state identity. However, this problem complicates the utility of the small state concept because it "is primarily … in the context of an international confrontation with great powers, or of small states as units in a context of a particular external problematique (globalisation) that the small state concept

---

[43]Cooper and Momani, "Qatar and Small State Diplomacy".

[44]Roberts, "Understanding Qatar's Foreign Policy Objectives", 237.

[45]Baehr, "Small States: A Tool for Analysis".

[46]Bukovansky, "American Identity and Neutral Rights", 209.

[47]The classic example is Wendt, *Social Theory of International Politics*.

[48]In brief, the neutral rights policy to which the United States subscribed entailed that belligerent states in times of war were not allowed to enter and search neutral ships for war material even if they were bound for enemy territory, a view which put the United States at odds with the great maritime powers in Europe in the early nineteenth century.

[49]Bukovansky, "American Identity and Neutral Rights".

can defend its utility".[50] In contrast to Bukovansky, our starting point is to consider how small states like Qatar arrive at a self-definition and identity given their size.

Ideas in foreign policy are usually defined as the filter through which actors give meaning to their own actions and the activities of others.[51] Thus, ideas of smallness emerge when perceptions about size become ingrained in diplomatic conduct and policy discourse. As small states develop deeper and more complex international ties, they find themselves enmeshed in differentiated relationships with other states. Once diplomatic exchanges are routinized, one emergent possibility for relational differentiation is size. This happens when a small state's anthropomorphic qualities such as its identity, interests and intentionality are gradually subsumed under the self-perception of being small.[52] In other words, small states start to play a unit-specific role when the perception of smallness infiltrates the calculations of decision-makers and officials. Even the most strong-minded national executive functions in an environment wherein collective ideas, such as smallness, strongly condition individual preferences and attitudes. Following Steinmetz and Wivel, this article defines smallness as emerging relationally in the context between the state and its external environment.[53] It is the consequence of being the weak part in an asymmetric relationship that makes smallness a useful concept.

In a differentiated social space based on size, the positioning of actors must be hierarchical. Max Weber famously defined hierarchy as a "clearly established system of super- and sub-ordination in which there is a supervision of the lower offices by the higher ones".[54] Weberian stratification theory offers a useful way of thinking about the place of small states in such hierarchical spaces. It becomes possible to speak about international society in terms of stratification when small states take subordinate positions in their routinized relations with larger and more powerful states and when hierarchical patterns persist over time. Thus, although meant in the first instance as a framework to describe the characteristics of bureaucracy, social stratification and hierarchy are features of social life that have an equally powerful bearing on the character of international relations.[55] John Hobson and Jason Sharman argue that hierarchies are themselves formed by 'social logics', which are recognised as legitimate by both the superordinate and subordinate parties.[56] As such, a differentiation based on size can be seen as an important ordering principle of international life.

What are the range of goals that may dominate policy circles in hierarchical spaces? Here, Weber develops a comprehensive scheme for the way in which hierarchical placement is articulated by social actors. He refers to the distribution of social power as emerging along three dominant axes: class (economy) as a result of access to the means of production; status, based on esteem (respect); and party (politics), derived from one's dominance over a legal or administrative system. As phenomena of the distribution of power, hierarchies based on class, status and party "presuppose a comprehensive societalization, and especially a political framework of communal action".[57] Stratification theory thus suggests that certain

---

[50]Knudsen, "Small States, Latent and Extant", 185.
[51]Gvalia et al., "Thinking Outside the Bloc".
[52]Wendt, The State as Person.
[53]Steinmetz and Wivel, Small States in Europe.
[54]Gerth and Mills, From Max Weber, 196.
[55]Lake, Hierarchy in International Relations.
[56]Hobson and Sharman, Hierarchy in World Politics.
[57]Gerth and Mills, From Max Weber, 195.

collective goals are not reducible to individual minds, but rather belong to categories that are themselves universal pursuits of human beings and, by implication, of states. While class refers broadly to the desire to accumulate material rewards, status may refer to the acquisition of such things as prestige, respect, honour or even moral clout. A key advantage of Weberian stratification is that it allows us to identify dominant structural dispositions of material and ideational origin, which are important in the domestic and international spheres of human agency.

In what sense do goals based on class, status and party inform hierarchically-situated small states? In an edited volume about Norway's quest for international status, Benjamin de Carvalho and Iver Neumann make two pertinent claims about weighing the relative importance of power and prestige in the goals pursued by small state actors. Their first claim is that "small powers suffer from status insecurity to an extent that established great powers do not, which makes the status game even more important to them".[58] Because great powers draw status from their advantage in military and economic capabilities in a way that is not open to small states, small states compensate by pursuing status-goods instead. Thus, small states in hierarchical environments are likely to affirm their status and seek recognition more frequently than other states.

The quest for distinguishability, esteem and acknowledgement in international affairs becomes more profound for small states because of an exceptional need to cope with marginality in conventional power terms. As such, status-seeking can be taken as a distinct category in the context of small state foreign policy because it serves the purpose of reclaiming subjectivity. It is precisely as a result of their systematic categorisation that small states seek recognition in spite of their size.

The second claim made by de Carvalho and Neumann is that "status is the condition of filling a place in a social hierarchy" and that the concept of status is "linked not to agency, but to structure."[59] Whilst status refers to the structural feature of the system in which small states operate, this is conceptually separate from status-seeking which is instead an attribute of agency. However, this delineation is problematic because both concepts are clearly related. A focus on status as a structural incentive alone is incomplete and limiting in its analytical utility, unless it is meant to affirm the enduring importance of status in the foreign policy of small states. It does not explain, for example, what particular shape status-seeking takes in some countries compared to others, why some status goals are more strongly pursued than others, and why small states exhibit important variations in seeking status. Greater analytical purchase is obtained in examining foreign policy change when status is treated not as a systemic property, but as a set of ideas explicitly connected to the practice of foreign policy by state elites.

The importance of historical variability in status-seeking is clearly borne out by the example of Qatar. Its turn towards greater international visibility and aggressive state branding was gradual. In the pre-independence days, Qatar's foreign policy was conducted by and through London and decisions were taken in the framework of British geopolitical needs. After the British withdrawal east of Suez in 1971, Qatar and Bahrain refused to join the other Trucial States in an enlarged Emirates. The pursuit of an independent path, however, was made subservient to the Riyadh-Doha connection, as the Qataris "looked to Riyadh

---

[58]Carvalho and Neumann, *Small State Status Seeking*, 1.
[59]*Ibid.*, 7.

implicitly for direction in policy matters and in terms of basic security" and "followed the typical foreign policy decisions taken by other Gulf countries".[60] A deterioration in the relations with Saudi Arabia in the early 1990s and the simultaneous emergence of a new ruling class in Doha made possible the idea that Qatar's future could diverge from that of Saudi Arabia and other GCC states. Reciprocal recognition of Qatar as an independent state and, more importantly, a small state was further entrenched by the time Qatar signed basing agreements with the US in 1992, setting Qatar on a path to pursue the unconventional and outlandish policies it has now become famous for. Qatar was born as a small state, but time was needed for Qatar to develop into a status-seeking actor.

The argument presented here therefore features ideas as a stimulus for structural change, but it explicitly recognises that multiple factors shape the emergence of long-term dispositions in foreign policy. Strategic circumstances in fact cannot be divorced from processes of collective idea-change, nor can material and ideational factors be analysed separately when discussing the foreign policy of small states. Class, status and party as possible determining frames for individual and collective action are nothing more than ideal-types, which need to be kept analytically distinct, even though they are not autonomous in empirical terms. Ideas are important, not because they trump other variables, but because they interact with them to form "a structure within which individual and group decision making takes place".[61]

Status-seeking and foreign policy change in Qatar

Weberian stratification theory reveals that small states are structurally pressured into pursuing status goals when their material capabilities are weak and cannot be improved. This theory provides an alternative account of the shifts and contradictions in Qatar's foreign policy. It also establishes that the structural incentive to pursue status only achieves its full causal potential when conceptions about the role and function of small statehood lead to shifts in the dominant ideas held by foreign policy actors. Small states seek status not only when their material capabilities are low, but especially when they frame their strategic ideas on the basis of their size. This latter claim allows us to pinpoint the sources of foreign policy change in Qatar.

Qatar's emergence as an influential actor in the Middle East is a much debated phenomenon across the IR and Middle East Studies literature. Much of this work focuses on the strategic calculations of Qatari decision-makers since the 1990s, showing how domestic leadership changes have functioned as key critical junctures in Qatar's foreign policy, including the pivotal transfer of power to Sheikh Hamad bin Khalifa Al-Thani in June 1995, and his abdication in favour of Crown Prince Sheikh Tamim bin Hamad Al-Thani in June 2013. The revitalisation of decision-makers from among the royal family, in this view, has ensured that the most qualified, judicious and shrewd have served in the foreign office in Doha.[62] This, in combination with the structural advantages that Qatar enjoys, such as the availability of massive oil and gas resources, the existence of a small and highly apolitical indigenous population and a cohesive and unitary polity, explains why a flexible and energetic foreign policy became possible.[63] Changes in foreign policy cannot be reduced to a

[60]Roberts, "Understanding Qatar's Foreign Policy Objectives", 234.
[61]Legro, *Rethinking the World*, 22.
[62]Kamrava, *Qatar: Small State, Big Politics*.
[63]Ulrichsen, *Qatar and the Arab Spring*, 104.

change in leadership alone, though, compelling us to look to the broader environment to provide the context for Qatar's regional and international ascendance.

Nevertheless, there are two major problems with the existing explanations for foreign policy change in Qatar that Weberian stratification theory might be able to account for more effectively. The first problem is that it is easy to slip into a highly teleological – almost ingratiating view – of Qatar's leadership, ascribing impressive qualities to the ruling elite as if only their miraculous stewardship were important in saving Qatar from international anonymity and geopolitical doom. This is problematic because Qatar's international visibility is as much influenced by the resources that it commands as it has been by the things that it desires, such as power and status. If Qatar's foreign policy is understood only as a function of its immanent qualities, explaining why Qatar's resources have been deployed to such great effect, then capacity is mistaken for intent. Foreign policy transitions in Qatar have not turned out the way they did without ideational context. Max Weber compared such ideational dynamics to switchmen working the railroad as "they point actors, like trains, down tracks in some directions, and divert them from others".[64] While the capabilities that Qatar commands, and the use of it, are important in accounting for Qatar's rapid evolution, they do not necessarily explain the specific nature and direction of this change.

The second problem is that existing accounts do not properly assign causal significance to status as an analytically separate condition in foreign policy. As illustrated by Weberian stratification, it is necessary to keep the behavioural expectations that spawn from smallness analytically separate first, from the question of what Qatar *can* do, and second, from the question of what Qatar *wants* to do. The reduction of status-driven goals to by-products of material factors creates significant problems in terms of accounting for foreign policy change in small states. While material and ideational goals are difficult to disentangle in empirical terms, Qatar's changing foreign policy in a number of areas achieves exactly that which is denied by the conventional view of small states: overcoming the security dilemma and dissolving the bounds of economic dependence. Moreover, this happens not because of vulnerability mitigation per sé, but because foreign policy change is acted upon by an ambitious foreign policy elite, strongly influenced by the hierarchical placement of their state in the international arena.

Status-driven visibility efforts are sometimes designed to be detrimental to the very goal of vulnerability mitigation. This makes Qatar's status-seeking qualitatively different from that of stronger and more powerful states. A full discussion of the manner in which this pans out is beyond the scope of this article, however, an overview of some aspects of Qatar's foreign policy involving a status-seeking perspective may be illuminating.

First of all, contrasting Qatar's mediating role in recent conflicts in Yemen, Lebanon, Palestine and Sudan to the manner in which mediation is traditionally pursued by countries such as Saudi Arabia, reveals a compelling divergence. Qatar's mediation is high-profile and bombastic, with a preference for mediation taking place out in the open rather than behind closed doors. Qatar's efforts are functional to its branding strategy, aimed at boosting Qatar's global reputation. But mediation is also a self-interested strategy intended to maximise influence by maintaining close ties and open lines of communication with friends and adversaries alike.

---

[64]Legro, *Rethinking the World*, 2.

Be that as it may, Qatar's mediation has had mixed results at best. Even in cases where there have been diplomatic achievements, those successes "are often checked by limited capabilities to affect long-term changes to the preferences of the disputants through power projection abilities, in-depth administrative and on-the-ground resources, and apparent underestimations of the complexities of the deep-rooted conflicts at hand".[65] While the inability to follow through on early accomplishments may be a sign of institutional overreach, it may also be the result of long-term policy success not being high on the list of Qatar's priorities.[66] It seems strange that Qatar would be willing to spend substantial financial resources to transport and host large diplomatic delegations for extended periods of time, when it is not properly equipped for the task of sustaining its activities with a serious institutionalised machinery focused on the long-term. Could this be a sign that Qatar is not really interested in being a serious mediator for its own sake, and that the main reason for its willingness to engage in such activities is the rewards that accrue from being *seen* as one?

Secondly, state branding in Qatar is not just a strategic move aimed at creating mutual interdependencies for security reasons. Qatar's soft power initiatives in the area of international media have, in fact, had a destabilising impact on its international alignments. More than any other organisation funded and controlled by Qatar, *Al Jazeera*, to take one example, regularly invites diplomatic controversy, sometimes even the scorn of regional and international partners. In the aftermath of the American invasion and occupation of Iraq after March 2003, Al Jazeera made a name for itself as one of the vocal critics of American policies in the region. Described by some US administration officials as anti-American, at one point there was even talk of US military personnel contemplating putting a stop to Al Jazeera's coverage of the Iraqi insurgency by bombing its headquarters in Doha.[67]

Lastly, Qatar's hedging strategy is deployed inconsistently and is not always risk-free. While Qatar maintains open lines of communication with friends and foes alike, it systematically goes out of step to emphasise its independent position, much to the annoyance of the great powers from which it seeks to stay independent. Qatar manages relations with Saudi Arabia on an eclectic basis, preferring in general to stay as independent as possible from its southern neighbour, but at times also displaying a clear willingness to act in concert with it. As a founding member of the GCC, Qatar has often used the collective body to influence Saudi perceptions about its own ambitions and to mend ties with it during tense periods.

Hedging is easily discarded as a policy orientation when status goods are at stake. In the activism displayed by Qatar in the context of the Arab Spring, Qatar was notably less interested in maintaining its honest broker role, and chose a strategy of taking sides, feeling that its international standing could not suffer the passivity exhibited by most other Gulf states. The perception that Qatar needed to be on the right side of history as the Arab Spring rocked the region, in fact cost Qatar dearly. Intervention generated resistance across the region, particularly on the Arabian Peninsula, leading to Saudi Arabia, the UAE and Bahrain recalling their ambassadors from Doha in March 2014.[68] By embracing change in the pursuit of an exaggerated sense of international visibility, Qatar also damaged its ties with the Syrian regime, Russia and Iran.[69] While a rapprochement with the remnants of Assad's

---

[65]Kamrava, "Mediation and Qatari Foreign Policy".
[66]Barakat, "Qatari Mediation", 2.
[67]Fromherz, *Qatar: A Modern History*, 109.
[68]"Gulf ambassadors pulled from Qatar over 'interference'", *BBC News*, 5 March 2014, http://www.bbc.com/news/world-middle-east-26447914
[69]Ulrichsen, *Qatar and the Arab Spring*, 145-171.

regime is now permanently out of the question, Qatar's Islamist clients are not fully satisfied with the aid they receive either.[70] The Arab Spring left few winners; the only winner left standing was the impression that Qatar, good or bad, was a small state to be reckoned with.

Conclusion

Focusing excessively on the security-inducing and dependency-creating tendencies of the international system risks painting a picture of small states as perennially trapped in material structures. The literature on small states recognises that such constraints may be overcome by skilful pursuit of statecraft, either by leveraging niche capabilities or through a foreign policy strategy that augments the power of small states through international institutions and norms. Qatar's expanding foreign policy is certainly made much more resilient by the alternative ways in which it manages to increase its influence. However, not all activities of small states are intelligible in terms of a focus on vulnerability and vulnerability mitigation.

Drawing on Weberian stratification theory, this article proposes a more relational understanding of small states, situating them in a stratified international context defined by size. As a result of their hierarchical placement, small states acquire an inherent tendency to overcome their disadvantage in conventional power terms through the pursuit of status. Thus, when ideas of smallness take hold, the desire for recognition, intended to overcome smallness, becomes an analytically relevant factor in processes of major foreign policy change. Qatar's emergence as an influential regional and international actor cannot be explained merely on the basis of its increased capabilities and competences, whether understood as an increase in hard, soft, smart or subtle power. Key in the transformation of Qatar has been the ascension of an ambitious foreign policy elite, who has seen Qatar's state-building inextricably linked to the projection of an autonomous and impactful foreign policy.

References

Baehr, P. "Small States: A Tool for Analysis". *World Politics* 27, no. 3 (1975): 456–66.

Barakat, S. *"Qatari Mediation: Between Ambition and Achievement"*, *Brookings Doha Center Analysis Paper 12*. Washington DC: Brookings Institute, November 2014.

Bennett, A., and C. Elman. "Case Study Methods". In *The Oxford Handbook of International Relations*, edited by C. Reus-Smit, and D. Snidal. New York: Oxford University Press, 2008.

Bukovansky, M. "American Identity and Neutral Rights from Independence to the War of 1812". *International Organization* 51, no. 2 (Spring 1997): 209–43.

Carvalho, B., and I.B. Neumann, eds. *Small State Status Seeking: Norway's Quest for International Standing*. London: Routledge, 2015.

---

[70]Kirkpatrick, "Qatar's Support Alienates Allies".

Cooper, A.F., and B. Momani. "Qatar and Expanded Contours of Small State Diplomacy". *The International Spectator* 46, no. 3 (September 2011): 113–28.

Cox, R.W. "Global Perestroika (1992)". In *Approaches to World Order*, edited by R.W. Cox, and T.J. Sinclair. Cambridge UK: Cambridge University Press, 1996.

David, S. *Choosing Sides: Alignment and Realignment in the Third World*. Baltimore, MD: Johns Hopkins University Press, 1991.

Doeser, F. "Domestic Politics and Foreign Policy Change in Small States: the Fall of the Danish 'Footnote Policy'". *Cooperation and Conflict* 46, no. 2 (June 2011): 222–41.

Elman, M.F. "The Foreign Policies of Small States: Challenging Neorealism in its Own Backyard". *British Journal of Political Science* 25, no. 2 (April 1995): 171–217.

Fromherz, A.J. *Qatar: A Modern History*. London: I.B. Tauris, 2012.

Galtung, J. "A Structural Theory of Imperialism". *Journal of Peace Research* 8, no. 2 (1971): 81–117.

Gerth, H.H., and C.W. Mills, eds. *From Max Weber: Essays in Sociology*. New York, NY: Oxford University Press, 1946.

Gvalia, G., D. Siroky, B. Lebanidze and Z. Iashvili. "Thinking Outside the Bloc: Explaining the Foreign Policies of Small States". *Security Studies* 22, no. 1 (2013): 98–131.

Gray, M. *Qatar: Politics and the Challenges of Development*. Boulder, CO: Lynne Rienner Publishers, 2013.

Handel, M. *Weak States in the International System*. London: Frank Cass, 1981.

Hanieh, A. *Capitalism and Class in the Gulf Arab States*. London: Palgrave Macmillan, 2011.

Harknett, R.J., and H.B. Yalcin. "The Struggle for Autonomy: A Realist Structural Theory of International Relations". *International Studies Review* 14, no. 4 (2012): 499–521.

Hey, J., ed. *Small States in World Politics: Explaining Foreign Policy Behavior*. London: Lynne Rienner, 2003.

Hinnebusch, R. *The International Politics of the Middle East*. Manchester, NH: Manchester University Press, 2003.

Hobson, J.M., and J.C. Sharman. "The Enduring Place of Hierarchy in World Politics: Tracing the Social Logics of Hierarchy and Political Change". *European Journal of International Relations* 11, no. 1 (March 2005): 63–98.

Ingebritsen, C. *Small States in International Relations*. Seattle: Washington University Press, 2006.

Ingebritsen, C. "Norm Entrepreneurs: Scandinavia's Role in World Politics". *Cooperation and Conflict: Journal of the Nordic International Studies Association* 37, no. 1 (2002): 11–23.

Kamrava, M. *Qatar: Small State, Big Politics*. New York: Cornell University Press, 2013.

Kamrava, M. "Mediation and Qatari Foreign Policy". *Middle East Journal* 65, no. 4 (Autumn 2011): 539–56.

Katzenstein, P.J. *Small States in World Markets: Industrial Policy in Europe*. New York, NY: Cornell University Press, 1985.

Keohane, R., and J. Nye. *Power and Interdependence*, 4th ed. New York: Longman, 2012.

Kirkpatrick, D.R. "Qatar's Support of Islamists Alienates Allies Near and Far". *The New York Times*, 7 September 2014. https://www.nytimes.com/2014/09/08/world/middleeast/qatars-support-of-extremists-alienates-allies-near-and-far.html

Knudsen, O.F. "Small States, Latent and Extant: Towards a General Perspective". *Journal of International Relations and Development* 5, no. 2 (June 2002): 182–98.

Lake, D. *Hierarchy in International Relations*. New York, NY: Cornell University Press, 2009.

Legro, J.W. *Rethinking the World: Great Power Strategies and International Order*. New York, NY: Cornell University Press, 2005.

Neumann, I.B., and S. Gstöhl. "Lilliputians in Gulliver's World?" In *Small States in International Relations*, edited by C. Ingebritsen, I. Neumann, S. Gstohl, and J. Beyer: 3–36. Seattle, WA: University of Washington Press, 2006.

Nonneman, G. "Determinants and Patterns of Saudi Foreign Policy". In *Saudi Arabia in the Balance: Political Economy, Society, Foreign Affairs*, edited by P. Aarts and G. Nonneman. New York, NY: New York University Press, 2005.

Nye, J.S. *Soft Power: The Means to Success in World Politics*. New York, NY: Public Affair, 2004.

Peterson, J.E. "Qatar and the World: Branding for a Micro-State". *Middle East Journal* 60, no. 4 (Autumn 2006): 732–48.

Roberts, D. "Understanding Qatar's Foreign Policy Objectives". *Mediterranean Politics* 17, no. 2 (2012): 233–9.

Snyder, J. *Myths of Empire: Domestic Politics and International Ambitions*. Ithaca, NY: Cornell University Press, 1991.

Steinmetz, R., and A. Wivel, eds. *Small States in Europe: Challenges and Opportunities*. London: Ashgate Publishing, 2010.

Ulrichsen, K.C. *Insecure Gulf: The End of Certainty and the Transition to the Post-Oil Era*. Oxford: Oxford University Press, 2015.

Ulrichsen, K.C. *Qatar and the Arab Spring*. Oxford: Oxford University Press, 2012.

Vital, D. *The Inequality of States: A Study of Small Power in International Relations*. Oxford: Oxford University Press, 1967.

Wallerstein, I. *The Capitalist World-Economy*. Cambridge UK: Cambridge University Press, 1979.

Walt, S.M. *The Origins of Alliances*. Ithaca, NY: Cornell University Press, 1987.

Waltz, K.N. *Theory of International Politics*. Reading, Mass.: Addison-Wesley, 1979.

Watson, A. *Diplomacy: The Dialogue Between States*. London: Eyre Methuen, 1982.

Wendt, A. "The State as Person in International Theory". *Review of International Studies* 30, no. 2 (April 2004): 289–316.

Wendt, A. *Social Theory of International Politics*. Cambridge: Cambridge University Press, 1999.

Worth, R.F. "Qatar, Playing All Sides, is a Nonstop Mediator". *The New York Times*, 9 July 2008.

Wright, S. "Foreign Policies with International Reach: The Case of Qatar". In *The Transformation of the Gulf: Politics, Economics and the Global Order*, edited by D. Held, and K.C. Ulrichsen: 303–4. London: Routledge, 2011.

Beyond Money and Diplomacy: Regional Policies of Saudi Arabia and UAE after the Arab Spring

Eman Ragab

ABSTRACT
The post-Arab Spring context created a window of opportunity for Saudi Arabia and the United Arab Emirates to reposition themselves in the region as countries capable of using not only money and diplomacy, but also military means in pursuing their regional policies. Their military interventions in Bahrain in 2011 and Yemen in 2015 uncover different aspects of the militarisation of their foreign policies. The permanence of the militarisation of their policies is, however, challenged by the type of interventionist state unfolding from these muscular policies, their domestic and regional legitimacy and the institutionalisation of this foreign policy pattern.

Five years after the 'Arab Spring' swept through the Arab region at the end of 2010, the Kingdom of Saudi Arabia and the United Arab Emirates (UAE) are among the most active players in the region. They are no longer concerned only with avoiding the wave of changes triggered by the Spring, but now pursue an active interventionist foreign policy in some Arab countries that they perceive as a threat to their national security and their role in the region.

The increasing activism in Saudi and Emirati regional policies is no longer based on money and diplomacy alone, as it used to be, but also on military means. They have intervened in Bahrain in 2011, in Libya in 2011, in Iraq and Syria against the so-called 'Islamic State of Iraq and Syria' (ISIS) since September 2014, and in Yemen since March 2015. In other words, the scope of these new military interventionist policies extends beyond Bahrain, once considered the only country in which they would be willing to intervene.[1]

While there are differences in the interests being served,[2] the level of military intervention, and the type of perceived threats that drive their policies, what is of interest is that all interventions have been within multilateral frameworks. These frameworks are either part of existing regional organisations, as is the case of the Gulf Cooperation Council (GCC)'s al-Jazeera Shield Forces and NATO's military operations, or they have been created by the United States and joined by the two countries, as in the case of the International Coalition

---

[1] Colombo and Ragab, "The Legitimacy Question in Saudi Arabia".
[2] On Saudi and Emirati interests in the context of the Arab Spring, see Ragab, "Tactical Alliance?". On Saudi interests, see Echagüe, "Saudi Arabia: emboldened yet vulnerable".

against ISIS, or created by Saudi Arabia, as in the case of the Arab Alliance, which is carrying out the military operations in Yemen.

This article argues that the growing militarisation of Saudi Arabia's and the UAE's foreign policies is repositioning the two countries in the region in terms of their status and regional roles, but that the outcome of this repositioning process is contingent on their ability to preserve the continuity of this foreign policy pattern.

To that end, the article examines specific aspects of the militarisation of Saudi and Emirati foreign policies in two cases: Bahrain in 2011 and Yemen in 2015. It then attempts to identify the drivers of this development by analysing the threats perceived by the ruling elites in both countries as reflected in their official discourse. The article also attempts to examine the outcome of the Saudi and Emirati foreign policies in terms of the type of regional role unfolding from the militarisation of their policies.

The article is divided into three sections. The first identifies the internal and external drivers of the Saudis' and Emirates' increasing reliance on military means in pursuing their foreign policies. The second section looks more deeply into this development by examining the roles of the two countries in Bahrain in 2011 and Yemen in 2015. In the third section, the challenges that could undermine the continuity of this pattern in Saudi and Emirati regional policies are discussed. The conclusion discusses the future of the Saudi and Emirati roles in the region.

The shift towards militarised foreign policies

Saudi and Emirati foreign policies in the pre-Arab Spring period were characterised by the absence of military means in the region. Thomas Richter and Khaled Almeziani, in their works on Saudi Arabia and the Emirates, used the term "quiet diplomacy" to describe their foreign policy actions.[3] According to Martin Adelmann, this meant extensive reliance on diplomatic means, and diplomatic efforts that "take place in behind-the-scenes negotiations" which "increase the chance of finding a diplomatic solution".[4] The two countries used diplomacy based on "compromises, direct negotiations [and] reasonable propositions" to "get the things done" and to secure a role for themselves.[5] In practice, it meant increasing reliance on financial tools, as well as on a broad network of personal relationships with the main policymakers and politicians in the world.[6] As argued by Bahgat Korany and Motaz Abdel Fattah, Saudi Arabia has used Islam and oil in pursuing its foreign policies in the region since the 1960s.[7] Gregory Gause argues that it also used "diplomatic balancing and its own transnational ideological networks".[8] The UAE, according to Almeziani, also used only two tools in its foreign policies after Khalifa bin Zayed Al Nahyan took power in 2004, foreign aid programs and its network of relations with the world's politicians to favour "conciliation, neighborliness, amicable relations with other countries and peaceful settlements of disputes".[9]

---

3 Richter, "Saudi Arabia"; Almezaini, *The UAE and Foreign Policy*.
4 Adelmann, "Quiet Diplomacy", 254.
5 Al-Mashat, "Politics of Constructive Engagement", 458; *Ibid.*; respectively.
6 Hubbard, "Saud al-Faisal of Saudi Arabia".
7 Korany and Fattah, "Irreconcilable Role Partners", 365–8.
8 Gause, "Saudi Arabia's Regional Security Strategy", 13.
9 Al-Mashat, "Politics of Constructive Engagement", 458.

Use of diplomatic means positioned Saudi Arabia as the only player in Arab affairs "capable of challenging the Iranian ambition in Iraq and Lebanon, with Egypt lagging behind owing to critical domestic problems".[10] Amir Abdullah bin Abdulaziz Al Saud's peace initiative of 2002 and his position towards the July 2006 war between Hezbollah and Israel are indicative of this.[11] He had a vision for active Saudi regional policies relying on "religious allure and *Realpolitik* to help shape its sphere of influence".[12] The UAE, on the other hand, was active in supporting the Palestinians financially and diplomatically, and proposed a political initiative to foil the potential US attack on Iraq in 2003 involving a "gradual transfer of power under the supervision of the UN and the Arab League and [an invitation to] Saddam to resign and to live in the UAE".[13] Later, the UAE opened up its territories to the Iraqi Sunni opposition groups.[14] According to Korany and Fattah, the vulnerability of these two countries caused by the transformations in their geopolitical environment following the US invasion of Iraq in 2003,[15] the increasing pressures from the US administration to initiate domestic political reforms, and the increasing influence of Iran in the region explain the adoption of this pattern of policies.

The uprisings that swept the region after 2010 triggered a wave of changes in the foreign policies of Saudi Arabia and the UAE. They were not concerned only with avoiding the spillover effects of the Arab Spring via subsidies or repression,[16] but started to pursue active interventionist policies in some Arab countries where events were perceived as a source of threat to their security.

There are two dimensions to this development. The first is the adoption of military interventionist policies towards other Arab countries. Saudi Arabia, the old player in the region, has become less reluctant to use its army in pursuing its regional interests. Together with the UAE, it sent its national army to Bahrain in 2011 under the umbrella of the al-Jazeera Shield Forces, and to Libya in 2011, along with Qatar, Morocco and Jordan, as part of the NATO Operation Unified Protector against former President Muammar Qadhafi,[17] and to Iraq and Syria against ISIS, along with Jordan, as part of the US International Coalition since September 2014 (expressed readiness in February 2016 to take part in ground operations in Syria if they take place[18]) and to Yemen under the umbrella of the Arab Coalition since March 2015.

---

[10]Korany and Fattah, "Irreconcilable Role Partners", 367.

[11]The Saudi peace initiative called on Israel to withdraw from all Arab territories it had occupied on 7 June 1967, recognise the independent state of Palestine with its capital in East Jerusalem, and agree to a just resolution of the refugees problem. In exchange, there would be Pan-Arab recognition of Israel's right to exist and to security. According to Korany and Fattah, this proposal "was the most momentous and far-reaching" ever put forward. In the case of Lebanon, Saudi Arabia blamed Hezbollah for having triggered the war with Israel, fully supported the Lebanese government, and at the same time criticised Israel's escalating policies. This position was unexpected, as many analysts thought that Saudi Arabia would fully support Hezbollah, following in the steps of Egypt. See *Ibid.*, 381–2, 373–7.

[12]*Ibid.*, 347.

[13]The initiative was first announced at the Arab Summit in March 2003, but was not supported by any Arab state. Al-Mashat, "Politics of Constructive Engagement", 472–3.

[14]On UAE foreign policy, see Almezaini, *The UAE and Foreign Policy,* 44–50.

[15]Korany and Fattah, "Irreconcilable Role Partners", 366.

[16]See Colombo and Ragab, "The Legitimacy Question in Saudi Arabia".

[17]NATO, "NATO and Libya"; Daalder and Stavridis, "NATO's Success in Libya"; *Foxnews*, "UAE Draws Praise From U.S. for Participation in Libya", 24 March 2011, http://www.foxnews.com/world/2011/03/24/uae-draws-praise-participation-libya.html.

[18]Emirati Minister of State of Foreign Affairs Anwar Gergash mentioned that "US leadership" would be a prerequisite for his country to take part in the ground operations. See also, Watkinson, "Syria conflict: UAE will join"; Maclean, "War with ISIS".

The second is that Saudi Arabia, with the support of the UAE, is becoming active in forming military coalitions through which they can carry out their interventionist policies. It formed the Arab Coalition in March 2015, joined by ten countries, in order to provide regional legitimacy for the intervention in Yemen. It also formed the Islamic Military Alliance to Fight Terrorism (IMAFT) in December 2015, joined by 34 Islamic countries, aiming at providing an umbrella under which it can counter terrorist organisations in Syria.[19] These two dimensions are manifestations of an unprecedented development in the two countries' military capabilities and their ability to coordinate with other countries.

Main drivers

In the context of the Arab Spring, two main drivers can help explain the militarisation of the Saudi and Emirati policies. The first is an internal development, that is, the shifting perceptions of the two countries regarding what represents a threat to their national security. According to the threat perceptions model, perceived threats are important factors in shaping the foreign policies of any country. For decades, Iran's 'imperialistic' policies have been framed in the official discourse of Saudi Arabia and to a lesser degree in that of the UAE as the main external threat.[20] For example, Saudi official discourse used to consider "the Iranian conspiracy" as the main explanation for political unrest in many Gulf countries after the Iraq-Iran war (1980–88).[21] It also portrayed the attempted coups in Kuwait and Bahrain in the 1980s as carried out by "pro-Iran opposition" groups.[22]

However, the 'spring' of armed conflicts in the GCC's neighbouring countries, namely Iraq, Syria and Yemen, turned these countries into new sources of threats. On the one hand, there are ISIS, Syrian and Yemeni refugees, the collapse of the central unified states, and the political advances of the Muslim Brotherhood (MB). On the other hand, there are threats emanating from Iran's policies in the region and its strategy of empowering Shiite political groups and their local 'allies' to control local authorities, increasing Tehran's role in settling the conflicts in the region and, in the future, the share of Iran's allies in the transitional governments once the conflicts are settled.[23] Thus, they consider the Shiite –Sunni conflict as the main threat to regional security and are acting in order to strengthen the Sunni pillar.

For the Saudis, threats emanating from Iran's policies are still important and need to be countered through militarised foreign policies. This is the case according to Saudi narrations not only in Bahrain, Iraq and Yemen, but also in Syria. For example, Brigadier General Ahmad Asiri affirmed that the continuous military exercises carried out by Saudi Arabia are "a clear message to Iran, that the countries in the region that support any hostile intentions and actions, will be firmly dealt with".[24]

For the UAE, the main perceived threat to its national security is the MB, and it is designated a terrorist organisation there. The local version of the MB, *al-Islah*, is not allowed to practice political activity. For instance, Dhahi Khalfan the head of Dubai police, pointed

---

[19]Browning and Irish, "Saudi Arabia announces 34-state alliance".
[20]Sadeghi and Ahmadian, "Iran-Saudi Relations: Past Pattern"; Kaye and Wehrey, "Containing Iran?".
[21]Cordesman, *Bahrain, Oman, Qatar, and the UAE*, 78.
[22]A coup d'état was attempted in Bahrain in December 1981 by elements the regime described as loyal to Iran. See *Ibid.*, 78. The same narration was confirmed by a number of Bahraini officials interviewed by the author in Bahrain and Cairo in December and March 2012. They prefer not to be named.
[23]Al Tamamy, "Saudi Arabia and the Arab Spring", 193–4; Salavatian *et al.* "Iran and Saudi Arabia", 141–9.
[24]Henderson, *Desert Stretch*.

out on 18 January 2012 that "[t]he MB threat to Gulf security is equivalent in importance to the Iranian threat".[25] According to Emiratis' perceptions, having the MB in power in any of the Arab Spring countries could inspire *al-Islah* to push for political change in the UAE. Thus, it took a firm position against providing any financial aid to Egypt during the MB's time in government from June 2012 to June 2013. At the time, the Emirates' foreign minister, Abdullah bin Zayed, criticised the MB for not respecting national boundaries and accused them of plotting to "undermine states' sovereignty". He called upon all GCC countries to cooperate to confront this threat.[26] According to a high-ranking Emirati security official, Qatari policies at the time were also perceived as a "source of threat" to the Emirates' national security. He stated that, "Qatar no longer provides strategic depth to the UAE as it should".[27]

The second main development is the power vacuum created by the 'priorities gap' between US President Barack Obama's administration (2008–16) and GCC countries. Obama preferred not to become deeply involved in the conflicts in the region, fearing a second 'Iraq 2003', and simply wanted to maintain the oil and arms sales.[28] The GCC countries considered these policies a setback in their relations with Washington, one that would open up room for Russia, Iran and its allies to play influential roles in ways that do not serve GCC interests. It also drove many politicians in the UAE and Saudi Arabia to assess the limits of US military support in case they faced a genuine threat to their national security from either ISIS or Iran.[29]

Finally, the occupation of Iraq in 2003 and its disastrous consequences, the complexities of the transition in Egypt since the fall of the Mubarak regime in 2011, and the ongoing armed conflict in Syria since 2011 have made it less realistic for Saudi Arabia and the UAE to be able to rely on these three countries, which used to be the traditional regional powers maintaining stability in the region. This motivated them to step in to fill the power vacuum, even if it requires using their own military arsenals.

As a result, these developments have created two intertwined priorities that are driving the increasing militarisation of Emirati and Saudi foreign policies: countering what is perceived as a threat to their national security and repositioning themselves as regional powers that cannot be overlooked or ignored when negotiating the future of the region with their old ally, the United States, or with the new player in the region, Russia.

The militarisation of the two countries' regional policies coincides in Saudi Arabia with a new vision engineered by the young Emir Mohammad Bin Salman, the deputy Crown Prince, who is keen on strengthening his position as the successor to his father, King Salman (who took power in Jan 2015), through assertive and muscular foreign policies. The 2030 vision announced by the young Emir in April 2016, in addition to providing a blueprint for the economic reforms required to walk away from the oil age,[30] redefines the structural pillars of strength needed for the country to play "the leading role in the Arab and Islamic world".[31]

---

[25]"UAE: Gulf States must Stop Plotters", *Gulf Times*, 9 October 2012.

[26]Ragab, "Tactical Alliance?", 109.

[27]Interview with a high-ranking UAE security official, Abu Dhabi, February 2014.

[28]See, for example, the speech of US Secretary of Defense Chuck Hagel at the 2014 Manama Dialogue, 7 December 2013, http://archive.defense.gov/speeches/speech.aspx?speechid=1824

[29]Al-Rasheed, "Saudi Arabia Pushes US toward Strike".

[30]Kinninmont, "Saudi Arabia Faces its Future".

[31]Saudi Vision 2030, 26 April 2016, http://vision2030.gov.sa/en

The UAE is also continuing to broaden its clout in the region by intervening in the main conflicts in neighbouring Arab countries, that is relying on military as well as financial tools and diplomatic means.[32] According to a high-ranking Emirati security official, since the Arab Spring, the UAE is ambitious to play an influential role in the region to "serve its national interests, containing the side effects of the Qatari policies towards the political future of the Muslim Brotherhood, and absorbing the tensions regarding the future of the region together with Saudi Arabia".[33] This has led to the creation of a "Saudi -Emirati pillar" based on a "strategic partnership".[34] The two countries launched a joint coordination council in May 2016 to coordinate their views and policies.[35]

Aspects of militarisation in the cases of Bahrain and Yemen

The cases of Bahrain in 2011 and Yemen in 2015 reveal important aspects of the militarised policies of Saudi Arabia and the UAE. The conflicts are perceived in different ways by the two countries in terms of both the type of threats emanating from them and the military interventions themselves.

Bahrain

Bahrain enjoys a special status due not only to its geographical proximity to the Eastern Province of Saudi Arabia, but also as a zone of historical confrontations and rivalry between Saudi Arabia and Iran. To a large extent, the influence of these two countries in Bahrain reflects the influence they can exercise in the Gulf region.[36] Historically, Saudi Arabia has shown a willingness to provide assistance to Bahrain, especially after the 1981 attempted *coup d'état*, carried out, as narrated by the regime, by pro-Iranian opposition figures.[37] During the mid-1990s, when unrest erupted in Bahrain, Saudi Arabia sent its troops to support the regime in confronting the opposition. In the economic field, Saudi Arabia provides Bahrain with important quantities of oil from the Abu Saafa field to fulfil its needs.[38]

The Emirati leaders are more pragmatic in their views towards Bahrain, but tend to act in accordance with Saudi policies and not stand against them because they understand that Bahrain is an integral part of Saudi national security concerns. What is important to them is to keep the situation there under control. Some Emirati officials feel Bahrain could "follow in the steps of Kuwait, and end up with failed governance, thus representing a model that no one in the Gulf wants to follow".[39]

Based on these perceptions, Saudi Arabia was in the lead in responding to the 14 February 2011 protests that evolved on the third day into a sit-in at the Pearl Roundabout. Since the

---

[32]The Emirates' leaked emails shows that they were trying to shape the transitional political settlement in Libya. For more, see Kirkpatrick, "Emirati Emails Could Threaten Peace".

[33]Interview with a high-ranking Emirati security official, who prefers not to be named, Abu Dhabi, February 2014.

[34]"Anwar Gargash: Emirati troops continue their fight along with Saudi Arabia until the Coalition announces the end of war", *CNN Arabic* (in Arabic), 16 June 2016; "Mohamed Bin Zayed Visits King Salman", *CNN Arabic* (in Arabic), 21 October 2016.

[35]"UAE and Saudi form joint council", *The National*, 16 May 2016.

[36]On the strategic importance of Bahrain to Saudi Arabia and Iran, see Mabon, "The Battle for Bahrain"; Wehrey *et al.*, *Saudi-Iranian Relations*, 53–4.

[37]Colombo and Ragab, "The Legitimacy Question in Saudi Arabia".

[38]"Bahrain is planning to increase the oil provided by Saudi Arabia day" (in Arabic), *Al-Arabiya net*, 3 November 2012, https://www.alarabiya.net/articles/2012/11/03/247383.html

[39]Interview with a high-ranking Emirati security official, who prefers not to be named, Abu Dhabi, October 2013.

cause of the demonstrations in Bahrain was judged to be the deterioration of the economic situation and social services, it provided Bahrain with a GCC package of USD 20 billion to be allocated to infrastructure and housing projects in the following years.[40] The situation continued nevertheless to deteriorate and a state of national emergency was called. In order to strengthen the ability of the Bahraini regime to "restore order and security" and "protect government facilities",[41] on 14 March 2011, the GCC's Peninsula Shield Force entered Bahrain.

Saudi Arabia led these forces and contributed about 1,200 soldiers; the UAE sent 600 police officers.[42] Saudi leaders were much keener than UAE leaders on maintaining the structure of power in Bahrain intact, thus avoiding any fundamental shift in favour of the opposition groups, as this would have weakened Saudi influence and strengthened Iranian influence in Bahrain. Emirati leaders, on the other hand, perceived the 2011 unrest in Bahrain as "another threat emanating from a failed democratic transition that can only be contained by rational management of the situation".[43] They were providing advice to the al-Khalifa family without any political agenda or intervention.[44]

The continuous presence of Saudi and Emirati troops in Bahrain in the following years nevertheless represented a source of concern for the Saudi regime, given that the largest share of the Peninsula Shield Force was provided by Riyadh. There was the prospect of becoming a target of the violent opposition groups in Bahrain, namely the '14 February' youth movement, especially after a permanent headquarters for these troops was established in that country.[45] Furthermore, while the role of these permanent forces was officially to protect the infrastructure, it seems they have at times become involved in confrontations with the opposition.[46]

It can be argued that this permanent presence, along with the appointment of Prince Muqrin bin Abdulaziz as the second Deputy Prime Minister during the era of King Abdullah,[47] resulted in a shift toward moderation in Saudi policies regarding Bahrain – from security intervention towards more political intervention – in an attempt to repeat the scenario of the Saudi-led political settlement in Yemen in 2011. It also coincided with increasing American pressure on the Saudi and Bahraini regimes to end the political crisis in the country peacefully. The change was mirrored in the appointment of Bahraini Crown Prince Salman as the First Deputy Prime Minister on 11 March 2013, a clear indication of

---

[40]"GCC decides to assist Manama and Muscat with $20 billion", *Asharq Al-Awsat* (in Arabic), 11 March 2011.

[41]Interview with Bahraini official who prefers not to be named, Bahrain, April 2012. Many Bahraini politicians considered the situation "a victory of the protesters over the regime". Interview with Bahraini leaders in the National Unity Gathering who prefer not to be named, Bahrain, March 2012.

[42]See Katzman, "Bahrain: Reform, Security", 95–101; "Kuwait Sends Navy Troops to Bahrain", *France 24* (in Arabic), 21 March 2011, http://www.france24.com/ar/20110321-bahrain-kuwait-qatar-saudi-arabia-protests-shiite-ship; "A Qatari Official: Qatari Troops Sent to Bahrain to Maintain Order and Security" (in Arabic), *Al Wasat* newspaper, 19 March 2011, http://www.alwasatnews.com/3116/news/read/532870/3116/news/read/532942/1.html; "GCC troops dispatched to Bahrain to maintain order" (in Arabic).*Al-Arabiya*, 14 March 2011: https://www.alarabiya.net/articles/2011/03/14/141506.html.

[43]Interview with a high-ranking Emirati security official, who prefers not to be named, Abu Dhabi, May 2014.

[44]Interview with a Bahraini leader in the National Unity Gathering, who prefers not to be named, Bahrain, March 2012.

[45]See, "A permanent headquarters for Peninsula Shield in Bahrain" (in Arabic), *Al Hayat* newspaper, 16 April 2013.

[46]For instance, in March 2014, an Emirati officer was killed by a bomb at *Daih* near Manama. Holmes, "Military intervention the world forgot".

[47]Prince Muqrin's appointment gave greater influence to the moderate faction in the House of Saud, which also includes Prince Miteb bin Abdullah, one of King Abdullah's sons and commander of the National Guard, whose paramilitary forces constitute the majority of the Peninsula Shield Forces units that intervened in Bahrain. They also played a role in supporting the King of Bahrain's call for national dialogue on 21 Jan 2013. Before this date, Bahraini Crown Prince Salman bin Hamad had called many times for dialogue with the opposition, but was not supported by the ruling family. Henderson, "The Bahraini royal policy". For details, see also Al-Hassan, *The Path of National Dialogue* (in Arabic).

a serious Saudi and Bahraini desire to find a political solution to the conflict between the Shiite opposition and the Sunni royal family.[48]

Not much political progress has been achieved since then however. After the death of King Abdullah in Jan 2015, King Salman maintained the presence of the permanent headquarter of the Al-Jazeera Shield Forces, but there is no evidence that they are helping the Bahraini regime to settle the conflict politically. Instead, the latter is becoming harsher in restricting the political activities of opposition groups. For instance, in May 2016, the activities of the main Shiite opposition group, *al-Wefaq*, were suspended and its funds frozen. Also, in June 2016, with the accusation of "creating a new generation that carries the spirit of hatred and of having links with sectarian and extremist political parties that adopt terrorism", the Bahraini court ordered the group to be dissolved.[49] The regime also stripped the leading Shia cleric, Sheikh Isa Qassim, of his citizenship, accusing him of "creating a sectarian atmosphere and of forming groups that follow foreign religious ideologies and political entities".[50]

Yemen

In the case of Yemen, the Saudi and Emirati responses to the conflict that erupted on 6 February 2015, when the Houthi groups announced their 'Constitutional Declaration' to overthrow Abd Rabbou Hadi's government, was a reflection of the perceived importance of Yemen, not only to their national security, but also to their regional roles.[51] For Riyadh, Yemen is a hornets' nest: if it breaks up, it will be hard to contain all the fragments. Apart from the Houthi who, as portrayed by Saudi Arabia and the UAE, are supported by Iran,[52] al-Qaeda and other terrorist groups enjoy a safe haven there, and are said to be using it as a base for launching "a regional plot" aimed at "destabilizing the countries in the region".[53] Houthi groups have attacked the Saudi cities of Najran and Jezan since the start of Decisive Storm, launched around 24 SSM missiles into the Kingdom, targeted security checkpoints and carried out military ambushes on the borders with Saudi Arabia.[54] According to Ali Omeir al-Shahrani, Najran's Civil Defence Spokesperson, the "cross-border militia rockets have at least partially damaged or destroyed 1,074 homes; 108 commercial stores were attacked and 420 civilian cars were burned".[55]

In the case of the UAE, the spillover effects of the conflict are also a central concern. The significant number of Yemeni workers in the Emirates' security institutions, especially the police, makes it possible that their internal interactions could be shaped by the dynamics

---

[48]"Appointing the Crown Prince as a Deputy Prime Minister gives hope to the opposition", *BBC Arabic* (in Arabic), 12 March 2013, http://www.bbc.co.uk/arabic/middleeast/2013/03/130312_bahrain_prince_nomination.shtml.

[49]"Bahrain court orders Shia opposition group to be dissolved", *The Guardian*.17 July 2016.

[50]*Ibid.*

[51]Usher, "Yemen crisis".

[52]"Al-Faysal: we are not at war with Iran"(in Arabic), *al-Raya* daily, 13 April 2015, http://www.raya.com/home/print/f6451603-4dff-4ca1-9c10-122741d17432/f6c1dbfd-1df9-4e64-bf7c-cb53481cb260

[53]"Saudi king: Yemen war launched to foil regional plot", *al-Arabiya*, 10 May 2015, http://english.alarabiya.net/en/News/middle-east/2015/05/10/Saudi-king-Yemen-war-launched-to-foil-regional-plot.html

[54]Knights and Mello, *The Saudi-UAE War Effort in Yemen (Part 2): The Air Campaign,* and *Gulf Coalition Operations in Yemen (Part 1): The Ground War,* respectively.

[55]Naar, "Najran citizens vow to stay".

of the conflict in Yemen in a way that would affect the Emirates' national security. Also, the future of the *al-Islah* party, the Yemeni MB, in any new power configuration after the conflict is an important issue as the UAE considers the political activism of the MB in a neighbouring country as a threat to its national security.

In accordance with these perceptions, in 2015, the UAE emerged as an important party in the Arab Coalition leading the military operations in Yemen. Its main mission was to train and support the 'popular resistance' groups, the pro-Hadi groups, in their military confrontations with the Houthi.[56] With time, its role changed from a country participating in the operations guided by the "leadership of King Salman"[57] to a co-leader of operations, in terms of both force numbers and the quality of operations it is carrying out inside Yemen. During the Decisive Storm Operation begun in March 2015, the UAE participated with 30 F16s and Merag 2000s.[58] Since then, it has deployed 1,500 of the UAE's elite military,[59] a significant number of special operation troops, national service conscripts, as well as troops from Colombia and Eritrea.[60] The total number of Emirati troops on the ground in September 2015 was estimated at 4,000, most of whom were of Omani origin.[61]

According to many reports, the UAE is leading ground operations in the south and the east[62] and managed to free Aden and Taiz in July 2016, while Saudi Arabia is leading operations in the north, targeting the strongholds and artillery of Saleh and the Houthi, as well as providing air support for the ground operations. Both also play important roles in the naval blockades around the Yemeni coasts.[63] In addition, they are setting up military bases in the Horn of Africa in order to monitor the strait of Bab al-Mandab. The UAE set up a military facility in Eritrea in 2015, and a military base in Somaliland in February 2017,[64] while Saudi Arabia is seeking to set up a military base in Djibouti.[65]

However, the future military role of the UAE is uncertain. Although Minister of State Anwar Gargash announced on 15 June 2016 that his country's role in the war in Yemen was over and that it was "monitoring political arrangements, empowering Yemenis in liberated areas" – an announcement that was retweeted by Crown Prince Mohamed Bin Zayed's official Twitter account – Gargash stated on 18 June that his statement had been "taken out of context and misinterpreted".[66] More recently, announcements of the death of three Emirati soldiers in Yemen on 4 and 17 Feb 2017[67] and the Emirates' participation in the

---

[56]"UAE supports the legitimate authority in Yemen and sends new troops"(in Arabic), *al-Bayan*, 29 April 2016.

[57]"Mohamed Bin Zayed praises King Salman's decisiveness and reaffirms support for the brothers", *The New Khaleej portal* (in Arabic), 27 April 2015, http://thenewkhalij.org/node/13418

[58]Knights and Mello, *The Saudi-UAE War Effort (Part 2)*.

[59]This group of soldiers is led by Australian General Mike Hindmarsh, who oversaw the guard's formation in early 2010. See Donaghy, "Mercenaries commanding UAE forces".

[60]Some national service conscripts were sent to fight in Yemen, but this was stopped in September 2015 after 45 Emirati conscripts were killed in a Houthi attack (*Ibid.*) For Colombians and Eritreans, see Hager and Mazzetti, "Emirates send Colombian mercenaries"; and Knights and Mello, *Gulf Coalition Operations (Part 1)*, respectively.

[61]"Emirati Brigade reveals the size of the UAE forces in Yemen"(in Arabic), *Ababiil.net*, 16 September 2015. http://ababiil. net/yemen-news/32734.html

[62]Knights, "The U.A.E. Approach to Counterinsurgency".

[63]Knights, "What did Gulf Coalition War Achieve?".

[64]Shafqat, "UAE to open second military base".

[65]"Djibouti finalizing pact soon for Saudi military base", *Al Arabiya English*, 18 January 2017, https://english.alarabiya.net/ en/News/gulf/2017/01/18/Djibouti-finalizing-pact-soon-for-Saudi-military-base.html

[66]"UAE: 'War is over' for Emirati troops in Yemen", *Al Jazeera online*, 17 June 2016, http://www.aljazeera.com/news/2016/06/ uae-war-emirati-troops-yemen-160616044956779.html; "My statement was taken out of context, UAE is continuing war in support of legitimacy in Yemen, says Gargash". *WAM*, 17 June 2016. http://wam.ae/en/details/1395296822308, respectively.

[67]Al-Masri, "UAE soldier killed".

first counterterrorism operation approved by the new US administration on 28 Jan 2017 targeting al-Qaeda in Yakla[68] reveal that its troops are still involved in the war.

Regarding a political settlement, the UAE and Saudi Arabia agree on the importance of a political settlement to the conflict on the basis of the 2011 Gulf initiative,[69] the outcome of the January 2014 National Dialogue, and UNSCR 2216.[70] The UAE is attempting, through its presence on the ground in Aden, to redefine the new power structure that will take shape after the conflict. The Emirates' main objective is to reduce the share of the Yemeni MB as much as possible by increasing the share of other parties, including those of Saleh and the Houthi group. The Saudis, on the other hand, are keen on maintaining the same balance of power that backed Hadi and marginalised the role of the Houthi. Thus, the UAE is more flexible regarding the Houthi than the Saudis, even though it has labelled it as a terrorist organisation, but is less flexible regarding the Yemeni MB.[71] Its political preferences have not been reflected, however, in the political talks with the Houthi that took place in Riyadh in May 2015, [72] and recommenced in Kuwait in April 2016. This is because they refuse to ally with the Yemeni MB and their allies,[73] whom they blame for having let Taiz fall into the hands of the Houthi.[74] The UAE seems to be in favour of the separation of the South, where it exercises an important influence after the battle for Aden, while the Saudis prefer a unified Yemen in accordance with the Gulf initiative and UNSC Resolution 2216.[75]

In order to deal with the humanitarian aspect of the conflict, in May 2015, Saudi Arabia established the King Salman's Center for Humanitarian Aid in Riyadh to provide assistance to the Yemeni people, and also opened a branch in Aden. Until August 2015, it had been funded by around USD 4 million. The UAE also provided aid to the approximately 1.1 million Yemenis, mainly in Aden, which amounted to around USD 202 million in 2015.[76]

Limitations and challenges

Bahrain and Yemen have been examined to try to unpack the developing pattern of militarisation of Saudi and Emirati foreign policies in the Arab region. Bahrain could be considered a 'normal' case, while Yemen represents the 'exceptional model', that is, one that is not expected to be repeated in other conflicts like Syria.

---

[68]"Two brave Emirati soldiers martyred". *Khaleej Times*.7 Feb 2014. Gibbons-Neff and Ryan, "Lesson for Trump's national security team".

[69]The initiative was proposed to put an end to the protest against Yemeni President Ali Abdullah Saleh. It led Saleh to leave the presidency in November 2011 and provided him with legal immunity as he transferred power to his deputy, Abd-Rabu Mansour Hadi. The initiative defined a transitional period during which a new constitution would be drafted, along with a plan to reconstruct the military, and presidential elections held. See *United Nations Web Portal*, "Agreement on the implementation mechanism for the transition process in Yemen in accordance with the initiative of the Gulf Cooperation Council (GCC)", 5 December 2011, http://peacemaker.un.org/sites/peacemaker.un.org/files/YE_111205_Agreement%20 on%20the%20implementation%20mechanism%20for%20the%20transition.pdf

[70]"The Saudi King gives the parties of the conflict in Yemen an opportunity to dialogue"(in Arabic), *Middle East Online*, 30 March 2015, http://www.middle-east-online.com/?id=197043; "King Salman: We are keen on reaching a political settlement in Syria and Yemen"(in Arabic), *Al-Arabiya online* , 16 November 2015. http://www.alarabiya.net/ar/saudi-today/2015/11/16/

[71]The UAE adopts the same stances towards Libya. See Kirkpatrick, "Emirati Emails Could Threaten Peace".

[72]"Riyadh Meeting. A Comprehensive Document to End the Conflict in Yemen"(in Arabic), *SkyNews Arabiya online*, 18 May 2015, http://www.skynewsarabia.com/web/article/746128/

[73]Donaghy, "Mercenaries commanding UAE forces".

[74]"UAE blames Muslim Brotherhood for lack of victory in Yemen", *Middle East Eye*, 24 November 2015, http://www.middleeast-eye.net/news/uae-blames-islamists-delay-against-rebels-yemen-province-979771572#sthash.vwlsy5jH.dpuf

[75]United States share the same stances with Riyadh. See Sharp, *Yemen: Civil War*.

[76]"The UAE is the Largest Aid Provider for Yemen" (in Arabic), *SkyNews Arabiya online*, 6 August 2015, http://www.skynews-arabia.com/web/article/765390/; "Total Emirati Humanitarian aid to Yemen amounts to 744 million Dirham" (in Arabic), *Emaratalyoum*, 13 August 2015, http://www.emaratalyoum.com/politics/issues/yemen-latest/2015-08-14-1.811405

However, the continued militarisation of their policies is hindered by two predicaments. The first is the importance of the multilateral frameworks as umbrellas under which they can exercise their muscular policies. According to Nolte, this strategy enables the emerging regional powers to "co-opt other states via positive incentives, it guarantees stability in the region, and it makes it more difficult to form counter-alliances inside the region or with states outside of the region".[77] Thus, Riyadh and Abu Dhabi are building coalitions to support their vision of the region, and make it difficult for countries that hold a different view, like Egypt, to build a counter-alliance. They are also providing the needed regional and international legitimacy for their military interventions.

For example, in Bahrain in 2011, Iran did not support the intervention, but as it was in the GCC framework, Iranian claims that the intervention was a "Saudi" move and an "occupation" could be refuted.[78] The Obama administration also criticised it, but did not "explicitly condemn" it; White House spokesman Jay Carney stated that it was "not an invasion".[79] In the case of Yemen, except for Iran, which called the intervention a "Saudi aggression" that will lead to "the expansion of terrorism",[80] no other country in the region opposed the intervention.

This strategy also assures the legitimacy of their acts outside of the GCC, the Arab League or the United Nations as it would be difficult for them to pass resolutions in these institutions legitimising and justifying their military intervention. For instance, Riyadh and Abu Dhabi announced the formation of the Arab Coalition two days before the Arab Summit in Cairo on 28 March 2015, and received support from Egypt, Sudan and other Arab countries, instead of seeking compromises within the framework of the Arab League to receive support for this action.

In addition, this strategy is a way of getting around the limited – but growing – military capabilities of Saudi Arabia and the UAE. In both Bahrain and Yemen, the Emirates' handled the shortage of manpower by hiring foreign soldiers.[81] In the case of the Arab Coalition, instead, the two countries were able to access resources available in other countries, ranging from soldiers who are professionally trained to others with combat experience.[82]

Given the importance of the multilateral frameworks, the challenge the two countries are facing is their ability to preserve them. The future of the Arab Coalition, for instance, is uncertain, especially with the increasing number of causalities on all sides. Also, to what extent they can rely on these multilateral frameworks to pursue their policies without compromising their national security priorities is debatable, as the UAE's main priority in Yemen is to limit the power of the MB in the new government, while the main concern of Saudi Arabia are the Houthis not the MB. Furthermore, could the multilateral frameworks actually lead to tensions regarding their regional roles? For example, the UAE is keen on leading the war in Yemen as a partner to Saudi Arabia in order to have a say in the political

---

[77] Nolte, "How to compare regional powers".

[78] "Bahraini forces disperse demonstrations in the second anniversary of Saudi occupation of Bahrain" (in Arabic). *Tabnak* (Iranian news agency), 18 March 2013. http://www.tabnak.ir/ar/news/11868/

[79] "US-Saudi Tensions Intensify with Mideast Turmoil", *The New York Times*, 14 March 2011, https://mobile.nytimes.com/images/100000000725835/2011/03/15/world/middleeast/15saudi.html

[80] "Stances of Iran and its Allies towards the Decisive Storm", *CNN Arabic* (in Arabic), 27 March 2015, http://arabic.cnn.com/middleeast/2015/03/27/yemen-iran-nasrullah

[81] Raising the issue of respect for international laws during combat, especially protection of civilians. See fn 89.

[82] Mukashaf, "Egypt and Saudi Arabia discuss maneuvers".

settlement. Saudi Arabia, on the other hand, is keen on maintaining its role as the main regional sponsor of the political settlement of the conflict in Yemen. These differences could lead to a tension between the two countries which would affect the future of their roles in Yemen and the region.[83]

A similar situation has materialized in the Islamic Alliance, initially formed by Saudi Arabia to combat ISIS in Syria. Contradictory views are emerging regarding the parties' roles in the alliance's main mission, and the list of terrorist organisations other than ISIS that the alliance is meant to counter in Syria.[84]

The second predicament is the gap between the acquisition of advanced military equipment and the professionalism of Saudi and Emirati troops. The military capabilities of both countries are developing in a remarkable way, in terms of new acquisitions and the ability to coordinate with American forces taking part in the air strikes in the south of Yemen,[85] or engaging in long-term ground combat. Indeed, Saudi Arabia and the UAE ranked second and fourth as major arms importers between 2010 and 2014, with a share of 5 percent and 4 percent of global arms imports, respectively.[86] They are the only Arab countries in this category.

The increase in their arms acquisitions is going hand in hand, however, with greater reliance on contracted soldiers to train forces, or act as senior security advisors, or merely infantry. It is not known how many foreigners work in their armies, but according to Anthony Cordesman, in Saudi Arabia they are "employed in key military specialties and technical areas within the Kingdom".[87] This is because both countries still lack a professional and efficient army, something that goes back to the fear among the ruling families to establish strong united national armies. Instead, their armies have always been built through controlled conscription, and are controlled by members of the royal family in order to reduce the likelihood of coups and enforce the internal legitimacy of the ruling family.[88]

In addition to the cost, the use of mercenaries raises problems of respect for international laws during combat, especially protection of civilians. According to UN Human Rights Chief Zeid Ra'ad Al Hussein, the air strikes and ground operations in Yemen had led to a civilian death toll estimated at 6000 by March 2016, half of which were civilians, which could qualify as an international war crime.[89] Indeed, Amnesty International called on Washington and London to halt the arm sales to the countries taking part in the conflict, following the 25 February 2016 European Parliament arms embargo on Saudi Arabia, and the Dutch parliament's 15 March 2016 call for the government of the Netherlands to stop arms transfers to Saudi Arabia.[90]

---

[83]See "Saudi-UAE relations tense following military action in Yemen", *Middle East Monitor*, 15 April 2015, https://www.middleeastmonitor.com/20150415-saudi-uae-relations-tense-following-military-action-in-yemen; Salisbury, "The UAE's Yemen Pivot".

[84]Browning and Irish, "Saudi Arabia announces 34-state alliance"; Aziz, "Purpose of Islamic Military Coalition".

[85]Schmitt, "United States Ramps Up Airstrikes".

[86]See *SIPRI Yearbook 2015*, http://www.sipri.org/yearbook/2015/10.

[87]Richter, "Saudi Arabia", 185.

[88]*Ibid.*, 182–5.

[89]"Yemen war: Saudi coalition 'causing most civilian casualties'". *BBC News*, 18 March 2016, http://www.bbc.com/news/world-middle-east-35842708; Mohamed and Shaif, "Saudi Arabia is Committing War Crimes".

[90]"Yemen: Reckless arms flows decimate civilian life a year into conflict", *Amnesty International*, 22 March 2016, https://www.amnesty.org/en/latest/news/2016/03/yemen-reckless-arms-flows-decimate-civilian-life-a-year-into-conflict/

Conclusion: are they leading regional powers?

Historically, playing an influential role in the Middle East required hard power.[91] The contention here is that in the post-Arab Spring period, being recognised as a regional power by the other countries in the region, as well as by the Western countries involved in the region's interactions requires not only hard power, but also soft power capabilities. Furthermore, it requires the ability to use them in maintaining and broadening one's clout in the region, along with "articulating the pretention of a leading position in the region".[92]

Saudi Arabia and the UAE have money, broad regional and international networks of influence, and now, more recently, are developing armies and a vision of their status and role in the region. For instance, they are paying the largest share of the Arab League's budget and dominating the main positions in the organisation and its specialised agencies.[93] They have developed strong networks of relationships with Western think tanks and universities.

Discussing the status of the two countries as regional powers raises four questions. The first is about the relationship between Saudi Arabia and the UAE. The UAE cannot be considered a follower of Saudi Arabia as the perceived threats to their national security and their visions of the region are different. Rather, they coordinate their regional policies despite seeking different regional roles.

The second question concerns the type of interventionist state unfolding from their active foreign policies, and whether these two countries have the ability to plan for the day after. In other words, will they have the capability to make peace after the military intervention or will they repeat the chaos created by NATO 's intervention in Libya in 2011? In Bahrain, they managed, more or less, to control the unstable situation with the aid packages provided through the GCC and on bilateral bases, and by building a permanent headquarters for the Shield Forces.

In Yemen, however, the popular resistance groups were unable to maintain control over the southern part of the country after being liberated from the Houthis, just as the Emirati troops did not succeed in establishing a system of governance able to strengthen the Hadi groups' control over the city. As a result, Al-Qaeda and ISIS are becoming increasingly active, unleashing further waves of conflict on the city. Brigadier General Ahmad Asiri, spokesman of the Arab Coalition, has not said much about future operations, except that there can be "no military solution" to the conflict.[94] Nevertheless, neither Saudi Arabia nor the UAE have put forward any political ideas other than those of the UN and those contained in the 2011 Initiative, which was one of the reasons for the failure of the five month-long Kuwaiti negotiations between the Houthis and the Hadi government.[95] Even though the Obama administration, Saudi Arabia, the UAE and the United Kingdom proposed a "renewed approach to negotiations with both a security and political track simultaneously working

[91] Nolte, "How to compare regional powers".

[92] *Ibid.*

[93] Interview with Ahmed Youssef Ahmed, professor of Political Science at the Faculty of Economics and Political Science, Cairo University, and former director of the Research Institute of Arab Studies , which is part of ALECSO, one of the Arab League's specialised organisations.

[94] Henderson, *Desert Stretch*.

[95] "UN: Yemen talks in Kuwait end, peace efforts to continue", *Al-Arabiya English*, 6 August 2016, https://english.alarabiya.net/en/News/middle-east/2016/08/06/Houthis-name-governing-body-in-Yemen.html

in order to provide a comprehensive settlement" a few days after the Kuwait talks,[96] it is still a stalemate with no genuine progress on either side.[97]

The third question is about the legitimacy of the militarisation of their policies. On the domestic level, these policies are perceived inside Saudi Arabia as an attempt by Mohammad Bin Salman to strengthen his position *vis-à-vis* Muhammad Bin Nayef, the Crown Prince, especially since the former shares foreign policy decision-making powers with King Salman.[98] For the UAE, disagreement inside the ruling family has been an issue ever since Operation Decisive Storm. Dhahi Khalfan, ex-head of Dubai police, on Twitter warned against a prolonged war that would turn Yemen into another failed state, and called for negotiations with Saleh and the Houthis. In response, the Emirati foreign minister's tweet asked him to trust the Emirates' leadership.[99]

On the regional level, there is no genuine opposition to the Emirati and Saudi resort to military means. Rather, countries that hold a different perception prefer to join the coalition rather than stand against it. An example of this is Egypt's participation in the Arab Coalition even though it still calls for a peaceful settlement of the conflict. Finally, the unwillingness of Saudi Arabia and the UAE to hold their soldiers accountable for any violations of international law during combat could delegitimise their intervention in Yemen regionally and internationally.

The fourth question concerns the institutionalisation of this pattern of foreign policy-making which is important in assuring the continuity. Saudi foreign policies used to be a reflection of the attitudes and perceptions of the King.[100] After the eruption of the Arab Spring, King Abdullah bin Abdelaziz was keen on securing the internal front and building a stable belt of monarchies able to counter the spillover effects of the Spring and of Iran's interventionist policies. The intervention in Bahrain and the support for the armed groups in Syria were the only two cases of Saudi interventionist policies during King Abdullah's reign. Since King Salman has risen to the throne, foreign policies decisions are shared with the Deputy Crown Prince, Mohammad Bin Salman, who tends to be more assertive and muscular. Thus, Saudi foreign policy is highly affected by the ambitions of the Crown Prince. The same is true for the UAE, where the role of Crown Prince Mohammed Bin Zayed is crucial in directing the country's foreign policy.[101] This makes institutionalisation much more difficult in that foreign policy decisions are being shaped and decided according to the attitudes and preferences of persons rather than institutions that could have other preferences and visions.

To conclude, on the basis of the foregoing, it seems that the increasing militarisation of Saudi and Emirati polices towards the conflicts in the region through multilateral frameworks will likely be transitional and contingent on their ability to compromise with other countries

---

[96]"US, UK, Saudi Arabia, UAE Find New Approach to Yemeni Conflict". *Sputnik News*, 25 August 2016, https://sputniknews.com/middleeast/201608251044637034-us-riyadh-yemen-uae/

[97]Oakford, "UN Email on Yemen Shows Difficulty".

[98]Young, *The Emerging Interventionists of GCC*. For criticism of Mohammad Bin Salman's policies in Yemen, see "AlWaleed Bin Talal Criticizes Bin Salman Publicly" (in Arabic), *Al-Minbar al-Araby*; and tweets by @mujtahidd (popular opposition Twitter account), https://twitter.com/mujtahidd/status/721639586842165249?lang=ar

[99]See the Twitter account of Dhahi Khalfan (@ Dhahi_Khalfan) and tweets on 12 May 2015.
Korany and Fattah, "Irreconcilable Role Partners", 363–77.

[100]*Ibidem*.

[101]According to Almeziani, the foreign policy of the UAE since the death of Sheikh Zayed in 2004 has been decided by the rulers and some members of the ruling family. See Almeziani, *The UAE and Foreign Policy*, 42–4.

in order to gain their support and cooperation. Also it is likely that the two countries will revise aspects of their militarised policies in light of the developments in the Arab region.

References

Adelmann, M. "Quiet Diplomacy: The Reasons behind Mbeki's Zimbabwe Policy". *Africa Spectrum* 39, no. 2 (2004).

Al-Hassan, O. *The Path of National Dialogue and Political Developments in Bahrain,* Reports, (in Arabic). Doha: al-Jazeera Center for Studies, 3 Dec 2013.

Al-Mashat, A. "Politics of Constructive Engagement: The Foreign Policy of the United Arab Emirates". In *The Foreign Policies of Arab States: The Challenges of Globalization*, edited B. Korany and A. E. Hillal. Cairo: The American University in Cairo Press, 2008.

Al-Masri, A. "UAE soldier killed in anti-Houthi operation in Yemen". *Anadhole news agency,* 17 Feb 2017. http://aa.com.tr/en/middle-east/uae-soldier-killed-in-anti-houthi-operation-in-yemen/752567

Almezaini, K. *The UAE and Foreign Policy: Foreign Aid, Identities and Interests*. London: Routledge, 2012.

Al-Rasheed, M. "Saudi Arabia Pushes US toward Military Strike in Syria". *Al-Monitor,* 2 September 2013. http://www.al-monitor.com/pulse/originals/2013/09/saudi-arabia-pushes-us-toward-military-strike-in-syria.html#

Al-Rashid, A. "The War in Yemen after a Year … a victory or a defeat?", *al-Bayan* (daily) (in Arabic), 5 April 2015.

Al Tamamy, S. "Saudi Arabia and the Arab Spring: Opportunities and Challenges of Security". In *Regional Powers in the Middle East: New Constellations after the Arab Revolts*, edited by H. Fŭrtig. NewYork: Palgrave Macmillan, 2014.

Beck, M. "The Concept of Regional Power as Applied to the Middle East". In *Regional Powers in the Middle East: New Constellations after the Arab Revolts*, edited by H. Fŭrtig. NewYork: Palgrave Macmillan, 2014.

Browning, N., and J. Irish. "Saudi Arabia announces 34-state Islamic military alliance against terrorism". *Reuters,* 15 Dec 2015. http://www.reuters.com/article/us-saudi-security-idUSKBN0TX2PG20151215?

Colombo, S., and E. Ragab. "The Legitimacy Question in Saudi Arabia in the Aftermath of the Arab Spring: Domestic and Regional Perspectives". Paper presented at the Annual Gulf Research Meeting, Cambridge University, UK 2–5 (July 2013).

Cordesman, A. *Bahrain, Oman, Qatar, and the UAE: Challenges of Security*. Boulder, CO: Westview Press, 1997.

Daalder, I., and J.G. Stavridis. "NATO's Success in Libya". *The NewYork Times*, 30 October 2011.

Donaghy, R. "Revealed: The mercenaries commanding UAE forces in Yemen". *The Middle East Eye*, 23 December 2915. http://www.middleeasteye.net/news/mercenaries-charge-uae-forces-fighting-yemen-764309832#sthash.BxVgL4U1.dpuf

Echagüe, A. "Saudi Arabia: emboldened yet vulnerable". In *Geopolitics and Democracy in the Middle East*, edited by K. Kausch: 80–6. Madrid: Fride, 2015.

Gause, F.G. "Saudi Arabia's Regional Security Strategy". In *International Relations of the Gulf*, Working Group Summary Report no. 1. Doha: Georgetown University School of Foreign Service in Qatar and Center for International and Regional Studies, 2009.

Gibbons-Neff, T., and M. Ryan. "In deadly Yemen raid, a lesson for Trump's national security team". *The Washington Post*, 31 Jan 2017. https://www.washingtonpost.com/news/checkpoint/

wp/2017/01/31/how-trumps-first-counter-terror-operation-in-yemen-turned-into-chaos/?utm_term=.f6faf1c69174

Hager, E., and M. Mazzetti. "Emirates secretly send Colombian mercenaries to fight in Yemen". *The New York Times*, 25 November 2015.

Henderson, S. *Desert Stretch: Saudi Arabia's Ambitious Military Operations*, Policywatch 2559. Washington DC: Washington Institute for Near East Policies, 16 February 2016. http://www.washingtoninstitute.org/policy-analysis/view/desert-stretch-saudi-arabias-ambitious-military-operations

Henderson, S. "The Bahraini royal policy and the US naval base". *Policy analysis*, Washington Institute for Near East Policies, 12 March 2013. http://www.washingtoninstitute.org/ar/policy-analysis/view/bahrains-royal-politics-and-the-u.s.-navy-base.

Holmes, A. "The military intervention that the world forgot". *Al-Jazeera*, 29 March 2014. http://america.aljazeera.com/opinions/2014/3/bahrain-uprisinginterventionsaudiarabiaemirates.html

Hubbard, B. "Saud al-Faisal of Saudi Arabia, Quiet Force in Middle East, Dies at 75". *The New York Times*, 9 July 2015. http://www.nytimes.com/2015/07/10/world/middleeast/prince-saud-al-faisal-longtime-saudi-foreign-minister-dies-at-75.html?_r=0

Katzman, K. *Bahrain: Reform, Security, and U.S. Policy*, CRS Paper. Washington DC: Congressional Research Service, 18 March 2016.

Kaye, D., and F. Wehrey. " Containing Iran?: Avoiding a Two-Dimensional Strategy in a Four-Dimensional Region". *The Washington Quarterly* (July 2009).

Kinninmont, J. "Saudi Arabia Faces Its Future in Vision 2030 Reform Plan". *Chatham House comment*, 29 April 2016. https://www.chathamhouse.org/expert/comment/saudi-arabia-faces-its-future-vision-2030-reform-plan#sthash.Jjkh8EYd.dpuf

Kirkpatrick, D. "Leaked Emirati Emails Could Threaten Peace Talks in Libya". *The New York Times*, 12 November 2015. https://www.nytimes.com/2015/11/13/world/middleeast/leaked-emirati-emails-could-threaten-peace-talks-in-libya.html?_r=0

Knights, M. "What Did the Gulf Coalition War Achieve in Yemen?", *Policy Analysis*. Washington Institute for Near East Policies, 9 April 2016. http://www.washingtoninstitute.org/ar/policy-analysis/view/what-did-the-gulf-coalition-war-achieve-in-yemen

Knights, M. "The U.A.E. Approach to Counterinsurgency in Yemen". *War on the Rocks*, 23 May 2015. http://warontherocks.com/2016/05/the-u-a-e-approach-to-counterinsurgency-in-yemen/

Knights, M., and A. Mello. *Gulf Coalition Operations in Yemen (Part 1): The Ground War*, Policywatch 2594. Washington DC: Washington Institute, 25 March 2016. http://www.washingtoninstitute.org/ar/policy-analysis/view/gulf-coalition-operations-in-yemen-part-1-the-ground-war

Knights, M., and A. Mello. *The Saudi-UAE War Effort in Yemen (Part 2): The Air Campaign*. Policywatch 2465. Washington DC: Washington Institute, 11 August 2015. http://www.washingtoninstitute.org/ar/policy-analysis/view/the-saudi-uae-war-effort-in-yemen-part-2-the-air-campaign

Knights, M., and A. Mello. *The Saudi-UAE War Effort in Yemen (Part 1): Operation Golden Arrow in Aden*, Policywatch 2464. Washington DC: Washington Institute, 10 August 2015. http://www.washingtoninstitute.org/ar/policy-analysis/view/the-saudi-uae-war-effort-in-yemen-part-1-operation-golden-arrow-in-aden

Korany, B. and M. A. Fattah. "Irreconcilable Role Partners. Saudi Foreign Policy between Ulama and US". In *The Foreign Policies of Arab States: The Challenges of Globalization*, edited B. Korany and A. E. Hillal. Cairo: The American University in Cairo Press, 2008.

Mabon, S. "The Battle for Bahrain: Iranian-Saudi Rivalry". *Middle East Policy* XIX, no. 2 (Summer 2012).

Maclean, W. "War with ISIS: UAE ready to send troops into Syria to fight insurgents". *The Independent*, 7 February 2016.

Mukashaf. M. "Egypt and Saudi Arabia discuss maneuvers as Yemen battles rage". *Reuters*, 14 April 2015. http://www.reuters.com/article/us-yemen-security-idUSKBN0N50TF20150414

Mohamed, R., and R. Shaif. "Saudi Arabia Is Committing War Crimes in Yemen". *Foreign Policy online*, 25 March 2016. http://foreignpolicy.com/2016/03/25/civilian-casualties-war-crimes-saudi-arabia-yemen-war/

Naar, I. "Najran citizens vow to stay despite indiscriminate Houthi rockets". *Al Arabiya English*. 28 August 2016. https://english.alarabiya.net/en/features/2016/08/28/Najran-citizens-vow-to-stay-despite-indiscriminate-Houthi-rockets.html

Nolte, D. "How to compare regional powers: analytical concepts and research topics". *Review of International Studies* 36 (2010).

North Atlantic Treaty Organisation (NATO). "NATO and Libya". 9 November 2015. http://www.nato.int/cps/en/natolive/topics_71652.htm

Oakford, S. "Leaked UN Email on Yemen Shows Difficulty of Negotiations — and Fears Over Al Qaeda's Growing Presence". *Vice News online*, 8 September 2015. https://news.vice.com/article/leaked-un-email-on-yemen-shows-difficulty-of-negotiations-and-fears-over-al-qaedas-growing-presence

Ragab, E. "Tactical Alliance? The Relationship between Egypt under el-Sisi, Saudi Arabia, and UAE". In *Egypt and the Gulf: A Renewed Regional Policy Alliance*, edited by R. Mason: 106–15. Germany: Gerlach Press, 2016.

Richter, T. "Saudi Arabia: A Conservative Player on the Retreat?" In *Regional Powers in the Middle East: New Constellations after the Arab Revolts*, edited by H. Fürtig. New York: Palgrave Macmillan, 2014.

Salisbury, P. "The UAE's Yemen Pivot Could Make Differences With Riyadh Unbridgeable". *World Politics Review*. http://www.worldpoliticsreview.com/articles/19184/the-uae-s-yemen-pivot-could-make-differences-with-riyadh-unbridgeable

Sadeghi, H., and H. Ahmadian. "Iran- Saudi Relations: Past Pattern, Future Outlook". *Iranian Review of Foreign Affairs* 1, no. 4 (Winter 2011).

Salavatian, H., A.S.N. Abadi and J. Moradi. "Iran and Saudi Arabia: the dilemma of security, the balance of threat". *Journal of Scientific Research and Development* 2, no. 2 (2015).

Schmitt, E. "United States Ramps Up Airstrikes Against Al-Qaeda in Yemen". *The New York Times*, 3 March 2017.

Shafqat, S. "UAE to open second military base in east Africa". *Middle East Eye,* 13 February 2017. http://www.middleeasteye.net/news/uae-eyes-military-expansion-eastern-africa-2028510672

Sharp, J. *Yemen: Civil War and Regional Intervention,* CRS Report 43960. Washington DC: Congressional Research Service (2 October 2015).

Usher, S. "Yemen crisis: Houthi rebels announce takeover". *BBC News*, 6 February 2015. http://www.bbc.com/news/world-middle-east-31169773

Watkinson, W. "Syria conflict: UAE will join anti-Isis ground operation despite Bashar al-Assad warning". *International Business Times,* 7 February 2016. http://www.ibtimes.co.uk/syria-conflict-uae-will-join-anti-isis-ground-operation-despite-bashar-al-assad-warning-1542462.

Wehrey, F., T.W. Karasik, A. Nader, J. Ghez, L. Hansell, and R.A. Guffey. *Saudi-Iranian Relations Since the Fall of Saddam: Rivalry, Cooperation, and Implications for US Policy*. Santa Monica: RAND Corporation, 2009.

Young, K. *The Emerging Interventionists of the GCC*. LSE Middle East Centre Paper Series/02. London: LSE Middle East Centre, December 2013.

Foreign Policy Activism in Saudi Arabia and Oman. Diverging Narratives and Stances towards the Syrian and Yemeni Conflicts

Silvia Colombo

ABSTRACT

Amid growing animosity and security concerns in the Middle East, the Gulf region appears to be on the way to becoming the new centre of gravity of regional equilibria. The increasingly active foreign policy postures of the Gulf Cooperation Council (GCC) countries is a key aspect of the new regional order in the making. Saudi Arabia and Oman are two examples of this trend. Their involvement in the Syrian and Yemeni conflicts reveals important differences regarding the aims, narratives, political and military postures, strategies and alliances pursued by Riyadh and Muscat and casts a shadow over the future of GCC cooperation and integration.

Six years after the Arab uprisings, the world is still grappling with the vast and deep repercussions of these momentous transformations. While most scholars agree on the fact that the Arab uprisings were first and foremost domestic phenomena, their regional and global ramifications cannot be overlooked. The unrest that flared up at the end of 2010 was caused by many years, if not decades, of ingrained authoritarianism, widespread corruption, repressive practices and a lack of social and economic opportunities, particularly for the young generations. At the same time, it set in motion a number of processes of change that have been unfolding over the past six years, altering the geopolitical equilibria in the Middle East. The Gulf Cooperation Council (GCC) countries have taken on a prominent role in the redefinition of the regional order through increasingly active foreign policy postures. On the one hand, most of them have been directly affected by the wave of change that has swept across the region. This is the case of Bahrain, Oman and Saudi Arabia.[1] These countries have all experienced more or less prolonged and wide-ranging protests against inequality and the lack of political outlets for expressing grievances, triggering domestic counter-reactions/'revolutions' entailing the deployment of a mix of limited political concessions, economic handouts and military interventions in the attempt to preserve the status quo.[2] On the other, the GCC countries have become enmeshed in Middle Eastern

---

[1] Hertog, "The Cost of the Counter Revolution"; Worrall, "Oman: The 'Forgotten' Corner"; and Matthiesen, *Sectarian Gulf*, respectively.

[2] Colombo, "The GCC and the Arab Spring".

regional and global affairs by influencing the changes (or lack thereof) taking place in some neighbouring countries, such as Syria and Yemen, and contributing to the re-structuring of the matrix of alliances in the region against the backdrop of the changing US engagement. In this regard, some of them have exploited the card of sectarian identities to advance their hegemonic interests in the region.

The coming to the fore of the GCC countries on the regional chessboard has not been a unidirectional process and cannot be regarded as a linear consequence of the 2011 uprisings. The trend has become more visible since then, but the uprooting of regional equilibria that followed the 2003 US-led invasion of Iraq had already laid the stage for the changes in the GCC countries' foreign policies. In the most recent phase, the emergence of the GCC countries as foreign policy heavyweights has been marked by bumps and U-turns, false starts and uncertainty, as well as conflicts and disagreements among the members of the regional organisation established in 1981. One of the most remarkable consequences of this trend is the extent to which it has endangered the cohesion of the group after an initial attempt back in 2011 to pursue a more united and coordinated course of action. Growing divisions among its members have become particularly evident in the past six years and are exemplified by the competition between Saudi Arabia and Qatar, which skyrocketed between 2011 and 2013 in connection to developments in Egypt, Libya and Syria. Another less documented and analysed occurrence is the way in which Oman has distanced itself from Saudi Arabia's regional hegemonic role by exploiting its increasingly autonomous foreign policy in the Middle East.

This article addresses the new foreign policy postures of the GCC countries on the regional chessboard and their implications for GCC cooperation and integration, both theoretically and empirically, by comparing Saudi Arabia's foreign policy with that of Oman in the context of the Syrian and Yemeni conflicts. By grasping the similarities and differences that characterise these two cases, it offers a contribution to the comparative academic and policy-oriented literature on the GCC countries' involvement in the Middle East following the Arab uprisings. Most importantly, the comparison between Saudi Arabia and Oman – whose mutual relations have traditionally been viewed through the lens of the literature on regional hegemony[3] – makes it possible to move away from some overly strict realist interpretations of the notions of 'power' and 'influence' and the ways they are projected by states to advance their foreign policy goals in the international system. Instead, it offers an alternative take on key IR concepts by highlighting the importance of domestic imperatives, ideational drivers and contingent factors in explaining foreign policy moves. What this article does not do is delve deeply into domestic decision-making dynamics in Saudi Arabia and Oman, even though it does acknowledge that GCC regimes are not black boxes or monolithic entities and that most of the foreign policy actions described in the following are the result of specific positions and preferences of specific actors within a given constellation of power.

The article is structured as follows. The first section articulates the theoretical and conceptual framework providing the tools for understanding the foreign policies of Saudi Arabia and Oman in the context of the post-Arab uprisings regional order. The second part analyses these foreign policies by delving into the Syrian and Yemeni cases. Before concluding, the

---

[3]Hurrell, "Hegemony, Liberalism and Global Order".

article discusses some implications of these trends for the two countries' bilateral relations and the prospects for enhanced GCC cooperation and integration.

Understanding the foreign policies of GCC countries

Omnibalancing

One of the most relevant features of the new regional order in the making and, more pointedly, one of the factors that has contributed to shaping it over the past half a decade is the increasingly active foreign policy posture of the GCC countries on the regional chessboard. From a geopolitical perspective, the decline of the 'old' regional order has coincided with an eastward shift of the centre of gravity – more precisely, towards the Middle East and Gulf region.[4] This area has become increasingly interconnected with other parts of the world economically and politically, leading some authors to speak of a "global Mediterranean".[5] Furthermore, this eastward shift has been marked by rising competition and often tensions among the GCC countries and their regional partners. As argued by Richard Youngs, the Middle East has become increasingly characterised by "an element of competitive multipolarity", meaning that there is no longer "a single dominant power but clusters of shifting coalitions between medium-sized powers".[6]

While a country like Saudi Arabia was already a key pillar of the 'old' regional order, the real novelty is represented by the rise – amid mixed fortunes – of the smaller GCC countries, namely Qatar, Oman and the United Arab Emirates (UAE). This development has been accompanied by a flurry of literature production scrutinising the decoupling of the notion of power from the size of a given polity.[7] In other words, with globalisation, the demographic and territorial size of a state can no longer be correlated with power capabilities. As pointedly argued by Kristian Coates Ulrichsen, "opportunities for small states abound as the link between size and power erodes".[8] Similarly, influence is not only the result of material factors, among which the most important ones in the case of the Gulf countries are oil and gas resources.[9] Instead, small states' power and influence can be projected through multiple channels, taking advantage of the leverage accorded by ideational factors and effectively mobilising specific circumstances and opportunities in their favour when confronting larger countries with greater geopolitical and military capabilities. Issues such as 'soft power', 'subtle power' and 'statebranding' become of crucial importance in explaining the ascent (and collapse) of rising foreign policy stars in the group of small GCC countries.[10] In this context, the literature on small states tends to draw a clear-cut dividing

---

[4]To simplify, the 'old' regional order, dating back to the years immediately after the Second World War and subsequently consolidated during the Cold War, was based on a division of the region into spheres of influence: the Western sphere, which included moderate states such as Egypt, Jordan and the Arab Gulf states, and the Eastern sphere or so-called 'non-aligned' countries, which included states firmly opposed to US hegemony in the region, such as Algeria, Libya and Syria. See Barnett, *Dialogues in Arab Politics*.

[5]Kausch, "Competitive Multipolarity in Middle East".

[6]Youngs, "Living with Old-New Security Paradigm", 17.

[7]Kamrava, *Qatar: Small State, Big Politics*; Peterson, "Qatar and the World"; Ulrichsen *Small States with Big Role*.

[8]Ulrichsen, *Qatar and the Arab Spring*, 4.

[9]Ulrichsen, *Insecure Gulf* and *The Gulf States*. It should also be recalled here that the downward trend in oil prices since late 2014 has negatively affected the fiscal balance of most GCC countries and necessitated corrective measures. See Callen *et al.*, *Economic Diversification in the GCC*.

[10]Hey, *Small States in World Politics*; Rickli and Almezaini, "Theories of Small States'", 8–30.

line between the foreign policies of Qatar, Oman and the UAE, on the one hand, and that of the regional hegemon, Saudi Arabia, on the other.

Yet, in order to grasp the rising trend of GCC countries more fully, the concept of small states is not useful and will therefore not be used here. First of all, being small (or big) is a relative feature and concept, and its use runs the risk of ascribing certain political behaviours to mere factors of size. Second, in order to make sense of differences and similarities in the foreign policy behaviours of the multifaceted GCC group, it is important to adopt a theoretical framework that can be applied to both large and small states – a theoretical framework that cannot but be rooted in the rich IR literature on GCC countries. In its realist and neo-realist incarnations, this literature has tended to view the foreign policies of most Middle Eastern countries, including GCC countries, as well as the creation of the GCC itself, as dictated by the perception of threats coming mostly from the capabilities of external actors.[11] Yet, some works criticise the notion of the nation-state as a unitary player and focus instead on state-society relations and domestic threats. Accordingly, regime survival becomes the key preoccupation of GCC rulers, among others.[12] What derives from these arguments is that, for GCC rulers, external actors can be both sources of threat and instruments for balancing against their own societies, as well as against those threats.[13] These arguments have been echoed by those who, from a constructivist perspective focusing on ideational factors and identity politics to frame the perception of threats, argue that the GCC leaders' priority is maintaining their own domestic political power.[14]

Thus, according to less strict realist interpretations, threat perceptions and the notions of power and influence – not exclusively at the material level – to deal with those perceptions see domestic and external security as inextricably linked. This is exemplified by the concepts of 'omnibalancing' and 'managed multi-dependence', which provide the theoretical umbrella overarching the analysis conducted here. Theories developed around these concepts highlight that variations in foreign policy may result from particular domestic configurations and preferences in addition to the constraints and opportunities provided by the external environment.[15] As the word omnibalancing suggests, this often entails a balancing act between potentially conflicting domestic imperatives which, in the case of the Gulf countries, boil down to regime survival, on the one hand, and the constraining and enabling effects, namely threats and opportunities, of the regional and international environments, on the other. As will be demonstrated in the following section, different sets of domestic conditions and preoccupations have significantly influenced the foreign policy courses of Saudi Arabia and Oman in the cases of the Syrian and Yemeni conflicts. With regard to the GCC countries, omnibalancing also takes on another meaning, that is the development of alliances away from an approach that has historically been exclusively focused on the United States. Overall, the concept of omnibalancing makes it possible to take into account the extent to which the GCC countries' foreign policies cannot be understood in isolation from domestic considerations and preferences, which are in turn defined not

---

[11]According to Stephen Walt's balance of threat theory, the GCC can effectively be interpreted as a balancing alignment "intended to limit potential pressure from both Iran and the Soviet Union". See Walt, *The Origins of Alliances*, 270.
[12]Ayoob, *The Third World Security Predicament*.
[13]Halliday, *Middle East in International Relations*; Ehteshami and Hinnebusch, "Foreign Policymaking in Middle East"; Wright, "Foreign Policy in GCC States".
[14]Barnett, "Institutions, Roles and Disorder".
[15]David, *Choosing Sides*; Nonneman, "Determinants of Saudi Foreign Policy" and *Analyzing Middle East Foreign Policy*.

only by size-specific factors and capabilities, but also by ideational variables and identity politics. This leads us to engage critically with the concept of (domestic) legitimacy under-pinning regime survival in order to understand foreign policy choices.

Legitimacy

All incumbent regimes, be they democratic or not, strive to cultivate belief in their legiti-macy as this enhances the stability and chances of regime survival.[16] Thus, as aptly recalled by Michael Hudson, it is no surprise that "the central problem of government in the Arab world [...] is political legitimacy".[17] Legitimacy is "the capacity of the system to engender and maintain belief that the existing political institutions are the most appropriate ones for the society".[18] As pointed out by Max Weber in his seminal work *Economy and Society*, a regime is legitimate when its subjects ultimately believe it to be legitimate. Popular perceptions are thus a central component of the legitimacy of a regime. However, other views argue that judging a regime's legitimacy on the basis of popular perceptions is not reliable and thus reject this argument as circular.[19]

Notwithstanding the difficulty in operationalising the concept of legitimacy, a number of typologies have been proposed to classify the process of legitimation, that is the process through which regimes continuously try to ensure and renew the bases of their legitimacy. The traditional one developed by Weber in 1978 defines legitimate rule as resting on either charismatic, traditional or legal-rational bases.[20] Charismatic legitimacy has to do with the extraordinary personal attributes of the leader; traditional legitimacy stems from the claim of upholding immemorial traditions; while legal-rational-based legitimacy derives from rules and institutions. This typology has inspired many authors to suggest alternative categories, such as allocative legitimacy, traditional-religious legitimacy, etc.[21]

To address the question of legitimacy in GCC countries, we will use the typology devel-oped by Tim Niblock, involving four bases of legitimacy.[22] The first basis of legitimacy stems from the articulation, manipulation, promotion and defence of a particular set of values important for the organisation of society. In the Saudi case, this ideology is epitomised by the 'religious-political' nature of the state, that is the constant projection of the Saudi monarchy as the protector of the Islamic faith. More concretely, the alliance between the Al Saud and the religious, and particularly Wahhabi, institutions has been used by several generations of rulers to acquire Islamic rulings that legitimise their decisions and consoli-date their power. Charismatic personal leadership is another source of legitimacy. The third basis of legitimacy according to Niblock's typology is defined as the acceptance of a ruler on grounds of family lineage, thus strengthening the House of Saud's right to rule. Finally,

---

[16] Weber, *Theory of Social Organization*. Many years later, Holger Albrecht and Oliver Schlumberger argued that all regimes – whether democratic or authoritarian – depend on a combination of repression, cooptation and legitimacy. See Albrecht and Schlumberger, "Waiting for Godot".

[17] Hudson, *Arab Politics*, 2.

[18] Lipset, *Political Man*, 77.

[19] Gause, *Kings for All Seasons*.

[20] Weber, *Economy and Society*, 953.

[21] Albrecht and Schlumberger distinguish between allocative legitimacy, traditional-religious legitimacy, legitimacy through ideology, and external legitimacy. See "Waiting for Godot", 376–7.

[22] Niblock, *Saudi Arabia*. The fifth basis of legitimacy identified by the author, the democratic/structural one, is not discussed as it is not of relevance for GCC countries. See also Herb, *All in the Family*; and Kostiner, *Middle East Monarchies*.

the last basis of legitimacy is the eudaemonic one. This is where the importance of oil and the rentier state paradigm comes in.[23] The impact of oil on politics, certainly a decisive one in the formation and destruction of coalitions and state institutions, is regarded by some authors as the most important determinant of the economic, institutional and political development of the oil producing countries of the Middle East. It is the main contention of these authors that

> within the context of the Arab oil states, under the conditions of the oil rentier economy, the state, through the provision of considerable welfare and economic gains (in the areas of education, public employment, health services, housing, the private sector, and the provision of public assistance and social welfare services), can play a crucial role, functionally, in the process of political legitimation.[24]

This approach clearly and directly links the process of political legitimation to the material satisfaction of the population's needs in terms of social policies and welfare programs. In order to perform its functional role in political legitimation, the rentier-state argument contends, two main premises need to be fulfilled. First, the typical conditions of the oil rentier economy need to be present, whereby substantial external rents accrue directly to the state, which is "the main financier of all social and economic activities, the major employer, the major single consumer, and the major developer".[25] Second, the achievements of the ruling elites in the provision of social benefits and welfare programs to the population require immediate and positive responses on the part of the latter in the form of acquiescence, compliance, acceptance or support of the former. Looking at the current development of the Saudi state, it is questionable whether the trade-off between welfare and patronage, and political acquiescence will be sustainable in the long run.[26] The challenge facing Saudi Arabia's ruling monarchy in the post-rentier state phase stems from the need to introduce real political reforms and effective measures to ease the sense of marginalisation felt by some groups of the population and to create a shared sense of economic and social justice. Although Niblock's typology of legitimacy has been developed with reference to Saudi Arabia, it can be applied almost entirely to Oman as well, with the significant exception of the first basis, thus there is no stringent religious justification underpinning the rule of the Al Qaboos.[27]

It is apparent that the four bases of legitimacy pertain above all to domestic factors. This typology does not take into consideration the impact of foreign policies on regime legitimacy, even though this has been proven to be of great significance.[28] Indeed, according to the foreign policy analysis literature, there is a cyclical relationship between domestic policies and foreign policies, which makes regime legitimacy not entirely a domestic game.[29] This begs the question to what extent the aforementioned domestic drivers of regime legitimacy are relevant in explaining foreign policy choices and their impact on regime legitimacy.

---

[23]Beblawi and Luciani, *The Rentier State*; Smith, "Oil Wealth and Regime Survival".
[24]Al-Dekhayel, *Kuwait*, 221.
[25]*Ibid.*, 28.
[26]Davidson, *After the Sheikhs*.
[27]Valeri, *Oman*, 71–118; Yom and Gause, "Resilient Royals".
[28]Holbig, "International Dimensions of Regime Legitimacy".
[29]Many studies assess the effectiveness of the external legitimation strategies used by authoritarian regimes; see for example Hoffmann, *International Dimensions of Authoritarian Legitimation*.

'Swing' states

The applicability of the concept of omnibalancing will be empirically tested in the next section examining the foreign policies of Saudi Arabia and Oman in the cases of the Syrian and Yemeni conflicts. It allows us to uncover the extent to which they have been filtered through domestic considerations and are meant to respond to domestic needs, in particular that of regime survival. This is one of the most important similarities between the two cases, the others being the crucial importance of ideational drivers and contingent factors in shaping Riyadh's and Muscat's foreign policy.

That said, it is equally important to pinpoint and explain the major differences in the foreign policy stances of the two countries. To do so, we refer to the concept of 'swing' state. Swing states have been described by Daniel Kliman and Richard Fontaine as powers "whose precise international role is in flux and whose mixed political orientation gives [them] a greater impact than [their] sheer size, population, or economic output would suggest".[30] Another aspect that characterises swing states is their flexible, issue-based approach, whereby they are able to walk a tightrope and balance competing and conflicting interests and allies in a pragmatic way.

Although this concept has not found much resonance in the IR literature about GCC countries, it is useful for conceptualising and explaining Oman's foreign policy track record in the Middle East. As will be demonstrated in the next section, not only has its foreign policy always displayed a certain degree of autonomy vis-à-vis the regional hegemon, namely Saudi Arabia, but it has also undergone a process of accentuation of its flexibility in the last six years, which largely explains Muscat's success in positioning itself as a key regional actor.

The same cannot be said for Saudi Arabia, whose flexibility has decreased significantly and become largely contingent on the role played by key figures in the country's leadership. In the past, Riyadh was able to maintain smooth relations with its traditional allies while its foreign policy contributed to enhancing the domestic legitimacy of the monarchy.[31] Since 2011, the more assertive stances adopted by the Saudi regime in the Middle East have put the country on a course that does not necessarily stand by its traditional and long-standing alliances within the Western camp. Oman, instead, has been able to match its relative geopolitical clout with the necessary flexibility and "a self-confidently proclaimed independence in foreign policy that potentially allows [it] to turn the tide on specific crises or dossiers".[32]

Saudi Arabia and Oman: comparing their foreign policies in Syria and Yemen

Saudi Arabia

As demonstrated elsewhere, the specific circumstances dictated by the changing geopolitical situation in the Middle East have led to a heightened sense of vulnerability in Saudi Arabia,[33]

---

[30]Kliman and Fontaine, *Global Swing States*; Kausch, *Promise of Middle Eastern Swing States*.

[31]For instance, by actively siding with the United States in the struggle against terrorism after the 9/11 events, Saudi Arabia was able to weaken Al-Qaeda's rhetoric and acts aimed at undermining the religious basis of the regime's legitimacy. Furthermore, the Saudi official discourse used to consider "the Iranian conspiracy" as the main explanation for political unrest in many Gulf countries after the Iraq-Iran war (1980–88). This was aimed at achieving two goals: first, promoting the status of Saudi Arabia in the region as the protector of 'Sunni Islam' against 'Shia Iran' and, second, delegitimising the opposition groups led by Shiites that demanded political change in, for example, Bahrain and Kuwait as well as at home. See Cordesman, *Bahrain, Oman, Qatar*, 78.

[32]Kausch, *Promise of Middle Eastern Swing States*.

[33]Colombo, "The GCC and the Arab Spring".

which stems from a number of elements. First, the feeling of encroachment by Iran on the geopolitical space controlled by the Saudi monarchy. This defining feature of the bilateral relations between the two countries since the end of the seventies has been heightened in the past six years as a result of the regional dynamics unleashed by the Arab uprisings and Iran's successful negotiation of the Joint Comprehensive Plan of Action (JCPOA), also known as the Iran nuclear deal, reached in Vienna in July 2015.[34] Second, the threat posed by the Muslim Brotherhood's electoral gains, and the emergence of 'Islamist democracies' in Egypt, Morocco and Tunisia between 2011 and 2013, challenging the Wahhabi establishment's exclusive religious credentials for leadership among Sunni Muslims. Last, the impact of the real or perceived disengagement of the United States from the Middle East. All this has come together to create a mix of uneasiness and fear, and a willingness to undertake autonomous foreign policy actions to guarantee the country's strategic interests and the regime's survival.[35] Saudi policies towards the Syrian and Yemeni conflicts can be assessed through this prism.

These policies have originated from different considerations. In the case of Syria, the need to be accredited as the regional hegemon has prevailed.[36] However, Saudi Arabia's role in the Syrian conflict has been rather ambiguous, particularly as concerns supporting and arming the opposition to Bashar al-Assad's regime and at the same time fighting the Islamic State in Syria (ISIS). Saudi Arabia has been directly sponsoring the Syrian opposition, including some radical elements, since the beginning of the conflict[37] – something that has at times put Riyadh into direct contrast not only with Doha but also with some Western capitals that were not so openly supportive of Saudi Arabia's narrative that "Al-Assad should go". But it was fighting ISIS after its rise in Syria in the summer of 2014 that brought to the fore a certain degree of incoherence between Riyadh's foreign policy goals in Syria, and the domestic preoccupations of the traditional bases of the Saudi regime's legitimacy. The strong reliance on the Wahhabi doctrine and preachers for domestic purposes seems to sit uneasily with Riyadh's proclaimed commitment to fighting ISIS in Syria and tackling the root causes of Sunni Islamic terrorism.

It may not be surprising then that this prompted the kingdom's attempt to divert the world's attention away from this incoherence by resorting to a more assertive foreign policy. To some extent, this could be seen, for example, in Riyadh's efforts to muster a platform of almost exclusively pro-Saudi Syrian opposition groups with a view to pushing for an interlocutor that could participate in the negotiation talks co-chaired by the United States and Russia in late 2015 and 2016. These partially successful attempts demonstrate Riyadh's willingness to pursue an autonomous foreign policy path while completely disregarding the need to coordinate with the other players that have a stake in the Syrian crisis, above all Iran. Nevertheless, it is in the context of the Yemeni conflict that the foreign policy tool has effectively been used to reinforce the crumbling legitimacy bases of the Saudi regime at the domestic level. The escalation of the conflict in Yemen in March 2015 represented a perfect opportunity for Riyadh to pursue its goals with the justification of defending the country's security and key strategic interests.[38]

---

[34]Saudi-Iranian relations as well as the impact of the JCPOA at the regional level are discussed in another contribution to this Special Issue. See the article by Riham Bahi, p. 89.

[35]Davidson, *After the Sheikhs.*

[36]Wehrey, *Sectarian Politics in the Gulf.*

[37]Schanzer, "Saudi Arabia Arming Syrian Opposition".

[38]Wehrey, *Sectarian Politics in the Gulf.*

This course of action was influenced by internal dynamics within the ruling elites, and in particular by the specific preferences and attitudes of Mohamed bin Salman Al-Saud, the Minister of Defence and Deputy Crown Prince since 2015, considered the mastermind behind the new Saudi foreign policy course.[39] The priorities pursued by this highly contested personality show that Saudi Arabia's foreign policy can vary to a certain degree depending on purely domestic factors. Although the perception of Yemen being a part of Saudi's national security concerns is not new, Mohamed bin Salam's decision to launch a military campaign in the country was remarkable. Operation Decisive Storm was launched in the wake of the outbreak of violence in March 2015 triggered by the capture of the capital Sana'a by the Houthi rebels from the north of the country. The official justification put forward for cobbling together a Sunni-based coalition under Riyadh's leadership – and with the more or less tacit support of external players, including the United States – was to contain any spillover of Yemeni instability into the rest of the Gulf region by restoring Yemen's internationally recognised government to power. This goal has, however, been couched in strong anti-Iranian language, thus adding an additional layer of sectarian tensions to what already look like tense regional affairs.[40] Since then, the Yemeni conflict has undoubtedly taken on a proxy-war dimension with crossfire-type accusations of meddling in Yemen's domestic affairs between the two most important regional players, Saudi Arabia and Iran, and has turned into one of the worst humanitarian crises in the Middle East.

Moreover, at the practical level, mixed-to-very-negative evaluations have been voiced about the ongoing military campaign, which has arguably further precipitated instability in the country and contributed to opening enormous spaces void of state control that have been occupied by Al-Qaeda in the Arabian Peninsula (AQAP).[41] At the Saudi domestic level, while the campaign has drained substantial resources and heightened the urgency of a more balanced and prudent use of the country's dwindling oil rents, thus raising doubts about its sustainability, it seems nevertheless to have contributed to propping up the monarchy's domestic legitimacy and diverting the majority of the Saudi population's attention away from internal problems.[42]

All in all, Saudi Arabia's foreign policy in the Syrian and Yemeni conflicts seems to be dictated by domestic preoccupations and personal preferences linked to the need to ensure regime survival, as well as by contingent factors stemming from the heightened sectarian tensions between Saudi Arabia and Iran. The result has been a mix of interventionist expansionism and proxy warfare to achieve political and security goals and ultimately reinforce the crumbling bases of the regime's legitimacy. It has dragged the region into a downward spiral of conflict and instability, given that other countries, including all GCC members except Oman, have felt under pressure to back Riyadh's foreign policy adventures and have entered into the fray. This has contributed to exacerbating tensions at the regional level as well as within the GCC itself, as will be explored in the following section.

---

[39]Mazzetti and Hubbard, "Rise of Saudi Prince".
[40]Purple, "Why Saudi Arabia is Hammering".
[41]Stephens, "Mixed success for Saudi operation".
[42]*Ibid.*

Oman

The case of Oman tells a different story, something that has attracted growing scholarly attention.[43] Since 1970, when Sultan Qaboos bin Said Al-Said deposed his father in a bloodless coup and initiated a new era for a country that faced severe domestic problems of political unrest, isolation and underdevelopment, Oman has made great strides in formulating its foreign policy vision. In the last 45 years, Qaboos has turned an isolated and unstable country into a proactive foreign policy actor in Middle East and global diplomacy.[44]

Immediately after his accession to the throne, Qaboos started to develop the idea of Oman as a regional power, the implementation of which meant tackling the unstable and fragile political and socio-economic domestic situation. On the foreign policy front, he established direct diplomatic relations with Arab and other states, and gained admittance to the League of Arab States (LAS) and the United Nations in 1971. Anchoring the country within broad regional and multilateral fora was to some extent instrumental in mitigating Oman's dependence on Great Britain, the former colonial power, and more recently the United States, for strategic and military assistance. Oman's autonomous foreign policy was evident in the forging of relations with Iran, a country that, contrary to Riyadh's perceptions, has always been regarded as a potential asset to the relatively small Sultanate. The two countries signed a border agreement on the Strait of Hormuz that remained in place even when the Shah was deposed by Ayatollah Khomeini in 1979. Around the same time, Sultan Qaboos showed public support for Egyptian President Sadat's peace efforts with Israel in 1977–78, an act that led to the country being ostracised by the other Gulf states.[45]

Even under these delicate circumstances, Oman stood firm in its continuous attempt to forge closer relations among the six countries of the Arabian Peninsula, laying the ground for what, in 1981, became the GCC. When the Gulf region became embroiled in conflict with the Iran-Iraq war of 1980–88, Oman worked to position itself as a (not always successful) impartial broker, retaining its diplomatic ties to both belligerent parties. Another foreign policy issue around which Sultan Qaboos tried to shape Oman's autonomous foreign policy was the Arab-Israeli conflict, for which Oman was ready to pursue mediation efforts and engage with Israel at a time when this was not considered an option by other Middle Eastern partners.

Therefore, Sultan Qaboos, in his role of absolute monarch, has been the real master behind the country's new foreign policy course.[46] Aside from its personalistic features, meaning that foreign policy has evolved almost solely on the basis of the Sultan's preferences and that some caution is therefore called for in light of the country's unclear succession prospects, this foreign policy has contributed to pursuing Oman's strategic goals of raising its status regionally (and globally), on the one hand, and fostering its long-term security, on the other.[47] In its foreign policy endeavours, Oman appears to be guided by neither religious or other types of ideology (although Ibadism, the moderate form of Islam dominant in the country is said to be behind its pragmatic approach to foreign policy[48]), nor short-term gains, but rather by a firm belief in the virtues of compromise, peaceful negotiations

---

[43]Jones and Ridout, *A History of Modern Iran*; Echague, *Oman: the outlier*.
[44]Allen and Rigsbee, *Oman Under Qaboos*.
[45]*Ibid.*
[46]Valeri, *Oman*, 71–118.
[47]Valeri, "Identity Politics and Nation-Building".
[48]Jones and Ridout, *Oman, Culture and Diplomacy*.

and mediation as essential ingredients in achieving the overall, long-term goals of Omani security and prosperity.[49] Key considerations informing them include the country's strategic Middle East location and important trade and population links to the Asian continent, making it much more an Indian Ocean than an Arabian Gulf state.

Thus, domestic imperatives as well as contingent and ideational factors, and not just mere material and size-related variables, have traditionally been the main driving forces behind Oman's foreign policy. Since then, a new, significant trend has emerged in foreign policy,[50] whereby Muscat is veering towards being a swing state, as defined in the conceptual section of this article. Oman is acting on the basis of a pragmatic, flexible and issue-based approach as a means to tailor its autonomous foreign policy to changing regional and global dynamics. Its ability to balance competing and conflicting dossiers, interests and partners – at both the multilateral and bilateral levels – can be observed in the ways in which Oman has dealt with the Syrian and Yemeni conflicts, resulting in the country's growing external clout.

In the case of Syria, already in January 2012, the foreign policy chief of the Sultanate, Omani Foreign Minister Yousef bin Alawi, was calling for a peaceful solution to the Syrian crisis.[51] To achieve this goal, he argued that the only way was to empower the LAS to propose a peace plan to be adopted by all Arab countries. This remained the official line of Omani foreign policy towards Syria in the following years, up until 2015. In the official discourse, Foreign Minister Bin Alawi argued on different occasions that Oman's policy was not to interfere in other countries' internal affairs, while underlining that it was playing an important role in dealing with the humanitarian crisis triggered by the conflict by providing humanitarian assistance and not arming groups, unlike the other GCC countries.[52] With the unfolding of the conflict and the increased level of violence, Muscat took on a more proactive role in 2015 by building a diplomatic bridge whereby the Al-Assad regime and the Syrian opposition could meet and negotiate an end to the hostilities. One of the first steps was to invite Syrian Foreign Minister Walid al-Muallem to Muscat in August 2015 to discuss prospects for peace, thus marking the first visit by the Syrian foreign policy chief to a GCC country since the Syrian conflict had erupted in 2011.[53] Unsurprisingly, the visit took place in the Arabian Gulf monarchy that is on best terms with Syria's main regional ally, Iran, as well as one that has maintained diplomatic relations with Damascus throughout the Syrian crisis (even though it voted to suspend Syria from the Arab League in November 2011).[54]

As demonstrated by Oman's successful contribution to brokering the Iran nuclear deal between the country and the P5+1 in July 2015,[55] the country's ability to conduct quiet diplomacy, straddling and bringing opposing camps closer to one another is evident also in the context of the Yemeni crisis. Not only has Oman taken an independent foreign policy stance, pitting itself against Saudi Arabia and the military coalition that has intervened in

---

[49]Ibid.; Jones, *Oman's Quiet Diplomacy*, Valeri, *Oman*, 71–118.
[50]O'Reilly, "Omnibalancing".
[51]"Oman: Syria crisis must be resolved through peace plan", *Aharamonline*, 28 January 2012, http://english.ahram.org.eg/NewsContent/2/8/33024/World/Region/Oman-Syria-crisis-must-be-resolved-through-peace-p.aspx.
[52]"Oman Says it will not Interfere in Syria's Internal Affairs", *Al-Monitor*, 4 October 2012, http://www.al-monitor.com/pulse/tr/politics/2012/10/oman-no-to-interference-in-syria.html#ixzz4EqJ5JNUX.
[53]"Oman's diplomatic bridge to Syria", *Al-Monitor*, 17 August 2015, http://www.al-monitor.com/pulse/originals/2015/08/oman-diplomatic-bridge-syria-moallem.html.
[54]For Oman, "the enemy (Iran) of my friend (the United States) may still be my friend"; see Lefebvre, "Oman's Foreign Policy".
[55]Rozen, "Inside the US-Iran diplomacy".

Yemen, but it has also launched direct verbal attacks against Riyadh's plans and policies in the country, describing them as "a sectarian project to confront Iran".[56] In this sense, Muscat has pursued a clear and alternative position vis-à-vis the other GCC states on the Yemeni conflict, which, in Sultan Qaboos' view, is more in line with the country's long-term security interests and quest for stability.[57] Rather than dropping bombs, Muscat has opted for trying to pressure the international community into pursuing a diplomatic solution to the rapidly deteriorating conflict. Oman has also emphasized that a negotiated settlement must come from the Yemeni people, and not from foreign governments.[58]

Calling on its regional partners not to interfere in Yemen's future, Qaboos offered a venue for peace talks. In May 2015, Oman facilitated and hosted a meeting in Muscat between the Houthi delegation, representatives of the Saudi-led coalition and US officials to explore a political compromise that could contribute to de-escalating the tensions and increasing regional stability.[59] At the same time, Oman is reported to have presented Riyadh and Tehran with a seven-point plan, the so-called 'Muscat principles', for achievement of a peaceful solution to Yemen's ongoing conflict.[60]

That the Omani regime has successfully used its foreign policy and growing diplomatic leverage to raise its regional and global profile as a means, ultimately, to enhance its legitimacy should not detract attention from the limits and contradictions of Oman's stance, particularly those stemming from the domestic context. In addition to the aforementioned personalistic nature of the country's foreign policy (to an even greater extent than in Saudi Arabia) deriving from the concentration of absolute powers in both domestic and foreign affairs in the hands of the Sultan, two further elements are worth discussing. First, as already mentioned in the introduction to the article, the country suffered its own period of domestic unrest in 2011 when hundreds of demonstrators took to the streets in the northern port city of Sohar demanding jobs and an end to corruption. Sultan Qaboos swiftly responded by firing 12 cabinet ministers and raising government salaries while agreeing to boost unemployment benefits and minimum wages by 40 percent.[61] While these measures restored calm in the country, resorting to traditional patronage measures to address structural socio-economic problems and buy-off dissent did not amount to a sustainable response. Nevertheless, since then, not many steps have been taken to move towards a more effective system of governance and a more viable set of state-society relations.[62] While this has not affected Oman's foreign policy course *per se*, it raises a number of doubts regarding the country's ability to uphold its stances vis-à-vis the region in the long run while navigating increasingly unsustainable and uncertain times domestically.[63]

Second, Oman's peace brokering actions should not be mistaken for a pacifist inclination as this would contrast with Oman's constantly growing trend in military expenditures.

---

[56]"Oman 'ready to help mediate' in Yemen war", *Gulf News*, 3 April 2015, http://gulfnews.com/news/gulf/oman/oman-ready-to-help-mediate-in-yemen-war-1.1485236v.

[57]Baabood, "Oman's Independent Foreign Policy", 107–122.

[58]*Ibid.*

[59]Barrett, "Oman's Balancing Act in Yemen".

[60]"Oman's role as a negotiator in Yemen conflict important: UAE defence official", *Muscat Daily*, 10 October 2015, http://www.muscatdaily.com/Archive/Oman/Oman-s-role-as-a-negotiator-in-Yemen-conflict-important-UAE-defence-official-4cnw#ixzz4ErDKQKvY.

[61]Jones and Ridout, *A History of Modern Oman*.

[62]Echague, *Oman: the outlier*.

[63]Baabood, "Oman's Independent Foreign Policy", 107–22.

According to *SIPRI Yearbook*, Oman is the country with the highest rate of military expenditure as a percentage of GDP in the world, with figures hovering around the double-digit level. This rate has been increasing steadily in the past decade and hit an all-time high of 15.9 percent in 2012.[64] The explanation for this can be found in the country's perception of a volatile and unstable regional environment as well as the potential threat of domestic unrest, prompting the Omani regime to participate in the more generalised arms race prevailing in the Middle East. In conclusion, although it would be inappropriate to speak of pacifism as the defining trait of Oman's identity, it can be demonstrated that the country's substantial military capabilities have neither dictated nor been used to implement Oman's long-term foreign policy interests and goals.

Eroding GCC integration prospects

The diverging stances and narratives that emerged in Saudi Arabia and Oman after the Arab uprisings and towards the Syrian and Yemeni conflicts have produced an earthquake not only in their bilateral relations but especially within the group of GCC countries. Bilateral relations between Riyadh and Muscat have grown increasingly tense since 2011 with repeated attempts by Saudi Arabia to recapture its leadership position within the group and counter the process of dispersal of power into a number of competing centres vying for increased influence. One such attempt was the proposal formulated by the late Saudi King Abdullah bin Abdulaziz Al Saud in December 2011 to augment the regional integration of GCC countries through the creation of a Gulf Union among the six members. It was met with a general lack of enthusiasm on the part of the other GCC countries over the course of 2012. Then, as Arabian Gulf leaders watched with astonishment as Islamist-based majorities and presidents rose to power in Egypt, Morocco and Tunisia, Saudi Arabia and Oman clashed on this issue at the December 2013 GCC Summit, with Omani Foreign Minister bin Alawi stating that Oman would simply withdraw from the body if the five other GCC members decided to form a union. The project has been abandoned since then. However, it opened a Pandora's box of significant disagreements regarding the questions of leadership within the group, on the one hand, and GCC future integration prospects, on the other.

Regarding integration prospects, a number of authors have argued that the GCC has effectively created a "pocket of stability within a given sub-complex" on the basis of the shared interests in preserving the member countries' security and status quo in response to an equally shared perception of acute external threats.[65] Elements of unity and convergence are thus highlighted to demonstrate that "the cacophony of Gulf states' foreign policies actually ends up by being constructive, thus maximizing rather than reducing the Gulf influence over the region".[66] The analysis presented here, however, has shown that the rifts and heightened competition among GCC countries against the backdrop of fast-changing domestic and regional dynamics have tarnished this 'pocket of stability', exposing the sense of threat and vulnerability of some of them.[67] This does not necessarily mean that the individual countries' influence on the regional chessboard has diminished. Nevertheless, it goes hand in hand with increased sub-regional fragmentation with regard to the most important

---

[64]*Sipri Yearbook 2015*, 394.
[65]Calculli, "Sub-regions and Security"; Khalifa Isaac, "Resurgence in Arab Regional Institutions?".
[66]Calculli, *Ibid.*, 62.
[67]Gervais, "Changing Security Dynamics".

foreign policy dossiers in the Middle East, including matters extending beyond the region, such as multilateral cooperation between the European Union (EU) and the GCC.[68]

Two blocks are clearly shaping. On the one hand, the Omani-Qatari axis with the external support of and in close coordination with Turkey – despite some recent, significant changes in its foreign policy posture – and Iran; on the other, Saudi Arabia and its staunchest allies, namely Bahrain and the UAE. Whether or not this corresponds to an insurmountable obstacle on the way to regional cooperation and a definitive halt to the process of sub-regional integration at the GCC level will be dictated by future events and moves. Meanwhile, it is undeniable that the major differences in foreign policy behaviour between Saudi Arabia and Oman have, in the short term, cast a shadow over the sustainability and future of intra-regional relations.

Conclusions

This article has aimed to describe and explain the similarities and differences in the foreign policies of Saudi Arabia and Oman towards the Middle East in general and the Syrian and Yemeni conflicts in particular. Both countries seem to be pursuing a certain degree of pragmatism and autonomy in developing their foreign policy courses as a result of their need to balance domestic and external imperatives to ensure regime survival and defend the status quo domestically. This is in line with the insights derived from the application of the concept of omnibalancing found in the IR literature in relation to GCC countries' foreign policy dynamics, as well as from some reflections stemming from the debate on regime legitimacy.

Moving from this conceptual framework, the importance of domestic variables in explaining foreign policy courses has been stressed. The domestic variables highlighted in the article pertain to the ideational sphere (e.g., the religious-political alliance with the Wahhabi establishment and doctrine in the Saudi case and Oman's firm belief in the virtues of compromise and moderation) and to some specific contingent circumstances created by the tectonic shifts following the outbreak of the Arab uprisings as well as broader regional and global changes (e.g., rising sectarian tensions, heightened sense of vulnerability/opportunity of engagement vis-à-vis Iran, rise of competitive multipolarity in the Middle East).

Yet, these factors do not suffice to explain the significantly diverging narratives and stances of Saudi Arabia and Oman towards the Syrian and Yemeni conflicts. Saudi Arabia has undertaken a more assertiveness and rather 'aggressive' foreign policy stance entailing the use of military power with the ultimate goal of defending itself from regional competitors and anchoring its role as regional hegemon in foreign policy facts. Oman, on the contrary, has invoked balance and used negotiation to increase the country's clout at the regional and global levels. To explain such differences, the article has grounded its empirical contribution in the concept of swing states, which has thus been further qualified and concretely applied to the Omani case. Away from traditional readings of the notions of 'power' and 'influence' derived from the mainstream realist and neo-realist IR literature, the weight of mere size-related facts and other material capabilities, including the country's geographic position and economic resources, has been balanced with an appreciation of Muscat's ability to combine potentially conflicting interests, allies and foreign policy motivations and instruments in

---

[68] Author's interviews with Saudi scholars and GCC policymakers, Doha, October 2013, and Muscat, November 2013.

an adaptable and issue-based approach to further its long-term strategic goals. As such, Muscat has demonstrated its desire to be ahead of the curve on many dossiers, particularly with regard to engagement with Iran.

Thus, the article projects new light onto the foreign policy dynamics of GCC countries, and explains Oman's successful achievement of a more prominent place on the regional chessboard, in opposition or to the detriment of the 'old' regional hegemon, Saudi Arabia. Finally, the comparative analysis shows how the important differences between the Saudi and Omani stances are impacting on sub-regional dynamics within the GCC and the prospects for further integration (or lack thereof).

References

Allen, C.H., and W.L. Rigsbee II. *Oman Under Qaboos: From Coup to Constitution, 1970–1996*. London and New York: Routledge, 2002.

Ayoob, M. *The Third World Security Predicament*. London: Lynne Rienner, 1995.

Albrecht, H., and O. Schlumberger. "Waiting for Godot: Regime Change without Democratization in the Middle East". *International Political Science Review* 25, no. 4 (2004): 371–92.

Al-Dekhayel, A. *Kuwait: Oil, State and Political Legitimation*. Reading: Ithaca Press, 2000.

Baabood, A. "Oman's Independent Foreign Policy". In *The Small Gulf States. Foreign and Security Policies Before and After the Arab Spring*, edited by K.S. Almezaini and J.-M. Rickli: 107–22. London and New York: Routledge, 2017.

Barnett, M.N. *Dialogues in Arab Politics. Negotiations in Regional Order*. New York: Columbia University Press, 1998.

Barnett, M.N. "Institutions, Roles and Disorder: The Case of the Arab States System". *International Studies Quarterly* 37, no. 3 (1993): 271–96.

Barrett, R. "Oman's Balancing Act in the Yemen Conflict". *The Middle East Institute online*, 17 June 2015. http://www.mei.edu/content/at/oman%E2%80%99s-balancing-act-yemen-conflict.

Beblawi, H., and G. Luciani, eds. *The Rentier State*. London, New York and Sydney: Croom Helm, 1987.

Calculli, M. "Sub-regions and Security in the Arab Middle East: "hierarchical interdependence" in Gulf-Levant Relations". In *Regional Insecurity after the Arab Uprisings. Narratives of Security and Threat*, edited by E. Monier: 58–81. Basingstoke: Palgrave MacMillan, 2015.

Callen, T., R. Cherif, F. Hasanov, A. Hegazy, and P. Khandelwal. *Economic Diversification in the GCC: Past, Present, and Future, International Monetary Fund Report*. Washington DC: IMF, 2014.

Colombo, S. "The GCC and the Arab Spring: A Tale of Double Standards", *The International Spectator* 47, no. 4 (2012): 110–26.

Cordesman, A.H. *Bahrain, Oman, Qatar, and the UAE: Challenges of Security*. Boulder, CO: Westview Press, 1997.

David, S. *Choosing Sides: Alignment and Realignment in the Third World*. Baltimore: Johns Hopkins University Press, 1991.

Davidson, C.M. *After the Sheikhs: The coming collapse of the Gulf monarchies*. London: Hurst, 2012.

Echague, A. *Oman: the outlier*, FRIDE Policy Brief. Barcelona: FRIDE, October 2015.

Ehteshami, A., and R. Hinnebusch. "Foreign Policymaking in the Middle East: Complex Realism". In *International Relations of the Middle East*, edited by L. Fawcett: 225–45. Oxford: Oxford University Press, 2013.

Gause, F.G. *Kings for All Seasons: How the Middle East's Monarchies Survived the Arab Spring*, Brookings Doha Center Analysis N° 8. Doha: Brookings, September 2013.

Gervais, V. "The Changing Security Dynamics in the Middle East and its Impact on Smaller GCC States: Alliance Choices And Policies". In *The Small Gulf States. Foreign and Security Policies Before and After the Arab Spring*, edited by K.S. Almezaini and J.-M. Rickli: 31–46. London and New York: Routledge, 2017.

Halliday, F. *The Middle East in International Relations: Power, Politics and Ideology*. Cambridge: Cambridge University Press, 2005.

Herb, M. *All in the Family: Absolutism, Revolution and Democracy in the Middle Eastern Monarchies*. Albany: State University of New York Press, 1999.

Hertog, S. "The Cost of the Counter Revolution in the GCC". *Foreign Policy*. 31 May 2011. http://mideast.foreignpolicy.com/posts/2011/05/31/the_costs_of_counter_revolution_in_the_gcc

Hey, J. *Small States in World Politics: Explaining Foreign Policy Behaviour*. London: Lynne Rienner, 2003.

Hoffmann, B. *The International Dimensions of Authoritarian Legitimation: The Impact of Regime Evolution*, GIGA article N° 182. Hamburg: GIGA, December 2011.

Holbig, H. "International Dimensions of Regime Legitimacy: Reflections on Western Theories and the Chinese Experience". *Journal of Chinese Political Science* 16, no. 2–3 (2011): 161–81.

Hudson, M.C. *Arab Politics: The Search for Legitimacy*. New Haven: Yale University Press, 1977.

Hurrell, A. "Hegemony, Liberalism and Global Order: What Space for Would-Be Great Powers?" *International Affairs* 82, no. 1 (2006): 1–19.

Jones, J. *Oman's Quiet Diplomacy*. Oslo: Norwegian Institute of International Affairs, 28 February 2014. http://www.nupi.no/en/News/Oman-s-quiet-diplomacy-and-Iran

Jones, J., and N. Ridout. *Oman, Culture and Diplomacy*. Edinburgh: Edinburgh University Press, 2013.

Jones, J., and N. Ridout. *A History of Modern Oman*. Cambridge: Cambridge University Press, 2013.

Kamrava, M. *Qatar: Small State, Big Politics*. Ithaca, NY: Cornell University Press, 2013.

Kausch, K. *The Promise of Middle Eastern Swing States*. Brussels: Carnegie Europe, 12 May 2016. http://carnegieeurope.eu/2016/05/12/promise-of-middle-eastern-swing-states/iy77

Kausch, K. "Competitive Multipolarity in the Middle East". *The International Spectator* 50, no. 3 (2015): 1–15.

Khalifa Isaac, S. "A Resurgence in Arab Regional Institutions? The Cases of the Arab League and the Gulf Cooperation Council Post-2011". In *Regional Insecurity after the Arab Uprisings. Narratives of Security and Threat*, edited by E. Monier: 151–67. Basingstoke: Palgrave MacMillan, 2015.

Kliman, D. M., and R. Fontaine. *Global Swing States: Brazil, India, Indonesia, Turkey, and the Future of the International Order*. Washington DC: GMF, 27 November 2012. http://www.gmfus.org/publications/global-swing-states-brazil-india-indonesia-turkey-and-future-international-order

Kostiner, J, ed. *Middle East Monarchies: The Challenge of Modernity*. Boulder, CO: Lynne Rienner, 2000.

Lefebvre, J. A. "Oman's Foreign Policy in the Twenty-First Century". *Middle East Policy Council* XVII, no. 1 (2010).

Lipset, S.M. *Political Man: The Social Bases of Politics*. London: Heinemann, 1960.

Matthiesen, T. *Sectarian Gulf: Bahrain, Saudi Arabia, and the Arab Spring that Wasn't*. Palo Alto, CA: Stanford University Press, 2013.

Mazzetti, M., and B. Hubbard. "Rise of Saudi Prince Shatters Decades of Royal Tradition". *The New York Times*, 15 October 2016. https://mobile.nytimes.com/2016/10/16/world/rise-of-saudi-prince-shatters-decades-of-royal-tradition.html

Niblock, T. *Saudi Arabia. Power, Legitimacy and Survival*. London and New York: Routledge, 2006.

Nonneman, G. *Analyzing Middle East Foreign Policies and the Relationship with Europe*. London and New York: Routledge, 2005.

Nonneman, G. "Determinants and Patterns of Saudi Foreign Policy: 'Omnibalancing' and 'Relative Autonomy' in Multiple Environments". In *Saudi Arabia in the Balance. Political Economy, Society, Foreign Affairs*, edited by P. Aarts and G. Nonneman: 315–51. London: Hurst & Co, 2005.

O'Reilly, M. "Omnibalancing: Oman Confronts an Uncertain Future". *Middle East Journal* 52, no. 1 (1998): 70–84.

Peterson, J.E. "Qatar and the World: Branding for a Micro-State". *Middle East Journal* 60, no. 4 (2006): 732–48.

Purple, M. "Why Saudi Arabia is Hammering Yemen". *The National Interest*, 12 April 2016. http://nationalinterest.org/feature/why-saudi-arabia-hammering-yemen-15748

Rickli, J.-M., and K. Almezaini. "Theories of Small States' Foreign and Security Policies and the Gulf states". In *The Small Gulf States. Foreign and Security Policies Before and After the Arab Spring*, edited by K.S. Almezaini and J.-M. Rickli: 8–30. London and New York: Routledge, 2017.

Rozen, L. "Inside the secret US-Iran diplomacy that sealed nuke deal". *Al Monitor*, 11 August 2015. http://www.al-monitor.com/pulse/originals/2015/08/iran-us-nuclear-khamenei-salehi-jcpoa-diplomacy.html

SipriYearbook 2015. *Armaments, Disarmament and International Security*. Oxford: Oxford University Press, 2015.

Schanzer, J. "Saudi Arabia is Arming the Syrian Opposition". *Foreign Policy*, 27 February 2012.

Smith, B. "Oil Wealth and Regime Survival in the Developing World, 1960–1999". *American Journal of Political Science* 48, no. 2 (2004): 232–46.

Stephens, M. "Mixed success for Saudi military operation in Yemen". *BBC News*, 12 May 2015. http://www.bbc.com/news/world-middle-east-32593749

Ulrichsen, K.C. *Qatar and the Arab Spring*. London: Hurst & Co, 2014.

Ulrichsen, K. C. *The Gulf States and the Rebalancing of Regional and Global Power*, Research paper. Houston: Rice University, 8 January 2014. http://bakerinstitute.org/media/files/Research/ec7b03d8/CME-Pub-GulfStates-010813.pdf

Ulrichsen, K.C. *Small States with a Big Role: Qatar and the United Arab Emirates in the Wake of the Arab Spring*, Discussion Article. Durham: HH Sheikh Nasser Al-Sabah Programme, 2012.

Ulrichsen, K.C. *Insecure Gulf: the End of Certainty and the Transition to the Post-Oil Era*. New York: Columbia University Press, 2011.

Valeri, M. "Identity Politics and Nation-Building under Sultan Qaboos". In *Sectarian Politics in the Persian Gulf*, edited by L.G. Potter: 179–206. London/New York: Hurst/Oxford University Press, 2013.

Valeri, M. *Oman. Politics and Society in the Qaboos State*. London: Hurst & Co, 2009.

Walt, S. *The Origins of Alliances*. Ithaca: Cornell University Press, 1987.

Weber, M. *Economy and Society*. Berkeley: University of California Press, 1978.

Weber, M. *The Theory of Social and Economic Organization*. New York: Oxford University Press, 1947.

Wehrey, F.M. *Sectarian Politics in the Gulf: From the Iraq war to the Arab uprisings*. New York: Columbia University Press, 2014.

Worrall, J. "Oman: The 'Forgotten' Corner of the Arab Spring". *Middle East Policy Council* XIX, no. 3 (2012). http://www.mepc.org/journal/middle-east-policy-archives/oman-forgotten-corner-arab-spring?print

Wright, S. "Foreign Policy in the GCC States". In *International Politics of the Persian Gulf*, edited by M. Kemrava: 72–93. Syracuse: Syracuse University Press, 2011.

Yom, S.L., and F.G. Gause. "Resilient Royals: How Arab Monarchies Hang On". *Journal of Democracy* 23, no. 4 (2012): 75–88.

Youngs, R. "Living with the Middle East's Old-New Security Paradigm". In *The Gulf States and the Arab Uprisings*, edited by A. Echague: 15–24. Geneva: FRIDE and the Gulf Research Centre, 2013.

The Evolution of Saudi Foreign Policy and the Role of Decision-making Processes and Actors

Umer Karim

ABSTRACT

Saudi Arabia has witnessed a centralisation of power in the office of the deputy crown prince, which has amounted to a shift in decision-making from consensual and deliberative to swift and adventurous, most markedly in foreign policy. This centralisation is coupled with an increase in institutionalisation. A new decision-making pattern and rising Iranian power in the region have affected the evolution of Saudi foreign policy. The Saudi crown prince's strict handling of Shia dissidents acknowledges the perceived extension of the Iranian threat to internal security. The relationship between these two princes and Saudi political competition with Iran will affect the evolution of Saudi foreign policy in a critical manner in the future.

The foreign policymaking of a state bears the mark of the system in which it functions, but it is also oriented by the internal dynamics of the state. The specific nature of the Kingdom of Saudi Arabia, lying at the crossroads of the Middle East, North Africa and South Asia, and home to Islam's holiest places, makes it one of the most politically and strategically important nations in the world.[1] Yet, the resurgence of Iran as a strong regional player is now challenging the regional power enjoyed by Saudi Arabia. In addition, Saudi Arabia has seen its political interests in the region diverge increasingly from those of the United States, a trusted and worthy ally and a long-time security guarantor of the Kingdom. The most evident manifestation of this is the American and European agreement with Iran over its nuclear program, with US President Barack Obama urging Saudi Arabia to "share the neighborhood" with Iran.[2] This US approach has heightened Saudi security concerns. The other major challenge for the Saudi state is the steep drop in oil revenues and the resultant burden on the economy. In a rentier state like Saudi Arabia, where the population has become accustomed to financial patronage from the state, such an economic downturn has implications for the internal security of the state, adding to the other political challenges facing the Saudi royalty.[3]

---

[1]Haykel *et al.*, *Saudi Arabia in Transition*, 1-10.
[2]Goldberg, "The Obama Doctrine".
[3]Hertog, "A Rentier Social Contract".

This was the state of affairs when King Salman replaced King Abdullah, after his death on 23 January 2015. The kingdom had two choices: either to accept President Obama's advice or to proactively counter Iran by itself, assuming a regional leadership role far less dependent on the US.

The questions this article will address are the role played by the new royal members in command in framing the threat posed by Iran and how the changes in the power hierarchy and decision-making processes in the Kingdom have translated into foreign policy strategies. The article will start with a description of Saudi foreign policymaking and its major determinants. This will be followed by a look at the changes in Saudi foreign policy under King Salman and the system in which decisions in different realms of government are taken. The focus of this endeavour is to highlight the structural changes in 1) the power hierarchy within the Saudi leadership, 2) the relationships between the new Saudi power-holders and their policy preferences in respective domains, 3) the decision-making process and how that has affected foreign policymaking. The implications of Iranian resurgence on Saudi foreign policy and how much that variable has contributed to transforming it will also be evaluated. For this purpose, the execution of Shia cleric Sheikh Nimr and the Saudi military intervention in Yemen will be analysed.

Saudi foreign policy

Former US Secretary of State Dean Acheson said, "the national purpose of the Kingdom of Saudi Arabia, like that of any other country, is to *survive, perchance to prosper*, but with the added proviso *under the Al Saud dynasty*".[4]

Traditionally, Saudi policymakers have always applied caution in regional overtures, adopted pragmatism, and strengthened relations with allied states, specifically the United States, to maintain stability and security, both internally and externally. This prudent approach was practiced in order to safeguard the sovereignty of the Saudi state and the survival of the Saudi regime. It manifested itself in the Saudi foreign policy goals, which include expanding regional influence to counter threats against territorial integrity, as well as containing supra-state ideologies that can threaten or question the legitimacy of the Saudi regime.

"Omnibalancing" has been practiced by decision-makers to balance out against external and internal threats. In order to counter an internal threat, support has been sought from external resources, and if an external threat becomes menacing, internal unity and legitimacy have been used to counter it. Saudi Arabia used this "pronghorn" approach to defend against external threats that emanated from Nasserite Egypt, Baathist Iraq and post-revolution Iran, as well as to resist against threats posed by supra-state movements like pan-Arabism and the Muslim Brotherhood.[5] These dynamics further intertwined the domains of internal and external policy.

This political context has been an evident hallmark of Saudi foreign policymaking. The Kingdom has adopted a cautious, calculated and pragmatic foreign policy to allay its security concerns. Yet it would be unwise to interpret Saudi foreign policy as stagnant. From the time of Ibn al-Saud and during the reigns of different Saudi monarchs, foreign policymaking has

---

[4] Eilts, "Saudi Arabia's Foreign Policy", 219.
[5] Nonneman, "Determinants of Saudi Foreign Policy", 318.

been evolving and adapting to the political developments in the region and world as well as to changing domestic dynamics.[6]

Being a powerful Gulf kingdom, Saudi Arabia has always been closely associated with other Gulf kingdoms and has institutionalised this association in the form of the Gulf Cooperation Council (GCC) in order to safeguard its security interests in the region.[7] The GCC platform provides Saudi Arabia with a pivotal power position on the Arabian Peninsula. It is the biggest contributor to regional GDP, accounting for 46 percent in 2013. Al-Mawali suggests that growth in the Saudi economy is not only linked to but further amplifies the economic growth of GCC nations.[8] In addition to this economic centrality, Saudi Arabia also leads the GCC in the security domain. It spearheaded the efforts to counter Arab Spring activism in the GCC by supporting the beleaguered Bahraini monarchy. This role has been further heightened by the Saudi-led military intervention in Yemen. In all its regional manifestations, Saudi Arabia attempts to use the GCC platform to add to its political weight and legitimacy.[9]

There have been ups and downs in the Saudi relationship with other GCC countries, the most notable case being Saudi tensions with Qatar. However, the political balance has been restored since the Saudi rapprochement with Qatar and its full support of Saudi intervention in Yemen.[10] GCC formation and its use as a strategic alliance for security purposes has been a chief part of Saudi policy. Indeed, former Saudi Ambassador to the United States, Prince Turki Al-Faisal, in his address to the 2015 annual Arab-US Policymakers conference, expressed the view that unity of the GCC and mutual cooperation are high on the Saudi foreign policy agenda. He also stressed that Saudi Arabia has a unique responsibility in this regard, which warrants a leading role for the Kingdom.[11]

Small-scale interventions on a limited level have been taken in the past. After the Arab Spring protests in Bahrain and Oman, GCC states showed strong concern and in March 2011 the Saudi government intervened in Bahrain to save its ally, showing that instability in the GCC is a red line for the Saudis.[12] Yet, intervention in Yemen in 2015 is the first large-scale military campaign conducted by GCC states, with Jordan and Morocco contributing with their air forces.[13] This endorses the view that Saudi foreign policy is gradually evolving from being cautious and calculated to more assertive and ambitious, and one that posits the Kingdom as the main power defending political interests in the Sunni Arab world.

Domestic determinants

Foreign policymaking in Saudi Arabia can be understood not only by examining the structural changes in the international political system, but also by observing the contestations in the sub-systemic or regional power circles, in particular the rise of Iran's political influence

---

[6]Eilts, "Saudi Arabia's Foreign Policy", 219.
[7]Members include Bahrain, Kuwait, Oman, Qatar, Saudi Arabia and the United Arab Emirates. Hinnebusch, *International Politics of Middle East*, 92.
[8]Al-Mawali, "Intra-Gulf Cooperation Council", 533-47.
[9]Dazi-Heni, *Can We Speak of a New Regional Order?*
[10]It is interesting that this change has occurred mainly due to a change in leadership in both countries, but this is beyond the scope of this article. For more information, see Ibish, "Qatar Changes Course".
[11]Al-Faisal, "Saudi Foreign Policy Vision".
[12]Ulrichsen, "Repositioning Saudi Arabia", 242.
[13]Knights and Mello, *The Saudi-UAE War Effort in Yemen*.

in the Middle East, as well as the internal political realities of the Saudi state.[14] Continuation of the rule of the House of Saud is the most important aspect of Saudi national life, and governmental policies in turn orient toward this goal.[15] Policymaking in the Kingdom is meant to strengthen and further the ruling regime and alleviate any challenges that could potentially threaten it. This is the base that connects the domains of domestic and foreign policy.[16] Foreign policy has to be oriented in such a manner that it not only promotes and protects Saudi political interests on the international stage, but also helps in achieving internal stability. It invariably touches the political, social, economic and religious domains that are in turn all linked with the Saudi regime and are an embodiment of its power.[17]

In this regard, it is the Saudi royalty that is central in foreign policy decision-making. At the top of the decision-making hierarchy sits the Saudi king himself, assisted by other princes in running the state. The nature of this hierarchy and power relationship between the members of the innermost core of Saudi royalty has differed for various Saudi monarchs, but this system of decision-making has prevailed over time. Nevertheless, institutional structures that have a predominantly bureaucratic setup like the Saudi Ministry of Foreign Affairs do exist and play an important role in coordinating and communicating with international audiences.

The Saudi state has a rentier character as it depends largely on oil revenues to maintain its budgetary obligations. Saudi Arabia is the leading oil producer in the world and has at times acted as a swing producer in terms of oil price.[18] The bounty deriving from the export of petro-chemical products is employed to give generous handouts and subsidies to Saudi citizens in order to maintain their political acquiescence and preserve power in the hands of the Saudi royalty. Oil, therefore, has become a very important variable in Saudi policymaking.

The most important domestic factor affecting foreign policy and its orientation, however, although with a limited role in the decision-making process itself is the Saudi religious establishment made up of members of the Al ash-Sheikh family, descendants of Mohammad ibn Abd al-Wahhab, the founder of Wahhabism. This religious elite, often called the *Ulema*, are the major drivers of legitimacy for the Saudi regime. Any foreign policy measure of a controversial nature or even domestic policy concerning some sensitive issue can be made more palatable to the populace by the clerical elite. A *fatwa* given by these clerics in support of a controversial foreign policy decision can lessen the internal opposition and become a way of garnering further support from society.[19] The Ulema create the frames of legitimacy for a ruler, but it must be understood that the legitimacy itself comes from the ideology of Wahhabism, which these Ulema can then exegete into a religious edict to support a government decision.

This religious interpretation becomes even more important in the case of a disagreement within the royal family. It has been suggested that it was the support of the Ulema for Prince Faisal against King Saud that decisively paved the way for his ascension to the Saudi throne.[20] In other cases, the support of the Ulema has been vital for Saudi monarchs

---

[14]Nonneman, "Determinants Saudi Foreign Policy", 315-7.
[15]Kamrava, "Mediation and Saudi Foreign Policy", 5.
[16]Ennis and Momani, "Shaping the Middle East".
[17]Hertog, *Princes, Brokers, and Bureaucrats*, 2-3.
[18]Echagüe, "Saudi Arabia: emboldened yet vulnerable".
[19]Gause, *Saudi Arabia in New Middle East*.
[20]Byman, "U.S.-Saudi Arabia counterterrorism relationship".

in orchestrating foreign policy measures that might have generated large-scale opposition at home. The rallying of the Saudi Ulema in favour of the Saudi government was most prominent when Saudi Arabia hosted the United States military during the First Gulf War.[21] The Ulema were there again to defend and legitimise the Saudi regime when the wave of Arab Spring protests started in 2011. This support was crucial in achieving low levels of dissent against the Saudi regime.[22]

The traditional decision-making process

Foreign policymaking in Saudi Arabia has always been a rather consensual affair. In order to understand it, an appreciation of the hierarchical power structure within the Al Saud family dictating the roles and positions of family members must be developed. After the removal of King Saud from the throne and the ascension of King Faisal, a new system of governance took shape in which all sectors of the family had some share of power.[23] In this system of governance, the king held absolute power and was fully autonomous in decision-making, yet he was surrounded by his brothers who also had substantial powers. Their status was regarded as almost equal to the king, with the king being *primus inter pares* among his brothers and half-brothers.[24] In this system, a decision was reached only after broad consultation between the King, the de facto prime minister, and the influential princes, who held the posts of crown prince, deputy crown prince, defence minister, foreign minister and interior minister. The head of the General Intelligence Presidency (GIP) was also involved, but to a lesser degree.[25] In the case of disagreement, the word of the King decided the matter.[26]

It is interesting to note that the personal agency of all these men at the helm of affairs had much weight in the policy decisions and strategies adopted. This decision-making process was quite different from an autocratic or dictatorial political system in which power is mostly the prerogative of one person or one position. The setup did not change much during the reigns of King Khalid, King Fahd and King Abdullah. In this manner, the traditional mechanism of policymaking in the Kingdom was a slow deliberative process.

Although each King pursued his own agenda and policy orientation, policies were transformed in a gentle and measured manner.[27] This was the most profound during the reign of King Abdullah. Iraq's defeat in the First Gulf War comprehensively removed a major threat to Saudi national security. The death of Ayatollah Khomeini and the arrival of new leadership in Iran also affected the Kingdom's foreign policy orientation considerably. The new geopolitical situation opened up possibilities for both countries to enhance their engagement. This ultimately resulted in a rapprochement between the two countries, centred on developing an understanding and acceptance of their political and ideological differences and simultaneously resolving to sit together and cooperate.

This departure from the traditional Saudi stance on Iran occurred as a result of, on the one hand, a change in the perceptions and policies of the Iranian leadership and, on the

---

[21] Al-Rasheed, *A History of Saudi Arabia*, 163.
[22] Gause, *Saudi Arabia in New Middle East*.
[23] Henderson, *After King Abdullah Succession in Saudi Arabia*.
[24] Korany and Fattah, "Irreconcilable Role-Partners?", 366.
[25] Altoraifi, "Understanding role of state identity", 197-8.
[26] Hinnebusch, "Introduction: The Analytic Framework", 381.
[27] Alajlan, "Vision 2030 offers hope".

other, a more central position of Crown Prince Abdullah in Saudi politics after King Fahd suffered from a stroke.[28] There were sections of the Saudi administration that were reluctant to pursue such a conciliatory approach towards Iran and were in favour of a more aggressive policy, especially in light of its advances in missile technology. The Ministry of the Interior also had concerns about the policy of normalising ties with Tehran, and this delayed the deliberations over a bilateral security accord. Eventually and gradually, however, the policy of rapprochement promoted by Crown Prince Abdullah prevailed.

There were also important domestic considerations that contributed to this policy orientation, but the role of leadership on both sides was critical. In Saudi Arabia, this policy remained unchanged, even after the Khobar bombing carried out by Hezbollah al-Hijaz, a terrorist group supported by the Iranian Revolutionary Guards.[29] This throws further light onto the resolve of Crown Prince Abdullah to pursue the policy of rapprochement vis-à-vis Iran. It is quite possible that if there had been another Saudi monarch, the decisions taken might have been quite different in response to such an incident.

New decision-makers and the centralisation of power

The ascent of King Salman to the Saudi throne has resulted in the adoption of a more assertive and interventionist foreign policy strategy to pursue national interests. This new royal elite and the new power hierarchy has essentially changed the very nature of decision-making in the Kingdom. Since ascension, King Salman has taken some steps that are unprecedented in the history of the Kingdom. He is the first person to have restructured the line of succession to the Saudi throne by removing his crown price, appointing his nephew as the new crown prince and his son as deputy crown prince.[30]

Crown Prince Muhammad Bin Nayef heads the Interior Ministry and the counter-terrorist infrastructure of Saudi Arabia. He also chairs the Council of Political and Security Affairs, a new administrative structure formed by King Salman. However, the crown prince has been overshadowed by the visibility, activism and power of his junior partner, the deputy crown prince. Deputy Crown Prince Mohammad Bin Salman is the Defence Minister and head of the Council of Economic and Development Affairs.[31] He is also the first chief of King Salman's royal court, which allows him to scrutinise people meeting the king.[32] He is the visible face of Saudi leadership worldwide and has visited the White House, NATO (North Atlantic Treaty Organisation) Headquarters and world capitals on official tours. He is evidently the 'voice' of the Kingdom.[33]

The appointment of Adel Al-Jubeir as the first non-royal foreign minister has further enhanced the power position of Prince Mohammad Bin Salman, as Al-Jubeir, unlike a royal

---

[28]Zuhur, *Saudi Arabia*, 62.

[29]On 25 June 1996, a truck filled with explosives was blown up outside a housing complex of US air force personnel in the city of Khobar. This resulted in the death of 19 American nationals and wounded 498 others. Altoraifi, "Understanding role of state identity", 199-204.

[30]Carey and Syeed, "Saudi Balancing Act Abandoned".

[31]Gause, "Saudi Arabia's Game of Thrones".

[32]Kirkpatrick, "Surprising Saudi Rises".

[33]In his interview with *The Economist*, he openly emphasised that the United States has a responsibility as the most powerful nation of the world and must act likewise. This was a clear message to the US that Saudi expectations, in terms of dealing with Iran, its actions in the Middle East and the nuclear deal had not been fulfilled. That Prince Mohammad Bin Salman said this was significant, as historically such messages were given either by the King or crown prince or by the foreign minister. "Interview with Muhammad bin Salman", *The Economist*, 6 January 2016. http://www.economist.com/saudi_interview.

position holder, has no specific constituency or power within the Saud family. Moreover, the head of the General Intelligence Presidency (GIP), Khalid bin Ali Al Humaidan, is also a non-royal.[34] Interestingly, all persons within the top leadership of Saudi Arabia belong to the Sudairi branch of the royal family, which means there has been an unprecedented accumulation of power by this specific branch of the family.

Doubts have been expressed about the health of King Salman and his functional capacity to govern actively.[35] This has amounted to a further increase in the power of the deputy crown prince and greater influence over all domains of policymaking and governance. The control of power has significant implications for foreign policy decision-making. Aggressive foreign policy initiatives like the military intervention against the Houthis in Yemen,[36] the formation of a 34-country Islamic Military Alliance against terrorism with the conspicuous absence of Iran,[37] and diplomatic initiatives to strengthen ties with Turkey and Qatar are seen as outcomes of the change in royal guard.[38]

The prominence of Prince Mohammad Bin Salman in all these affairs warrants two questions about Saudi policymaking. The first is about the role of Saudi crown prince in this policymaking, how much is he involved and what is the nature of his relationship with Prince Mohammad Bin Salman. The other question is more focused on Saudi foreign policy and inquires whether the departure of Saudi foreign policy from a pragmatic to a more belligerent line is largely due to a change in Saudi royalty and its decision-making model or a change in the nature of the rising political and security challenges posed by Iran.

Reasons for an aggressive foreign policy

The young Prince's domain

Prince Mohammad Bin Salman possesses a unique degree of power, unparalleled in Saudi history, with virtual control over the Foreign, Defence, Finance and Petroleum Ministries. An important development has been greater involvement of bureaucrats and advisors in decision-making and policy formation.[39] The rise of Brigadier General Ahmad Al-Assiri as advisor to the deputy crown prince and as spokesperson of the Defence Ministry is one such case. He has been advocating the Saudi policy line, especially with respect to Yemen, to world media outlets. The other notable case is the rise of Adel Al-Jubeir, a long-time Saudi diplomat, as the first non-royal to become a foreign minister.[40] Both cases reveal the unique degree of trust the royalty has in their capabilities, but more significantly, the breaking of the taboo that a non-royal cannot reach these positions. This phenomenon is less notable in the financial and economic sectors in which there has always been a relatively larger technocratic influence. Nonetheless, it can be said that role of advisors and consultants is another key feature of the new decision-making process in the Kingdom, even though all these developments take place with the consent and under the wing of Prince Mohammad Bin Salman.

---

[34]Henderson, "Princely Personalities Sidelined in Saudi Arabia".
[35]Sullivan, "Before he was king".
[36]Bahout *et al.*, "Saudi Arabia's Changing International Role".
[37]Jenkins, "A Saudi-Led Military Alliance".
[38]Cafiero and Wagner, "Turkey and Qatar's Burgeoning Strategic Alliance".
[39]Saab, "Can bin Salman Reshape Saudi Arabia?".
[40]Karam, "Saudi Arabia's new foreign minister".

Only the mega governance structure of the Saudi Interior Ministry is under the direct control of Crown Prince Mohammed Bin Nayef, and it is the only potential arena of governance in which policymaking is not the domain of Prince Mohammad Bin Salman.[41] This division of power also shows that the Saudi political system in which different princes held onto different positions of power has now been reshaped into one in which, after the king, only the crown prince and the deputy crown prince hold the kind of power that can change policy orientations. This points to a considerable degree of centralisation and a significant shift in the decision-making process itself - centralisation that has paved the way for Prince Mohammad Bin Salman to pursue an aggressive foreign policy. In part, this approach can be attributed to a desire on the part of the prince to achieve quick results. Being a young man in his early thirties and without significant experience, the prince is known for his hawkish demeanour. However, one must not ignore the fact that his father, King Salman, bestows full confidence on him and approves of his policies.[42]

The Iranian variable

The influence of Iran has risen significantly in all Gulf countries after the American invasion of Iraq and the Arab Spring protests. On the contrary, the Saudis have lost much of their clout in all these countries, posing a threat to their standing in the region.

The American invasion of Iraq in 2003 effectively paved the way for Iran to expand its sphere of influence inside Iraq. Iran historically had strong ties with Shia political movements in Iraq and exploited these links to further its political clout. This Iranian influence could not effectively translate into Iraqi politics as long as the US was present in Iraq, during which time the Iraqi government was relatively successful in playing both sides off against each other. However, the US withdrawal from Iraq allowed Iran to strengthen its foothold. In the Iraqi elections of 2010, Iranian manoeuvring was instrumental in uniting various Shia political forces to form a government more amenable to Iran.[43] Nevertheless, Iraqi political forces treaded a delicate balance in terms of following their own interests and those of Iran. Iran was probably more successful in its support for Shia armed militias. These groups were trained and financed by the Iranian Republican Guard Corps - Quds Force (IRGC-QF).[44]

The next change in the regional balance of power came through the Arab Spring protests in 2011. Close Saudi ally President Hosni Mubarak of Egypt was toppled by mass protests and the royalty in Bahrain also faced a massive uprising that threatened its rule. Saudis eventually intervened military to save the Bahraini monarchy.

The uprising against Syrian President Bashar Al-Assad presented a different picture for Saudi Arabia. As an ally of Iran, Assad's downfall would threaten Iran's political power in the Levant and its strategic link to Hezbollah in Lebanon. Iran thus used the IRGC, Hezbollah and a plethora of Shia militias to bolster Assad.[45] Saudi Arabia, on the other hand, alongside Turkey and Qatar, backed Syrian rebels, but the lack of a coherent strategy, diverging goals

---

41 Riedel, "The Prince of Counterterrorism".
42 Henderson, "Saudi Arabia's 'Inexperienced Youngster'".
43 Kagan *et al*, "Iranian Influence in the Levant", 70.
44 Eisenstadt *et al.*, "Iran's Influence in Iraq", 3-12.
45 Ansari and Tabrizi, "The view from Tehran", 3-11.

amongst these backers and complex local dynamics resulted in a failure to oust the Assad regime from power.[46]

In Yemen, the takeover of Sanaa by Shiite Houthi rebels in alliance with former President Ali Abdullah Saleh altered the traditional Saudi influence over Yemeni politics. Historically, Saudi Arabia had relations with all actors in the Yemeni political fabric. The Yemeni President Saleh was backed by Saudis in the 1970s and 1980s, but his stance on the Iraqi invasion of Kuwait damaged the relationship in the 1990s. It was restored in 2000 and the Saudis understood that only Saleh could guarantee a stable Yemen. Saudi Arabia was also a primary source of economic aid to Yemen.[47]

The extent of support and linkages between Iran and the Houthis is debatable and it has been argued that Iranian support is not so crucial that the Houthis would collapse without it.[48] The Saudis, instead, see the current conflict in Yemen as an Iranian effort to convert the Houthis into a strong paramilitary force in Yemen that can challenge the Yemeni state and become a source of trouble for Saudi Arabia along the Saudi-Yemen border.[49] On the other hand, Iran has questioned the legitimacy of the government of President Abdrabbuh Mansour Hadi and the GCC-brokered agreement which transferred power to President Hadi from Ali Abdullah Saleh. Iran is of the view that the Houthi takeover of Sanaa is a just manifestation of frustration and bitterness of Yemenis against a government that was imposed on them. Iranian religious authorities view Houthi actions as akin to those of the 1979 Islamic revolution in Iran. The offices of the Supreme Leader and Iranian President equally condemned the Saudi intervention in Yemen and have blamed the Saudis for playing the sectarian card in the conflict. There was even speculation in some circles that the Saudi intervention in Yemen was an attempt to jeopardise the negotiations between Iran and the P5+1 on the Iranian nuclear program.[50]

Saudi Arabia's stance has been generally negative towards the Iranian nuclear deal, widely known as the Joint Comprehensive Plan of Action (JCPOA), which Iran signed with the P5+1 countries (United States, Russia, China, France, United Kingdom and Germany) as well as the European Union. Initially, Saudi officials felt that the nuclear deal would have positive effects on regional security by ending the threat posed by Iran's nuclear program. However, on 6 April 2015, Adel Al-Jubeir, Saudi ambassador in Washington at that time and later foreign minister, expressed scepticism about the nature of the agreement intended by the P5+1 and Iran. Veteran Saudi commentators and the press have been much more hostile towards the nuclear deal.[51] As the lifting of sanctions implies Iran's return to the international market, Saudi Arabia is worried that this will provide Iran with the economic resources to further its position in regional affairs and strengthen its proxy elements. The agreement becomes an incremental source of concern for Saudis when they see it against the backdrop of a waning US commitment to their political interests in the region. Therefore, the US relationship with Saudi Arabia has also contributed negatively to the Saudi stance on the JCPOA.[52]

---

[46] Pierret, "State Sponsors and Syrian Insurgency", 22-8.
[47] Horton, *The Unseen Hand*.
[48] Juneau, "Iran's policy towards the Houthis".
[49] Hariri Center, "Challenges to Yemeni Peace Process".
[50] Selvik, *War in Yemen*.
[51] Pasha, "Saudi Arabia and Nuclear Deal", 392-7.
[52] Einhorn and Nephew, "The Iran nuclear deal".

Case studies of change

The change in Saudi decision-making is an independent variable and cannot be linked to regional politics or the current confrontation with Iran. It is, however, a major factor at play affecting the orientation of a new proactive Saudi foreign policy. The relationship between the Saudi crown prince and the deputy crown prince, the level of Crown Prince Muhammad Bin Nayef's influence on Saudi foreign policy and his views about the strategies pursued by his younger cousin are key to understanding how this new Saudi decision-making process works and how it will dictate foreign policymaking in the future. Two important political events will be analysed to investigate this question.

Execution of Sheikh Nimr al-Nimr

A very important political event that shook the entire region and had an extremely negative impact on Saudi-Iran relations was the execution of the dissident Shia cleric Sheikh Nimr al-Nimr, followed by the execution of a number of Al-Qaeda operatives.

First, it is essential to understand who among the current Saudi royals was most likely to be behind this decision. Sheikh Nimr had been a fierce critic of the late Prince Nayef, the father of the current crown prince. He was the Interior Minister of Saudi Arabia for more than thirty years and had conducted numerous crackdowns in the restive Eastern Province, mainly against Shia activists. Following the protests in 2011 against the Saudi royalty, the Interior Ministry forces arrested Sheikh Nimr on charges of instigating unrest. After his execution, protests erupted in Qatif, mainly against the crown prince.[53]

Therefore, it is likely that the decision to execute Sheikh Nimr had the full backing of the crown prince, if it was not he, himself, who ordered it.[54] It can be implied from the stature of Sheikh Nimr that his execution was meant to send a strong message to Iran, the main regional backer of the Shiite political unrest in Saudi Arabia's Eastern Province. The Saudi leadership clearly meant to signal that any political attempt to destabilise the Kingdom would be handled with severity regardless of the political repercussions. It also contained a message to the Shia dissenters in the Kingdom that anti-regime rhetoric would not be tolerated.

Immediately after the executions, protests started in Iran, and the Saudi High Commission in Tehran as well as the Saudi Consulate in Mashad were set on fire by protestors. This reaction increased bilateral tensions and resulted in the cutting of diplomatic relations between the two countries.[55] This response in Iran was condemned worldwide and Iranian authorities later admitted that it was not appropriate. Thus, an event inside Saudi Arabia had political implications for the whole region and linked the domains of internal security and foreign policy. The event also highlighted that, in addition to the quest for security against an external threat, Saudi policymakers give equal importance to internal threats.

---

[53]Kerr, "Mohammed Bin Nayef".

[54]Sheikh Nimr is not the only prominent Shia dissident to have been arrested by the Saudi Interior Ministry. In August 2016, it was also successful in capturing and bringing to Saudi Arabia Ahmed Ibrahim al-Mughassil, the brains behind the 1995 Khobar towers attacks. He had been in the top ranks of the Saudi Hezbollah (*Hezbollah Al-Hijaz*) and thus a source of valuable information about Iranian intelligence operatives and activities in the Gulf region. Riedel, "Saudi executions signal royal worries".

[55]Parsi, "Will the U.S. fall for Saudi Arabia".

It can be argued that the crown prince and deputy crown prince are in agreement in terms of the main regional threats to Saudi security. Their actions in their respective domains are against actors that are inherently linked. However, this does not mean that they necessarily agree with each other in terms of the strategies to be adopted in their respective domains to counter Iran and the actors backed by it. This dynamic will be explored further in the next case.

Saudi military intervention in Yemen

The second important political episode was the Saudi decision to intervene militarily in Yemen to push Iran-backed Houthi rebels out of Sanaa and other cities.[56] This move was a clear message that Iranian political machinations through its proxies in the Saudis' backyard were intolerable. It should be noted that when forces loyal to former Yemeni President Ali Abdullah Saleh and the Houthi rebels took over the Yemeni capital in September 2014, forcing President Abdrabbuh Mansour Hadi to flee towards Aden, there was no retaliation or action from Saudi Arabia. This shows that Saudi decision-makers had a different perception at that time regarding events unfolding in Yemen. The new royalty under King Salman is more concerned about the changing balance of power in the region. Specifically, the threat posed by Iran to Saudi Arabia's regional standing is taken much more seriously by Prince Mohammad Bin Salman. The centralisation of multiple power domains in his person has also made decision-making swifter, with Saudi Arabia launching air raids immediately after the attack of Houthi and Saleh forces on Aden.[57]

The intervention in Yemen affected the public discourse in the same way as the execution of Sheikh Nimr did. It latter resulted in the severing of Saudi ties with Iran and aggravated bitterness in Saudi society against Iran, but the intervention in Yemen also resulted in the unification of thinking about Iran in the Saudi public sphere and generated a fervent backing for the Saudi regime in its endeavour. Even the Islamists of the Sahwa movement supported these actions. Saudi leadership very intelligently used the sectarian underpinnings of these political events to consolidate domestic public opinion in its favour.[58]

In addition to intervening in Yemen, Prince Mohammad Bin Salman has also embarked on a campaign to form a multi-national Islamic alliance to fight terrorist entities in the Muslim world.[59] These initiatives by the ambitious Saudi deputy crown prince reveal two different things. First of all, his interest in further strengthening and developing Saudi armed forces and a regional leadership role for them, thereby enhancing his personal power profile. The involvement in Yemen may be seen as the first step in this regard. They also point to an institutional power competition of the Ministry of Defence with the mighty infrastructure of the Saudi Ministry of the Interior, in the hands of Crown Prince Muhammad Bin Nayef, and the Saudi Arabian National Guard (SANG), under the command of late King Abdullah's son, Prince Mutaib Bin Abdullah.

The lack of the crown prince's involvement in any of the events related to the Yemen war and his absence during the mega anti-terror exercise 'Northern Thunder' is intriguing. This could be either at the start of the strategies pursued by the deputy crown prince. Or this

---

[56]Riedel, "The would be king".
[57]"Saudi Arabia launches air strikes in Yemen", bbc.com, 26 March 2015, http://www.bbc.co.uk/news/world-us-canada-32061632
[58]Matthiesen, *Domestic sources of foreign policy.*
[59]Jenkins, "A Saudi-Led Military Alliance".

could be evidence of a power hierarchy in which both the crown prince and the deputy crown prince hold absolute power in their own respective domains without any checks and balances.

Challenges

The vast power capital and influence of Prince Mohammad Bin Salman is changing the nature of decision-making in the Kingdom. The traditional, more consultative system of decision-making resulted in a pragmatic, cautious and non-interventionist foreign policy. Through such an approach, any serious differences in policymaking within the royal family were settled before they became public.[60] These characteristics of the Saudi decision-making processes and foreign policy are changing under the current power hierarchy. Decision-making is now more rapid and centralised, but more concentrated in the hands of only a few.

The crown prince and the deputy crown prince might agree on the need to adopt aggressive policies in the realm of security, but if such strategies are non-productive in terms of achieving security and damaging economically in the long run,[61] they might generate discord among these key power players and have the potential to create domestic unrest amongst the Saudi public. Saudi Arabia's budget deficit was 15 percent of GDP in 2015. The economic downturn resulted in austerity measures and the cutting of subsidies.[62] This was a clear indication that the Kingdom was facing a tough economic situation. Nevertheless, it continued the military intervention in Yemen, aggravating these economic problems. The war, considered 'unwinnable', has been a major drain on Saudi resources. The country has been spending a huge amount on its war effort in Yemen. One estimate suggests that Saudi Arabia spent USD 5 billion on its Yemen campaign in twenty months.[63] Karen Young puts the joint GCC costs in one year of conflict at USD 15 billion.[64] Saudi Arabia has also spent huge amount in terms of its defence budget generally, which for the fiscal year 2017 is projected to be 191 billion riyals or approximately USD 50 billion.[65] The citizens are feeling the brunt of subsidy cuts in oil, electricity and water and have started questioning the usefulness of such a costly war.[66]

The role played by Iranian aspirations in the development of this foreign policy is also significant and cannot be ignored. However, the dividends of this hawkish policy vis-à-vis Iran are still to be seen. There are no signs that the current foreign policy course set by Saudi rulers will change. In case of Yemen, there has been retrospection and admission in Saudi circles that this war will not end easily or in a short time span. The air campaign has not been as useful as expected and the Saudi coalition has been unable to sow internal discord among the Houthis and their tribal allies. This effectively means a continuation of the conflict.[67]

One cannot help but wonder whether, had the policy towards Iran been different under King Salman, the nature of the Saudi-Iran relationship might not be different too.

---

[60]Korany and Fattah, "Irreconcilable Role-Partners?".
[61]Carey, "The Saudi Town on the Frontline".
[62]McDowall and Torchia, "Saudi plans spending cuts".
[63]Horton, "An Unwinnable War".
[64]Young, "Counting the Cost".
[65]Fateha and Fattah, "Main Features of Saudi Arabia".
[66]Carey and Almashabi, "The Soft Pinch of Austerity".
[67]Young, "A Rough Patch".

Another aspect of the new power hierarchy in Saudi royalty is the increased control of government positions and key places by the Sudairi branch of the Saud family. The King, crown prince and deputy crown prince are all Sudairis and so are the governors of important provinces. Prince Mutaib Bin Abdullah, son of late King Abdullah, is the only non-Sudairi to hold the important post of the head of SANG.[68] This is problematic for other royal factions who have been cut off from policymaking in general and foreign policymaking in particular. It has in fact already led to concerns within the royal family that the new rulers may lead the Kingdom to disaster, and calls by some "unnamed" princes to overthrow the ruling elite.[69]

Furthermore, the re-ordering of the Saudi economy in the form of Vision 2030 will usher in enormous change. Vision 2030 is broadly structured around decreasing Saudi dependence on oil. The major goals include selling about 5 percent of shares of the Saudi oil giant, Aramco, and setting up a sovereign wealth fund that can be used to invest in other sectors. Other key aspects include ensuring a transparent economic environment to encourage foreign investment, improving governance and reducing unemployment.[70] Such a focus on transparency and abating corrupt practices to improve governance will inadvertently affect the influence and monopoly enjoyed by branches of the Saud family in some sectors of government and subsequently may lead to discord within the family.

Conclusion

Saudi Arabia plays a very important role in regional and world politics. Structural changes in the political environment of the region and changes in leadership in the Kingdom have been instrumental in its adoption of a more robust and activist foreign policy. The Saudi leadership is clear in admitting the importance of the Iranian challenge. It views the upheaval and disorder in its Eastern Province as connected to Iranian political manoeuvrings in the region and a threat to domestic order. There is also an understanding in Saudi power circles that the implications of this increase in Iranian power will be catastrophic for the interests of Saudi Arabia in the region.

This has led to the formation of domestic and external security policies that more effectively contest Iranian designs in Middle East and stability inside the kingdom and are more in line with the changing geopolitics of the region. One result has been an Iran-centric foreign policy under King Salman. This has led to a worsening of relations between Saudi Arabia and Iran. Till now, there has been no significant attempt by the two nations to settle their problems politically.

Saudi Arabia has been most critical of Iran's policy of supporting sectarian non-state actors in the Middle East to achieve its foreign policy goals. To some extent, these goals can be summed up as the return of the 'export of revolution' policy. This time, however, the IRGC, the main force for attaining these goals, has crafted a different strategy which advocates not to take over states themselves, but to make them vulnerable by nurturing armed non-state actors who can challenge the writ of state and pressure governments into changing their policies. Hezbollah in Lebanon and the Badr Militia of the Supreme Islamic Council of Iraq (SICI) in Iraq are examples of this strategy. Iran on the other hand, views

---

[68]Pollack, "Welcome to Sudayri Arabia".
[69]Miles, "Saudi royal calls for regime change".
[70]Fattah *et al.,* "Saudi Blueprint for Life After Oil?".

all conflicts in the Middle East as stemming from the teachings of Wahhabism. Iranian Foreign Minister Jawad Zarif views Saudi Arabia as a state sponsor of such extremist actors and accuses it of playing the "Iranian card" to involve its allies in wars in Syria and Yemen. He frames Iran's actions in the Middle East and its support for Shia militias as a response to Saudi attempts to destabilise its allies in Syria and Iraq.[71]

Saudi relations with the United States were downhill during the entire second term of President Obama. The election of Donald Trump came as a surprise for everyone except the Saudis, who are positive about him. Some people on his team, especially Defense Secretary (retired) General James Mattis and Trump's son in law and senior advisor, Jared Kushner, have expressed a need to contain Iranian ambitions in the region.[72] It can be expected that the tensions in the Saudi-US relationship will ultimately be resolved and replaced by a more healthy working relationship.

Apart from the Saudi rapprochement with Turkey and Qatar, and increased cooperation with them in Syria, the new Saudi foreign policy has not yielded any major success. Evidently, Turkey has drawn closer to Saudi Arabia and moved away from Iran recently, but this is mainly due to the Turkish-Iranian clash of interests in Syria and not specifically to Saudi Arabia. Regional capitals including Baghdad, Sanaa, Damascus and Beirut that were under Iran's sway before the current royalty's ascension remain that way. Egypt's friendly posture towards the Syrian regime of Bashar Al-Assad and Pakistan's refusal to send its forces to participate in the military intervention in Yemen remain significant failures.

At the same time, foreign policy measures taken under the lead of the deputy crown prince, specifically the military intervention in Yemen, have drained considerable Saudi resources without there being any end in sight or any chance of a political settlement that the Saudis can boast about as their victory. This means that the war will go on and as the conflict is prolonged, the questions for those who undertook it will also increase. This looks like the point at which the views of the crown prince and the deputy crown prince will differ.

The Saudi crown prince has much more experience than the deputy crown prince and it can be assumed that he may have had concerns over the decision to intervene in Yemen without first exhausting other channels or resources to coerce or pressure the Houthi rebels or Saleh into a political solution.[73] It is of note that, after the Yemen war, Saudi Arabia has avoided undertaking further military interventions, especially in Syria, even though Turkey has been pushing for a more active Saudi engagement in Northern Syria in support of its actions on the ground against ISIS.[74] This points to some revision with respect to using this specific method to solve foreign conflicts.

On the internal security front, the crown prince seems to be fully in control and bent upon dealing strictly with any attempt by Shia (or Sunni) actors to instil chaos and destabilisation. Yet, the deputy crown prince's hold on the Kingdom's financial matters might complicate matters between the two men in the future. The Saudi Interior Ministry demands a huge budget, but the deputy crown prince could consider devoting more resources to the Defence Ministry which falls under his remit. Such an event would have all the potential to create discord and hostility between the two royals.

---

[71]Ostovar, "Sectarian Dilemmas in Iranian Foreign Policy".
[72]Young, "A Rough Patch".
[73]Al-Muslimi, "How Can Yemen Find Peace?".
[74]Gurbuz, "Erdoğan's Gulf Tour".

The relationship between the crown prince and the deputy crown prince will evidently determine the future of Saudi Arabia, but the biggest factor is the King himself. As long as he is on the throne, the current power setup will probably work as it is, and it is unlikely that Saudi Arabia will change its foreign policy trajectory. King Salman has full confidence in his son Prince Mohammad Bin Salman and has given him uncensored power in his actions. Since there are no other royals in any significant ministerial position, the consultation circle which once was quite broad has structurally narrowed and is likely to remain that way. The decision-making circle within the Kingdom will continue to be made up of the King, the crown prince and the deputy crown prince. This will ensure the continuity of the present decision-making system. Any substantial change in the future can only happen if one of the three men is removed.

References

Alajlan, A. "Vision 2030 offers hope to many in Saudi Arabia - but this is why I'm less optimistic". *The International Business Times,* 25 August 2016. http://www.ibtimes.co.uk/mohammed-bin-salmans-vision-2030-ambitious-saudi-arabias-problems-are-bigger-one-man-1577995.

Al-Faisal, T. "Saudi Foreign Policy Vision: 'Unity, Stability, and Responsibility'". Speech at SUSRIS. Washington DC, 14 October 2015. http://susris.com/2015/10/15/saudi-foreign-policy-vision-unity-stability-and-responsibility-prince-turki-alfaisal/.

Al-Mawali, N. "Intra-Gulf Cooperation Council: Saudi Arabia Effect". *Journal of Economic Integration* 3, no. 3 (September 2015): 532–52.

Al-Muslimi, F. "How Can War-Torn Yemen Find Peace". *Carnegie-mec.org,* 21 January 2016. http://carnegie-mec.org/2016/01/21/analysis-how-can-war-torn-yemen-find-peace-pub-62557.

Al-Rasheed, M. *A History of Saudi Arabia.* Cambridge: Cambridge University Press, 2010.

Altoraifi, A. "Understanding the Role of State Identity in Foreign Policy Decision-Making: The Rise and Demise of Saudi-Iranian Rapprochement (1997-2009)". PhD dissertation, The London School of Economics and Political Science, 2012.

Ansari, A., and A.B. Tabrizi. "The View from Tehran". In *Understanding Iran's Role in the Syrian Conflict,* edited by A.B. Tabrizi, and R. Pantucci: 3–11. London: Royal United Services Institute, August 2016.

Bahout, J., P. Cammack, D. Livingston, M. Muasher, K. Sadjadpour, T. Volpe and F. Wehrey. "Saudi Arabia's Changing International Role". *Carnegieendowment.org,* 18 April 2016. http://carnegieendowment.org/2016/04/18/saudi-arabia-s-changing-international-role/ixec.

Byman, D.L. "The U.S.-Saudi Arabia counterterrorism relationship". *Brookings.edu,* 24 May 2016. http://www.brookings.edu/research/testimony/2016/05/24-us-saudi-counterterrorismbyman?cid=00900015020089101US0001-052401.

Carey, G. "The Saudi Town on the Frontline of Yemen's War". *Bloomberg.com,* 22 December 2015. https://www.bloomberg.com/news/articles/2015-12-21/in-one-saudi-town-gunfire-all-day-brings-yemen-war-near-home.

Carey, G., and D. Almashabi. "The Soft Pinch of Austerity in Saudi Arabia Could Backfire". *Bloomberg.com,* 17 August 2016. https://www.bloomberg.com/news/articles/2016-08-16/as-saudi-austerity-starts-to-bite-a-testing-time-for-its-prince.

Carey, G., and N. Syeed. "Saudi Balancing Act Abandoned as King Imposes Rapid Change". *Bloomberg.com,* 1 May 2015. https://www.bloomberg.com/news/articles/2015-04-30/salman-abandons-saudi-royal-balancing-act-to-impose-rapid-change.

David, S. "Explaining Third World Alignment". *World Politics* 43, no. 2 (January 1991): 233–56.

Dazi-héni, F. "Can We Speak of a New Regional Order Driven by the Gulf States after the Arab Spring?" *Mediterranean YearBook 2016.* Barcelona: IEMed, 2016. http://www.iemed.org/observatori/arees-danalisi/arxius-adjunts/anuari/med.2016/IEMed_MedYearBook2016_Gulf%20States%20New%20Regional%20Order_Fatiha_Dazi.pdf.

Echagüe, A. "Saudi Arabia: emboldened yet vulnerable". In *Geopolitics and Democracy in the Middle East*, edited by K. Kausch: 77–88. Madrid: FRIDE, 2015.

Eilts, H.F. "Saudi Arabia's Foreign Policy". In *Diplomacy in the Middle East: The International Relations of Regional and Outside Powers*, edited by L.C. Brown: 219–44. London: I.B.Tauris, 2004.

Einhorn, R., and R. Nephew. "The Iran nuclear deal: Prelude to proliferation in the Middle East?", *Brookings.edu,* 31 May 2016. https://www.brookings.edu/research/the-iran-nuclear-deal-prelude-to-proliferation-in-the-middle-east/.

Eisenstadt, M., M. Knights and A. Ahmed. *Iran's Influence in Iraq. Countering Tehran's Whole-of-Government Approach*, Policy Focus no. 111. Washington, DC: Washington Institute for Near East Policy, April 2011. http://www.washingtoninstitute.org/uploads/Documents/pubs/PolicyFocus111.pdf.

Ennis, C.A., and B. Momani. "Shaping the Middle East in the Midst of the Arab Uprisings: Turkish and Saudi foreign policy strategies". *Third World Quarterly* 34, no. 6 (July 2013): 1127–44.

Fattah, Z., V. Nereim., D. Almashabi and D. Khraiche. "What's In Saudi Arabia's Blueprint for Life After Oil?". *Bloomberg.com,* 26 April 2016. https://www.bloomberg.com/news/articles/2016-04-25/key-elements-of-saudi-arabia-s-blueprint-for-life-post-oilGause.

Fateha, A., and F. Zainab. "Main Features of Saudi Arabia 2017 Budget, 2016 Performance". *Bloomberg.com,* 22 December 2016. https://www.bloomberg.com/news/articles/2016-12-22/main-features-of-saudi-arabia-s-2017-budget-2016-performance.

Gause, F. G. "Saudi Arabia's Game of Thrones: King Salman amasses power". *Foreignaffairs.com,* 2 February 2016. https://www.foreignaffairs.com/articles/saudi-arabia/2015-02-02/saudi-arabias-game-thrones.

Gause, F. G. *Saudi Arabia in the New Middle East,* Council Special Report no. 63. New York: Council on Foreign Relations, December 2011. http://www.cfr.org/saudi-arabia/saudi-arabia-new-middle-east/p26663.

Goldberg, J. "The Obama Doctrine - The U.S. president talks through his hardest decisions about America's role in the world". *The Atlantic,* April 2016. https://www.theatlantic.com/magazine/archive/2016/04/the-obama-doctrine/471525/.

Gurbuz, M. "Erdoğan's Gulf Tour: Reassurance without Substance". *Arabcenterdc.org,* 21 February 2017. http://arabcenterdc.org/policy_analyses/erdogans-gulf-tour.

Haykel, B., T. Hegghammer, and S. Lacroix. *Saudi Arabia in Transition*. Cambridge: Cambridge University Press, 2015.

Henderson, S. "Saudi Arabia's 'Inexperienced Youngster'". *Policy analysis*, Washington Institute for Near East Policies, 21 April 2015. http://www.washingtoninstitute.org/policy-analysis/view/saudi-arabias-inexperienced-youngster.

Henderson, S. "Princely Personalities Sidelined in Saudi Arabia". *Policy analysis*, Washington Institute for Near East Policies, 30 January 2015. http://www.washingtoninstitute.org/policy-analysis/view/princely-personalities-sidelined-in-saudi-arabia.

Henderson, S. *After King Abdullah Succession in Saudi Arabia,* Policy Focus no. 96. Washington D.C.: The Washington Institute for Near East Policy, August 2009. https://www.washingtoninstitute.org/uploads/Documents/pubs/PolicyFocus96_Henderson.pdf.

Hertog, S. "A Rentier Social Contract: The Saudi Political Economy since 1979". *Mei.edu,* 22 February 2012. http://www.mei.edu/content/rentier-social-contract-saudi-political-economy-1979.

Hertog, S. *Princes, Brokers, and Bureaucrats: Oil and the State in Saudi Arabia*. London: Cornell University Press, 2010.

Hinnebusch, R. *The International Politics of Middle East*. Manchester: Manchester University Press, 2003.

Hinnebusch, R. "Introduction: The Analytic Framework". In *The Foreign Policies of Middle East States*, edited by R. Hinnebusch, and A. Ehteshami: 1–27. Boulder: Lynne Rienner, 2003.

Horton, M. "An Unwinnable War: The Houthis, Saudi Arabia and the Future of Yemen". *Terrorism Monitor* 14, no. 22 (11 November 2016).

Horton, M. "The Unseen Hand: Saudi Arabian Involvement in Yemen". *Terrorism Monitor* 9, no. 12 (24 March 2011). https://jamestown.org/program/the-unseen-hand-saudi-arabian-involvement-in-yemen/.

Ibish, H. "Qatar Changes Course". *The New York Times,* 29 June 2015. http://www.nytimes.com/2015/06/30/opinion/qatar-changes-course.html?_r=0.

Jenkins, B. M. *A Saudi-Led Military Alliance to Fight Terrorism: Welcome Muscle in the Fight Against Terrorism, Desert Mirage, or Bad Idea?*, PE-189-R. Santa Monica: Rand Corporation, 2016. http://www.rand.org/pubs/perspectives/PE189.html.

Juneau, T. "Iran's policy towards the Houthis in Yemen: a limited return on a modest investment". *International Affairs* 92, no. 3 (May 2016): 647–63.

Kagan, W.F., A.K. Majidyar, D. Pletka and M.C. Sullivan. "Iranian Influence in the Levant, Egypt, Iraq and Afghanistan", *The American Enterprise Institute and the Institute for the Study of War,* May 2012. http://www.aei.org/wp-content/uploads/2012/05/-iranian-influence-in-the-levant-egypt-iraq-and-afghanistan_171235465754.pdf.

Kamrava, M. "Mediation and Saudi Foreign Policy". *Orbis* 57, no. 1 (Winter 2013): 152-70.

Karam, J. "Saudi Arabia's new foreign minister: The king's confidante". *Al-Arabiya.net*, 30 April 2015. http://english.alarabiya.net/en/views/news/middle-east/2015/04/30/Saudi-Arabia-s-new-foreign-minister-The-king-s-confidante.html.

Kerr, S. "Mohammed bin Nayef, Saudi strong man in a power struggle". *FT.com,* 8 January 2016. https://www.ft.com/content/0d299e2e-b533-11e5-8358-9a82b43f6b2f.

Kirkpatrick, D.D. "Surprising Saudi Rises as a Prince Among Princes". *The New York Times,* 6 June 2015. https://www.nytimes.com/2015/06/07/world/middleeast/surprising-saudi-rises-as-a-prince-among-princes.html?_r=0.

Knights, M., and A. Mello. *The Saudi-UAE War Effort in Yemen (Part 2): The Air Campaign*, Policy analysis. Washington DC: The Washington Institute for Near East Policy, 11 August 2015. http://www.washingtoninstitute.org/policy-analysis/view/the-saudi-uae-war-effort-in-yemen-part-2-the-air-campaign.

Korany, B., and M.A. Fattah. "Irreconcilable Role-Partners? Saudi Foreign Policy between the Ulama and the US". In *Foreign Policies of Arab States: The Challenge of Globalization,* edited by B. Korany, H. Ali, and E. Dessouki: 343–97. Cairo: American University in Cairo Press, 2014.

Matthiesen, T. *The domestic sources of Saudi foreign policy: Islamists and the state in the wake of the Arab Uprisings,* Brookings Working Paper. Washington DC: Brookings Institution, August 2015. https://www.brookings.edu/wp-content/uploads/2016/07/Saudi-Arabia_Matthiesen-FINAL.pdf.

Mcdowall, A., and A. Torchea. "Saudi plans spending cuts, reforms to shrink budget deficit". *Reuters,* 28 December 2015. http://www.reuters.com/article/us-saudi-budget-idUSKBN0UB10D20151228.

Miles, H. "Saudi royal calls for regime change in Riyadh". *The Guardian,* 28 September 2015. http://www.theguardian.com/world/2015/sep/28/saudi-royal-calls-regime-change-letters-leadership-king-salman.

Nonneman, G. "Determinants and Patterns of Saudi Foreign Policy: 'Omnibalancing' and 'Relative Autonomy in multiple environments". In *Saudi Arabia in the Balance: Political Economy, Society, Foreign Affairs,* edited by P. Aarts and G. Nonneman: 315–51. London: C. Hurst & Co, 2005.

Ostovar, A. "Sectarian Dilemmas in Iranian Foreign Policy: When Strategy and Identity Politics Collide". *Carnegieendowment.org,* 30 November 2016. http://carnegieendowment.org/2016/11/30/sectarian-dilemmas-in-iranian-foreign-policy-when-strategy-and-identity-politics-collide-pub-66288.

Parsi, T. "Will the U.S. fall for Saudi Arabia's deliberate provocation in killing of Shi'ite cleric?". *Reuters.com,* 4 January 2016. http://blogs.reuters.com/great-debate/2016/01/04/will-the-u-s-fall-for-saudi-arabias-deliberate-provocation/.

Pasha, A.K. "Saudi Arabia and the Iranian Nuclear Deal". *Contemporary Review of the Middle East* 3, no. 4 (September 2016): 387–404.

Pierret, T. "State Sponsors and the Syrian Insurgency: The Limits of Foreign Influence". In *Inside wars: local dynamics of conflicts in Syria and Libya*, edited by L. Narbone, A. Favier, and V. Collombier: 22–8. Florence: European University Institute, 2016.

Pollack, K. "Welcome to Sudayri Arabia". *Brookings.edu,* 30 April 2016. http://www.brookings.edu/blogs/markaz/posts/2015/04/30-saudia-arabia-salman-yemen-pollack.

Riedel, B. "The man who would be king in Saudi Arabia". *Brookings.edu,* 10 May 2016. http://www.brookings.edu/research/opinions/2016/05/10-saudi-who-would-be-king-riedel.

Riedel, B. "Saudi executions signal royal worries". *Al-monitor.com,* 4 January 2016. http://www.al-monitor.com/pulse/originals/2016/01/saudi-arabia-iran-execution-nimr-al-nimr-concerns-stability.html.

Riedel, B. "The Prince of Counterterrorism". *Brookings.edu,* 29 September 2015. http://csweb.brookings.edu/content/research/essays/2015/the-prince-of-counterterrorism.html.

Saab, B.Y. "Can Mohamed bin Salman Reshape Saudi Arabia?". *Foreignaffairs.com,* 5 January 2017. https://www.foreignaffairs.com/articles/saudi-arabia/2017-01-05/can-mohamed-bin-salman-reshape-saudi-arabia.

Selvic, K. *War in Yemen: the view from Iran,* Expert Analysis. Oslo: Norwegian Peacebuilding Resource Centre, October 2015. http://noref.no/var/ezflow_site/storage/original/application/3aa838bcc38767deb0af8f2125e20f36.pdf.

Sullivan, K. "Before he was king, Salman was the family disciplinarian who put princes behind bars". *The Washington Post,* 23 January 2016. https://www.washingtonpost.com/world/salman-is-known-for-mediating-saudi-royal-disputes/2015/01/22/1bc8dc1a-a2b0-11e4-b146-577832eafcb4_story.html.

Ulrichsen, K.C. "Repositioning Saudi Arabia and the Gulf Cooperation Council States in the Changing Global Order". *Journal of Arabian Studies* 1, no. 2 (December 2011): 231–47.

Young, M. "A Rough Patch - In an interview, Princeton University's Bernard Haykel discusses Saudi Arabia's multiple challenges". *Carnegie-mec.org,* 27 February 2017. http://carnegie-mec.org/diwan/67977.

Young, K.E. " Counting the Cost – Military Expenditure in the GCC". *The Arab Gulf States Institute in Washington,* 16 November 2015. http://www.agsiw.org/counting-the-cost-military-expenditure-in-the-gcc/.

Zuhur, S. *Saudi Arabia.* Santa Barbara: ABC-CLIO, 2011.

Iran, the GCC and the Implications of the Nuclear Deal: Rivalry versus Engagement

Riham Bahi

ABSTRACT
The Joint Comprehensive Plan of Action, also known as the Iran nuclear deal, is consequential for Middle East regional security. It has raised a number of concerns for Arab Gulf states in relation to an emboldened Iran after sanction relief and the perceived shift of the US away from supporting its traditional allies in the Gulf. The international recognition and incorporation of Iran into regional power constellations resulting from the deal will intensify Saudi-Iranian rivalry to assert dominance. This rivalry and competition will increase in the short run, however, regional crises are expected to highlight the need for dialogue and engagement on regional affairs.

The period since 2011 has been particularly tumultuous for Middle East regional politics. The initial optimism of the early pro-democracy uprisings of the 'Arab Spring' gave way to resurgent terrorism, civil wars and a (re)turn toward authoritarianism. These developments have altered regional power balances, shaken regional alliances and alignments and instigated a new round of competition over regional leadership, especially between Saudi Arabia and Iran, dubbed the 'Arab cold war'. Saudi-Iranian rivalry has further intensified after the signing of the nuclear agreement between Iran and the world's major powers.

Since its completion in Vienna on 14 July 2015, the Joint Comprehensive Plan of Action (JCPOA) has been the focus of much heated debate between supporters and opponents. In the JCPOA, also known as the 'nuclear deal' between Iran and the P5+1 group of world powers – the US, UK, France, China and Russia, plus Germany – Iran promised to curb its nuclear program in exchange for the lifting of certain sanctions imposed on it and the freeing up of ten billion dollars in oil revenues and frozen assets.[1] Proponents of the nuclear deal argue that it successfully ended the nuclear dispute between Iran and the United States, guaranteeing that Iran's nuclear capacity will remain peaceful under international monitoring, and averted a disastrous military conflict in a region already enmeshed in civil wars, economic turmoil and Islamic state terrorism. It also allows the United States and Iran to work on issues of shared interests in the Middle East, such as solving conflicts in Iraq and

---

[1] "Iran Nuclear Deal: Key Details", *BBC News*, 16 January 2016, http://www.bbc.com/news/world-middle-east-33521655.

Syria and cooperating against the Islamic State. A clear benefit of the nuclear deal has been the prevalence of diplomacy and peace over military action. Moreover, lifting the sanctions on Iran is supposedly going to have a positive impact on the global economy as Iran managed to become the second largest economy in the Middle East-North Africa (MENA) region in recent years, despite sanctions.[2]

On the other hand, sceptics of the nuclear deal argue that it strengthens Iran's regional role. The Arab Gulf states are particularly sceptical and consider it a destabilising factor in the region. The nuclear deal highlights the divergent strategic views of the United States and its traditional Arab allies. The GCC states are concerned that Iran's rapprochement with the West, especially the United States, will allow Iran to expand its influence in the region at the expense of their security and sovereignty. The nuclear deal, so they say, will embolden Iran, enrich it with oil revenues and enable it to advance its hegemonic project to dominate the region, undermine GCC security and sovereignty through its proxies in Iraq, Syria, Lebanon and Yemen and intervene in the domestic affairs of Arab Gulf states.[3] GCC states claim that, since the deal, Iran has escalated its aggressive statements and actions.[4]

Ayatollah Khamenei, the final arbiter of the nuclear deal in Iran, has not clearly endorsed the JCPOA, but he has not condemned it either; he has remained neutral, maintaining an anti-Western rhetoric for domestic purposes. He has asserted that the deal will not open Iran up to the United States.[5] In violation of United Nations Security Council resolution 2231, Iran has conducted ballistic missile tests in October and November 2015 and again in March 2016[6] and has continued hostile acts across the region. In a meeting on 10 January 2016, the Arab League backed Saudi Arabia in its dispute with Iran and denounced what they labelled as "hostile acts and provocations of Iran". This support came after attacks on the Saudi diplomatic mission in Iran.[7] Arab diplomats used this opportunity to issue a statement warning Iran against interfering in the internal affairs of Arab states.[8]

The United States, on its part, has been limiting its security engagement in the Middle East and the nuclear deal with Iran is perceived as part of the new US security approach to the region. At a meeting in Camp David in May 2015, the United States tried to assure the Arab Gulf states that the deal mainly aims at denying Iran the ability to obtain nuclear weapons,[9] but it is also meant to allow the United States and Iran to work together to solve regional problems. This approach has alarmed the US' Arab allies because it leaves them uncertain of their place in this new regional order.

Consequently, Arab Gulf states have been trying to adjust to these major changes in regional politics and security by taking charge of their own security in the form of

---

[2]Iran ranks second in the world in natural gas reserves and fourth in proven crude oil reserves. It has well developed processing and manufacturing capabilities, a strong industrial base, an educated workforce and a potential consumer market of over 77 million. "Lifting of Iran sanctions is 'a good day for the world'", *The Guardian*, 16 January 2016, http://www.theguardian.com/world/2016/jan/16/iran-prepares-for-lifting-of-sanctions-and-the-end-of-decade-long-isolation.
[3]Al Shayji, "Nuclear Iran Worries GCC".
[4]*Ibid.*
[5]Devine, "Iran Versus ISIL", 30.
[6]Al Otaiba, "One Year after Iran Nuclear Deal".
[7]Which were a reaction to the execution of the Saudi Shia cleric Nimr al Nimr the day before.
[8]"Arab League backs Saudis in Iran row", *Al-Jazeera*, 11 January 2016, http://www.aljazeera.com/news/2016/01/arab-league-backs-saudis-iran-row-160110150424144.html.
[9]"Obama to back Gulf allies against any 'external attack'", *Al-Jazeera*, 15 May 2015, http://www.aljazeera.com/news/2015/05/obama-holds-security-talks-gulf-arab-leaders-150514170745879.html.

strengthening or shifting regional alliances. Furthermore, they have been diversifying their extra-regional alliances by reaching out to Russia and China.

The purpose of the more aggressive foreign policy on the part of Saudi Arabia and its Arab allies in the short run can be seen as an attempt to overcome their weaknesses and vulnerabilities. However, the argument put forward here is that the growing mistrust and uncertainty can only be addressed through engagement and dialogue. The series of regional shocks, the Arab Spring, the Syrian civil war, the rise of the Islamic State and the Iran nuclear agreement can push in the direction of regional dialogue to manage those perceptions. Hence, rivalry and competition will increase in the short run, hopefully paving the way for dialogue and engagement in the future.

The article is divided into six parts. The first describes the 'regional power approach' as the theoretical framework most suited to analysing the power competition in the Middle East region. The next two parts examine the 'new' regional cold war between Iran and Saudi-Arabia that has escalated as a result of the nuclear deal, and show how it is taking place in the context of the US 'rightsizing' its role in the Middle East. This is followed by a section that looks at Iran-Saudi rivalry and its implications for regional alignments. The fifth part illustrates how the nuclear deal with Iran introduced a new era of multilateralism that could be borrowed to deal more effectively with regional problems such as the civil war in Syria. The last part provides some conclusions on the prospects of regional dialogue and engagement.

Theoretical framework

This article adopts the 'regional power' approach which is a major offshoot of regionalism. The scholarly debate in international relations is currently discussing the rise of regional powers in order to postulate the move towards "a multiregional system of international relations".[10] In a regionalised world order, "regions are neither wholly self-contained entities nor purely extensions of global dynamics".[11] It is important to distinguish between the concept of regionalism before and after the end of Cold War. During the Cold War, international relations focused on regional politics through the lens of global affairs and the East-West conflict. After the Cold War, the concept of regional power has looked at "the momentum of regions and actors within it".[12] More than before, regional affairs are being shaped by regional actors. However, not all the world's regions enjoy the same degree of relative autonomy *vis-à-vis* global structures and actors.

The concepts of regionalism and regional powers could be instrumental in analysing the nuclear deal with Iran and the consequent regional power competition in the Middle East resulting from the deal. Increasingly, with the shift towards a multipolar world order, there are very few regions with only one dominant power. The norm has rather become competing power centres and contested leadership.[13] Hence, this has also become characteristic of the Middle East. The rise of a number of competitors has shaped the Middle East into

---

[10]Nolte, "How to compare regional powers".
[11]Acharya, *End of American World Order*, 80.
[12]Beck, "The Concept of Regional Power", 2.
[13]Nolte, "How to compare regional powers".

a multipolar region in which it is no longer possible for a single actor to act as a regional hegemon or as a provider of regional stability and security.[14] Furthermore, many scholars highlight that the peculiar economic and political trajectories of the modern Middle East make it impossible for the emergence of one single regional power.[15] Regional powers, especially and Iran and Saudi Arabia, have sought to take advantage of the ongoing power shifts in the Middle East to raise their political profile by pursuing broader regional agendas.

Like other regional theories, the 'regional security complex' theory addresses the regional level of analysis of international relations between the state and the international system. The theory points to the existence of regional sub-systems as objects of analysis. As a region, the Middle East qualifies as a regional security complex, which is highly penetrated by external actors, above all the United States. Regional security and stability are vital concerns for regional security complexes, especially in conflict-ridden regions such as the Middle East, where security and stability are interlinked with global security.[16] Barry Buzan and Ole Wæver defined a regional security complex as a "set of units whose major processes of securitization, desecuritization, or both, are so interlinked that their security problems cannot reasonably be analysed or resolved apart from one another".[17] In the Middle East, "regionalization of conflicts has been realized, but it has failed to generate durable regional structures for conflict prevention and conflict management". Any peaceful settlement in a particular region requires comprehensive regional engagement.[18] However, in the Middle East security complex, interdependencies do not imply cooperation, and institutional cooperation has remained limited. Alliances and cooperation shape and reshape themselves across areas of conflict.

Regional security complexes are shaped not only by material factors, but also by ideational factors. For the Middle East security complex, the inclusion/exclusion schemes are constructed through interactions distinguishing between Arabs and Persians, and between Sunni and Shiite Muslims. The negative identification of the 'other' paves the way for securitisation processes, in which the 'other' is portrayed as an existential threat, justifying the use of extraordinary means to achieve security, thereby creating the security dilemma prevalent in the region.[19]

According to Martin Beck, the Middle East as a region has the following major features:

> high power dispersion, preponderance of competitive rather than cooperative behaviour and hard power rather than soft power use; the command of only low global-power capabilities and the lack of usage of resources for regional development by regional actors; and the distinct role of the United States as a quasi-regional power.[20]

The Middle East is a multipolar system in which regional powers, such as Egypt, Israel, Turkey and Saudi Arabia have very strong ties with the United States. Iran was part of the pattern until the 1979 Islamic Revolution.

If regional security complexes are defined by "a high level of threat/fear which is felt mutually among two or more major states", then this definition militates against the prospect of regional engagement between Iran and its Arab neighbours. However, regional

---

[14]Pinfari, *Of Cats and Lions*.
[15]Lustick, "Absence of Middle Eastern Great Powers".
[16]Coskun, "Regionalism and Securitization", 91.
[17]Buzan and Wæver, *Regions and Powers*, 141.
[18]Coskun, "Regionalism and Securitization", 91.
[19]*Ibid*.
[20]Beck, "The Concept of Regional Power", 5.

security complexes feature an "intense interdependence of national security perceptions".[21] As a result, this interdependence can lead to cooperative arrangements among regional actors in order to manage security problems. Regional security arrangements such as the Gulf Cooperation Council (GCC[22]) are important factors in the definition and analysis of regional security complexes. These arrangements are sub-regional alliances that define the line of regional rivalry and polarisation, but also help in stabilising the security complex by promoting a balance of power *vis-à-vis* the rival actors and in reducing conflicts within their own membership.[23]

Alternative arrangements could also help moderate and reduce rivalry within the complex by helping actors regulate their behaviour, promote stability in their mutual expectations, and develop formal and informal models of cooperation. There are calls for setting up a regional security arrangement in the Middle East similar to the Conference on Security and Cooperation in Europe (CSCE[24]), since it was successful in promoting regional confidence-building between Eastern and Western Europe during the Cold War. An alternative regional security arrangement in the Gulf region might have the capacity to moderate the central rivalry between Saudi Arabia and Iran within the security complex.

The Arab Spring has led to a new constellation of rising regional powers and a new round of regional leadership competition. Saudi Arabia and Iran are engaged in heated rivalry and proxy conflicts in order to assert regional leadership and block their rival from rising. This leadership competition is one of the key factors defining the Middle East security complex today.

A nuclear deal amidst a regional cold war

The nuclear agreement between the US and Iran focused on limiting Iran's nuclear capabilities but did not take the stability of the Middle East or the security of Iran's Arab neighbours into consideration. Iran's Arab neighbours believe that they should have been consulted about the deal and its implementation.[25] It has been perceived in the region as an enabler of Iran's ascendance to regional leadership. It gives Iran the ability to regain its frozen financial assets, increasing its capacity to project power throughout the region, and facilitates a strong return of Iran to the global oil market. Therefore, the JCPOA concerns not only Iran and the major powers, but also Saudi Arabia and its allies in the GCC and has led to more tensions and mistrust between Iran and Saudi Arabia.

Escalating conflicts and rivalry in the Middle East are provoking an arm race, especially in Yemen where Iran is backing the Houthi opposition to the Saudi-supported government, and in Syria, where Iran is supporting embattled Syrian President Bashar al-Assad, while Saudi Arabia is sending weapons to groups opposing his government. Saudi Arabia's arms purchases have skyrocketed as a result and Saudi Arabia is now the world's second largest weapons importer.[26]

---

[21] Acharya, "Regional Security Complexes".
[22] Members include Bahrain, Kuwait, Oman, Qatar, Saudi Arabia and the United Arab Emirates.
[23] Acharya, "Regional Security Complexes".
[24] A European intergovernmental security grouping which first met in Helsinki in 1973 and later developed into the Organisation on Security and Cooperation in Europe.
[25] Shabneh, *Implications of a Nuclear Deal*.
[26] Stockholm International Peace Research Institute (SIPRI), "Increase in arms transfers driven by demand in the Middle East and Asia", 20 Feb 2017, https://www.sipri.org/media/press-release/2017/increase-arms-transfers-driven-demand-middle-east-and-asia-says-sipri

Prevalent among GCC states is the perception that the US under President Barrack Obama was eager to pivot to Asia at the expense of the Middle East. However, Iran-Saudi rivalry has complicated US attempts to rebalance to Asia by destabilising the region.

Gregory Gause argues that "the best framework for understanding the regional politics in the Middle East is as a cold war in which Iran and Saudi Arabia play a leading role".[27] The current confrontation has an important sectarian element but to reduce it to a 'Sunni-Shia' fight is an oversimplification of regional dynamics. Saudi Arabia and Iran are playing a 'balance of power' game, in which they are using sectarianism to reach out to regional allies. This Iran-Saudi rivalry can be "understood by appreciating the links between domestic conflicts, transnational affinities, and regional state ambitions".[28] Gause argues that the weakening of Arab states, more than Islamism or sectarianism, has created the battlefield of the new cold war in the Middle East.[29]

Curtis Ryan notes that the new Saudi-Iranian struggle for regional hegemony has manifested itself in "competitive interventions with a pronounced sectarian tone".[30] This sectarian tension is not the driving force behind regional international relations. Rather, the material and ideational struggle is simply manipulating sectarian and ethnic tensions in a struggle for power with devastating results for the Middle East as a region.[31]

The Arab Spring and the subsequent rise of political Islam provided Iran with the opportunity to claim leadership of the Muslim world. Iran tried to provide an interpretation of the Arab Spring as a delayed extension of the Iranian Revolution. This interpretation would have given Iran a prominent role in leading by example, while the rise of political Islam would have served Iran's interest by neutralising the Arab-Persian divide.[32] To be accepted as a regional leader that could safeguard regional security, it tried to forge an inclusive identity that would appeal to major actors in the region, drawing attention away from the exclusive Persian/Shia identity. Iran constantly stresses its merits in its resistance against imperialism and Zionism compared to the pro-Western attitude of most Arab regimes. This interpretation did not resonate, however, with the Arab revolutionaries and was challenged from the beginning. Inconsistent Iranian reactions toward various revolutionary movements were perceived regionally as "selective measures employed in pursuance of Iran's own hegemonic ambitions".[33]

Yet, Iran's regained self-confidence has been not so much a result of this narrative as of the "blatantly weak and unpopular Arab governments unable to counter the Iranian offensive".[34] Iran's influence is based upon its excellent relations with Hezbollah, stable contacts with the Palestinian resistance, strong roots within the region's Shiite communities, tremendous natural resources, and ability to exert massive influence on the events in Iraq, where it is supplying considerable arms to Shiite forces. Iran has been playing "a leading role in the creation of an 'axis of resistance', which includes Tehran, Baghdad, Damascus, Beirut, Ramallah, and Gaza".[35] In responding to the Arab Spring uprisings, Iran crowed over the fall of Mubarak in Egypt, supported the demonstration in Bahrain and stood against the one

---

[27]Gause, *Beyond Sectarianism*, 1.
[28]*Ibid.*
[29]*Ibid.*
[30]Ryan , "Regime security and shifting alliances".
[31]*Ibid.*
[32]Fürtig, "Iran: Winner or Loser?", 23.
[33]*Ibid.*, 38.
[34]*Ibid.*, 28.
[35]*Ibid.*

in Syria, supporting Assad with arms, money and military assistance. In fact, the uprising in Syria, Iran's strategic ally, was a major concern for Iran. Losing Syria would have constituted a strategic defeat, as it would have lost the ability to influence events in the Eastern Mediterranean and lost access to Hezbollah in Lebanon. However, Iran's actions in Syria have undermined Iranian claims of supporting the people's will and the Islamic awakening narrative of the Arab Spring.[36]

Similarly, the Iran-Saudi rivalry explains the various Saudi reactions to Arab Spring uprisings. Saudi Arabia intervened directly to suppress the uprising in Bahrain and to contain it in Yemen, and supported it in Syria. In all these cases, Saudi Arabia was concerned with its regime security and Iran's increasing influence. Likewise, given the geographic proximity and the common borders, and the presence of a Shiite majority in Bahrain, the success of the uprising in Bahrain would have meant a direct threat to the ruling regime in Saudi Arabia. Saudi Arabia feels threatened by the unrest in Bahrain, Yemen and Saudi Arabia's Eastern Province and sees itself "encircled by the Shia crescent that stretches from Iran across southern Iraq through Syria and into southern Lebanon".[37]

A post-American order in the Middle East

Under the Obama administration, US policy toward the region consisted of two elements: US retrenchment and the Iran nuclear deal. The United States began to retrench from the Middle East in favour of an accelerated pivot to Asia. According to Marc Lynch, the United States was "rightsizing" its role in the Middle East by reducing its massive military and political investment in the region.[38] This was a balancing act that sought to ensure US domestic security and secure US regional interests without dragging the US into regional conflicts and wars. The rightsizing policy, however, was met with great concern in "a region hard-wired for the exercise of American power",[39] especially after the United States' role and credibility in the region were already affected by the 2003 invasion of Iraq and its destabilising ramifications in the region.

At the same time, President Obama undertook a major initiative that he also considered vital to the United States' national security, that is bringing the negotiations on stopping Iran's nuclear program to a positive conclusion. A top priority for the Obama administration, it was seen as part of a long-term strategy of engagement to limit Iran's 'hostile' regional influence and reintegrate a more moderate Iran into the global political economy.[40] The nuclear agreement also provided the United States and Iran with an opportunity to cooperate against the Islamic State. It did not mean that the US was willing to concede the Middle East as an Iranian sphere of influence. However, the US failed to convince its Arab allies of its intentions and strategy and the rift between the US and GCC countries, especially Saudi Arabia, has grown wider.

---

[36]*Ibid.*,33.
[37]Devine, "Iran Versus ISIL", 30.
[38]Lynch, "Obama and the Middle East".
[39]*Ibid.*
[40]Gause, *Beyond Sectarianism.*

The bilateral Saudi-American relationship has always been an important element of regional stability. Thus, the US took several steps, including Obama's visit to Riyadh in March 2014, to assure Saudi Arabia and other Arab Gulf states that the nuclear deal was not a geopolitical 'grand bargain' confirming Iranian regional dominance. The US pressed Iraq to avoid further integration into Iran's sphere of influence.[41] At a meeting in Camp David in May 2015, the United States tried to reassure the Arab Gulf states that the accord was aimed only at denying Iran the ability to obtain nuclear weapons. The US has supported the Syrian opposition and maintained close alliances with Arab Gulf states. Due to Saudi Arabia's limited military capabilities, the US has reinforced its security connection with the Kingdom.[42] In 2015, the US authorised the sale of USD 5.4 bn worth of Patriot missiles and related equipment to Saudi Arabia. Since 2010, the Obama administration has authorised a record USD 60 bn in military sales to Saudi Arabia.[43]

In line with its interest, the US has always played a role in preventing an independent regional power from gaining prominence. However, it is unlikely that the United States will maintain this role and continue to shape regional politics for various reasons. Not only has it been focusing more on domestic affairs recently and lost major allies in the region, particularly Mubarak in Egypt, but anti-Americanism is also spreading in the region as is scepticism about and rejection of the US' leading role there.

Thus, the outcome of the nuclear deal has been a security dilemma. The deal has actually complicated the US' balancing strategy and intensified the tension among Gulf states and between the US and its Arab allies. Moreover, the deal has transformed the unipolar system in the region into a system of great power competition, in which China and Russia have been trying to fill the gap left by the diminished US role.

Saudi-Iranian power rivalry: implications for regional alignment

Saudi Arabia and Iran have been arch-enemies since the 1979 Islamic Revolution, when Iran announced that it would export its revolution and type of government to Arab Gulf states. Before that, both countries had normal diplomatic relations because they were both conservative monarchies. As US allies, they worked together to prevent the spread of Soviet influence in the region.

Religious tension is only one of the reasons for this longstanding rivalry, with Saudi Arabia representing the Sunni Wahhabi sect of Islam and Iran representing the Shiite sect. This sectarian division is embedded in regional politics as both countries compete for Islamic leadership. However, the competition between Iran and Saudi Arabia also extends into the internal politics of Arab states. For example, both countries are in competition in Lebanon's domestic politics as Iran supports the Shiite Hezbollah and Saudi Arabia supports the Sunnis and Christians. Historically, the Iran-Iraq war (1980-88), in which Saudi Arabia helped Iraq against Iran, further deteriorated bilateral relations between them. It is important to note, however, that relations between Saudi Arabia and Iran improved during the presidency of the Iranian reformist president, Muhammad Khatami, in the early 2000s, when Saudi Arabia and Iran signed an agreement on regional security (April 2001).

---

[41] *Ibid.,* 23.
[42] *Ibid.,* 26.
[43] "Kerry to Discuss Iran Nuclear Deal with Egypt and Qatar", *Al-Jazeera*, 1 August 2015, http://www.aljazeera.com/news/2015/08/kerry-discuss-iran-nuclear-deal-egypt-qatar-150801100543056.html.

Saudi Arabia and other GCC states did not feel strong enough militarily to defend their territorial integrity and sovereignty. Therefore, in the context of the strong US involvement in the Middle East, when regional powers occasionally found themselves in a situation in which they had to choose whether to bandwagon with the United States or join up with another regional power, they generally chose to bandwagon with the United States. Arab Gulf states were dependent on the United States for their security.

Now, with the US retrenchment and the nuclear agreement with Iran, GCC state fear abandonment by their main patron and have been forced to take responsibility for their own security. Consequently, shifting alliances and alignments have become a key policy to ensure GCC security. Saudi Arabia is trying to lead "an essentially Sunni and Arab alliance against Iranian inroads in Arab politics".[44] The Iran nuclear deal has led to a deepening of the already-existing alliance of Saudi Arabia, UAE, Egypt, Jordan and other GCC states, including Qatar.[45]

A newly hawkish Saudi Arabia has demonstrated its willingness to use military force to try to roll back Iran's influence in the Gulf. The Saudi-led Arab intervention in Yemen has brought GCC forces into direct conflict with the Iran-backed Houthi militia. Saudi Arabia has also undertaken a major initiative to unite Sunni states even outside the Gulf area in an anti-Iran alliance. To this end, it has reached out to former antagonists, such as the regional Muslim Brotherhood movement, including Hamas; forged an alliance with Sudan; and strengthened its relations with Turkey.[46]

In turn, these responses to the perceived threats of the nuclear deal have deepened the security dilemma in the region. The rise in defence spending and the regional arms race are making an already volatile region more unstable. Instead of halting nuclear proliferation in the region, Saudi Arabia and the UAE have now shown interest in acquiring nuclear energy.[47] Ultimately, this will have negative effects on the prospects for peace in the region, inciting fear and lack of trust among states and making it more difficult to pursue reconciliation and engagement. Regional powers have another option, however, and that is to cooperate with one another. If regional powers were to cooperate among themselves, a "regional concert" could emerge.[48] So far, this option has never been tried because regional powers are concerned with relative gains. They fear that cooperation might empower their competitors. Even the United States frequently took advantage of power rivalries between regional powers in order to keep any one of them from attaining a position able to challenge it as the most powerful actor in the Middle East.[49]

Multilateralism and the prospect of Iran-GCC rapprochement

Regional politics in the Middle East is the result of a complex interplay of extra-regional and intra-regional factors. No regional power is likely to emerge in the Middle East as long as all contenders for regional leadership – Egypt, Iran, Saudi Arabia and Turkey – are concerned with preventing the advancement of their competitors. However, this regional competition,

---

[44]Ryan, "Regime security and shifting alliances".
[45]Ibid.
[46]Council on Foreign Relations, "The Middle East after Nuclear Deal".
[47]Ismail, "Iran's Nuclear Program", 260.
[48]Beck, "The Concept of Regional Power", 8.
[49]Ibid., 9.

especially the competition between Iran and Saudi Arabia, is likely to exacerbate regional problems such as terrorism, sectarianism and instability. A concert of regional powers, which focuses on security and economic cooperation, instead of the current political/sectarian competition, could help alleviate existing tensions, as well as concerns about the security of the ruling regimes.

An appreciation of Iran's weight and interests is long overdue. Iran can no longer be ignored or marginalised. The JCPOA already acknowledged Iran as an important regional player. The many destabilising trends in the region can only be stopped through Iran's engagement with other regional powers, similar to Iran's engagement with international powers in the JCPOA. Therefore, the nuclear deal with Iran is a good starting point, but it is not enough to bring peace and prosperity to the Middle East.

A dialogue between Iran, Saudi Arabia and the other GCC countries could encourage them to adopt reconciliatory approaches in managing their regional relations. A regional dialogue/conference among regional powers for regional security and cooperation could help reduce tensions. The Conference for Security and Cooperation in Europe which took place in the 1970s is a successful example and could serve as a blueprint for regional security and cooperation.[50] The political dialogue should include regional issues such as terrorism, Syria and Yemen. This complex political dialogue should be complemented with confidence-building negotiations on issues such as refugees, energy, trade and investment. Calls for this initiative should preferably come from within the region and not from the outside.

In spite of all the problems, the Iran nuclear deal is an important milestone in strengthening the idea of collective action to solve regional problems and could introduce a new era of multilateralism in the region. Multilateralism proved to be effective in the case of the Iran nuclear deal. Sanctions on Iran really began to work when countries other than the United States joined in and the negotiations with Iran required the participation of the P5+1 to work. Multilateral initiatives are also needed to deal with regional problems such as the civil war in Syria and the fight against the Islamic State.

Arab Gulf states have maintained diplomatic relations with Iran, which makes direct dialogue possible. In April 2015, Iran's Javad Zarif called for regional dialogue to "address the causes of tension in the wider Persian Gulf region".[51] Without such a dialogue, there is a high risk that the differences between Iran and GCC states over the emerging regional order will continue to play out violently in various states in the region. Moreover, the conflict can spread beyond state actors. Already the Islamic State is capitalising on the Sunni-Shiite division.

An improvement in Saudi-Iran relations would enhance the chances for political settlements in Syria, Iraq, Lebanon and Bahrain. However, there are obstacles to this multilateral approach, especially the lack of direct contacts between Iran and Saudi Arabia since Riyadh severed ties in January 2016 following the attacks on its diplomatic mission in Iran. Yet, the biggest obstacle to Iran-Saudi rapprochement can be found in the domestic politics of both countries. Gregory Gause argues that "in Iran, it is the power of a particular player in the domestic political game, the IRGC [Islamic Revolutionary Guard Corps], which has ideological and organizational interests in an aggressive regional policy".[52] Saudi Arabia has

---

[50]Hanelt and Koch, "A Gulf CSC".
[51]Zarif, "A Message From Iran".
[52]Gause, "Saudi-Iranian Rapprochement?".

hardened its stance against its Shiite minority and taken steps to suppress public unrest and guard against future demonstration by introducing Vision 2030, aimed at creating more jobs and developing private sector industry.

Another significant obstacle to Saudi-Iranian rapprochement is "the weakness or collapse of state authority in so many Arab states. The political vacuums in Lebanon, Syria, and Iraq invite regional intervention".[53] Regional peace is unlikely without both countries resolving to resolve their differences.

Rapprochement is not impossible, but it is unlikely that it will take the form of an alliance. If at all, it will be in the form of a mutual understanding to ease tensions in order to solve regional problems. The Iran nuclear deal will hopefully have a moderating impact on domestic politics in Iran. With the possibilities offered by the nuclear deal, Iran will be focusing on domestic economic development and reintegration into world economy. This may strengthen moderate forces under Hassan Rouhani, thereby increasing the chances of a Saudi-Iranian rapprochement. Rouhani has stated that improving relations with Gulf neighbours is a top priority of his foreign policy. He has expressed the desire to return to normal relations with Saudi Arabia, but this would depend on Saudi policy toward Syria and whether Saudi Arabia is willing to scale down its support for the rebels.

Divisions within the GCC are also an important factor to be taken into consideration. There are important differences among the GCC members in terms of their attitudes toward Iran, indicating that relations are not simply determined by religious or ethnic differences. Iran has strong ties with other Gulf countries such as the UAE and Oman. Iran and the UAE are major trading partners. Iran-UAE trade amounted to around USD 3 billion (87.3 percent of Iran's total commercial dealings with all Arab countries in 2001).[54] Unlike Saudi Arabia, Oman and Qatar have reacted to the Iranian nuclear deal by making clear their intentions to explore a more open relationship with Iran in the economic, energy and security sectors. Moreover, the rise of the Islamic State in Iraq and Syria – a threat to both the GCC and Iran – is prompting some Gulf Arab rulers to consider exploring deeper cooperation with Iran in security sectors.[55] Iran has been reaching out to the Gulf Cooperation Council since 2013. So far, it has been focusing on Oman, Qatar and Kuwait and will gradually try to convince Saudi Arabia that accommodation is possible. It sees improving relations with the GCC as a way to consolidate the diplomatic gains made by signing the nuclear deal. Furthermore, if Iran were to succeed, Israel would be marginalised as the sole voice calling for Iran's isolation.

Conclusion

The Joint Comprehensive Plan of Action or Iran nuclear agreement reached between Iran and the P5+1 is consequential for regional security, especially Iran-GCC security relations with tensions between Iran and Saudi Arabia at the center. Regional conflicts and proxy wars and how they are managed will determine the security landscape of the region.

The nuclear agreement has raised a number of concerns related to regional security. First, Iran could use the sanction relief (estimated at about USD 100 bn) to support proxies

---

[53] *Ibid.*
[54] Shama, *Egyptian Foreign Policy,* 131.
[55] Cafiero and Wagner, "Iran Exposes Myth of GCC Unity".

in the region. Second, the agreement could be *perceived* as a sign that the United States is shifting away from supporting its traditional allies in the Gulf toward Iran. In response to these concerns, GCC countries, especially Saudi Arabia, have been pursuing an assertive foreign policy with the objective of achieving regime security, the key driver of alliance politics in the Middle East. It is trying to lead a Sunni alliance against Iranian inroads in regional politics. Because of the concern that the agreement with Iran can amount to a US realignment away from Gulf partners and allies, GCC countries have also sought to diversify international partners with a pivot to China as well as Russia so as not to rely only on the US.[56] Yet, regional security remains an elusive objective even when Arab Gulf states work together because they have different security threats in mind (Iran for Saudi Arabia and Bahrain, and the Muslim Brotherhood for the UAE).

The Middle East after the agreement will feature international recognition and incorporation of Iran into regional power constellations, which will intensify rivalry to assert dominance. This article has argued that although rivalry and competition will continue to increase in the short run, it could and should pave the way for dialogue and engagement on regional affairs in the long run. Arab Gulf states will be compelled to engage in a dialogue with Iran in the light of the numerous vulnerabilities facing their countries, including state weakness, growing instability, and political division with the GCC.

The growing mistrust and uncertainty can only be addressed through engagement and dialogue. The many regional shocks – the Arab Spring, the Syrian civil war, the rise of the Islamic State and the Iran nuclear agreement – can all push in the direction of dialogue to manage regional dynamics. The nuclear agreement also gives the US leverage in influencing the conflicts in the Middle East. A conference for regional security and cooperation modeled upon the Conference on Security and Cooperation in Europe could help alleviate tensions.

References

Acharya, A. *The End of American World Order*. USA: Polity Press, 2014.

Acharya, A. "'Regional Security Complexes' in the Third World: Stability and Collaboration" http://www.amitavacharya.com/sites/default/files/Regional%20Security%20Complexes%20in%20the%20Third%20World.pdf.

Al Otaiba, Y. "One Year after the Iran Nuclear Deal". *Wall Street Journal*, 3 April 2016. http://www.wsj.com/articles/one-year-after-the-iran-nuclear-deal-1459721502.

Al Shayji, A. "Nuclear Iran Worries GCC States more". *Gulf News*, 6 September 2015. http://gulfnews.com/opinion/thinkers/nuclear-iran-worries-gcc-states-more-1.1579489.

Beck, M. "The Concept of Regional Power as Applied to the Middle East". In *Regional Powers in the Middle East: New Constellations after the Arab Revolts*, edited by H. Fürtig. New York: Palgrave Macmillian, 2014.

Buzan, B., and O. Wæver. *Regions and Powers: the Structure of International Security*. Cambridge: Cambridge University Press, 2003.

---

[56]For more on GCC relations with Russia, see the article by Shumilin and Shumilina in this issue, 115

Cafiero, G. and D. Wagner. "Iran Exposes the Myth of GCC Unity". *The National Interest*, 7 September 2015. http://nationalinterest.org/feature/iran-exposes-the-myth-gcc-unity-13787

Coskun, B. "Regionalism and Securitization: The Case of the Middle East". In *Beyond Regionalism? Regional Cooperation, Regionalism and Regionalization in the Middle East*, edited by C. Harders and M. Legrenzi. New York: Routledge, 2016.

Council on Foreign Relations. "The Middle East After the Iran Nuclear Deal". 7 September 2015. http://www.cfr.org/middle-east-and-north-africa/middle-east-after-iran-nuclear-deal/p36963.

Devine, J. "Iran Versus ISIL". *Insight Turkey* 17, no. 2 (Spring 2015): 21–34.

Fürtig, H. "Iran: Winner or Loser of the 'Arab Spring'?" In *Regional Powers in the Middle East: New Constellations after the Arab Revolts*, edited by H. Fürtig. New York: Palgrave Macmillian, 2014.

Gause, F. G. *Beyond Sectarianism: The New Middle East Cold War*, Analysis Paper No. 11. Doha: Brookings Doha Center, 2014.

Gause, F. G. "Saudi-Iranian Rapprochement? The Incentives and Obstacles". *Brookings Institution*, 17 March 2014.

Hanelt, H., and C. Koch. "A Gulf CSC Could Bring Peace and Greater Security to the Middle East, spotlight europe # 2015 / 02. Guetersloh: Bertelsmann Stiftung, 2 July 2015.

Ismail, M. "Iran's Nuclear Program: Regional Implications and Possible Outcomes". *Asian Politics & Policy* 7, no. 2 (April 2015).

Lustick, I. "The Absence of Middle Eastern Great Powers: Political 'Backwardness' in Historical Perspective". *International Organization* 51, no. 4 (Autumn 1994): 653–83.

Lynch, M. "Obama and the Middle East: Rightsizing the U.S. Role". *Foreign Affairs* (September/ October 2015).

Nolte, D. "How to compare regional powers: analytical concepts and research topics". *Review of International Studies* 36, no. 4 (October 2010): 881–901.

Pinfari, M. *Of Cats and Lions: Egypt and Regional Security Governance in the Middle East*, Paper No. 48. Florence: Robert Schuman Centre for Advanced Studies Research, 2014.

Risen, T. "Arms Sales Boom Amid Iran, Saudi Arabia Proxy Wars". *U.S. News*, 22 February 2016. http://www.usnews.com/news/blogs/data-mine/2016/02/22/arms-sales-boom-amid-iran-saudi-arabia-proxy-wars.

Ryan, C. "Regime security and shifting alliances in the Middle East". *Project on Middle East Political Science (POMEPS)*. 20 August 2015. http://pomeps.org/2015/08/20/regime-security-and-shifting-alliances-in-the-middle-east.

Shabneh, G. *The Implications of a Nuclear Deal with Iran on the GCC, China, and Russia*, Report. Doha: Al Jazeera Center for Studies, 14 June 2015.

Shama, N. *Egyptian Foreign Policy from Mubarak to Morsi: Against National Interest*. New York: Routledge, 2013.

Zarif, J. "A Message From Iran". *The New York Times*, 20 April 2015. http://www.nytimes.com/2015/04/20/opinion/mohammad-javad-zarif-a-message-from-iran.html?_r=0

US-Arab Gulf Relations amidst Regional and Global Changes

Dania Koleilat Khatib

ABSTRACT

The Arab Gulf has long enjoyed privileged relations with the United States. Being home to the world's largest oil reserves, the US saw it in its strategic interest to keep Arab Gulf states in its camp during the Cold War. The relation developed over the years to include other areas of cooperation such as in the military, economic and even academic fields. However, many factors today challenge this relationship. In the face of the US' evident retrenchment from the region, the Arab Gulf is showing more inter-GCC cooperation, and Saudi Arabia is trying to forge alliances independently from the US. At the same time, Arab Gulf countries are intensifying their lobbying efforts in the US.

The United States and the Arab Gulf countries, especially Saudi Arabia, have enjoyed a longstanding, positive relationship. The Arab Gulf acquired strategic importance due to the fact that it sits on the world's largest proven oil reserves, essential to US interests. Therefore, the US has always been on the Arab Gulf's side against all threats. The US helped confront the wave of Arab nationalism in the fifties; supported Iraq, which shielded the Arab Gulf during the Iraq-Iran war; and came to the rescue of Kuwait during the military invasion of Saddam Hussein. During the Cold War, keeping the Arab Gulf countries in its camp was a main pillar of the US' policy of containing the Soviet Union.

At the same time, Arab Gulf countries have relied on their strategic value to get leverage from the US. In addition to political support, Arab Gulf countries have enjoyed military cooperation with the US. The relationship, however, has had a schizophrenic aspect to it. For example, the Saudis have relied on the US for their protection, and yet they have not wanted to be seen as a client state:[1] indeed, the American military presence in Saudi Arabia, considered a holy land, gave Bin Laden the pretext to start Al Qaeda. Therefore, American favouritism has been both a privilege and a curse for the Saudis.[2] The wealth that oil exports brought to the Gulf region also allowed it to become an important market for American businesses. While the two original components, security and oil, remain the backbone of the relationship, oil still is *the* point of gravity of all aspects of the relationship. Nevertheless, with the drop in oil prices and the austerity measures the governments are

---

[1]Safran, *Saudi Arabia: the ceaseless quest.*
[2]Van Auken, "Terrorism is imperialism's own creation".

implementing, the Arab Gulf has become less attractive as a market to businesses and enterprises seeking profit.[3]

Relations between Arab Gulf states and the US have not always been smooth. The Saudis have confronted the US on several occasions. The most prominent instances were the oil embargo of 1973 and King Fahd's threat to shut down production if Israel did not retreat from Lebanon in 1982. More recently, Qatar defied the US when it opened a representation office for the Taliban in Doha.[4] Despite those occasional frictions in which the different countries showed defiance to US authority, Arab Gulf states have never shifted alliance. Yet, these relations face new challenges today as the US retreats from the region, Russia takes a more assertive role and Iran re-enters the regional power constellation. Today, the US has adopted a passive attitude of endorsing the winner instead to trying to forge the course of events. In order to reverse this trend and re-engage the US in the region, Arab Gulf states should work on garnering support domestically inside the US, much in the way Israel keeps the US committed to its support by engaging with large groups of Americans.

The article will initially examine the US-Arab Gulf relationship, its foundation, its history, and will then discuss the geopolitical as well as internal changes (also in the US) that have affected it. This is followed by an anlysis of the Arab Gulf reaction to American retrenchment. The conclusion highlights the prospects for such a relationship.

The paradigm of US-GCC relations

Saudi Arabia's strategic value

The value of oil as a source of energy alternative to coal emerged following the Second World War. The Arab Gulf became the centre of attention of the two major powers, the Soviet Union and the United States, and the US saw it in its national interest to prevent the Soviets from reaching the oil fields in the Arab Gulf.[5] This gave Arab Gulf countries strategic importance.

Under President Richard Nixon, the 'two pillars' policy revolved around balancing power between Iran and Saudi Arabia.[6] The Shah was Nixon's favourite ally due to his Western tendencies and his effort to Westernise Iran. However, the overthrow of the Shah and the embargo imposed on Iran following the 1979 Islamic Revolution, which removed Iran as a source of oil, increased the importance of Saudi Arabia.

After the two oil shocks (1973 and 1979), an oil shortage came to be viewed by the US administration as a threat to national security.[7] As a result, protection of the Gulf was embodied in the Carter doctrine, announced by President Jimmy Carter in his State of the Union Address in 1980. It stated that oil was of strategic importance to the US and that the United States would use military force, if necessary, to defend its national interests in the Arab Gulf.[8] The US commitment to the protection of Gulf oil fields was maintained by subsequent administrations.

---

[3]Carey and Deema, "Austerity Could Backfire".
[4]Ahmed, "Gulf States Shape Washington Game".
[5]Lateef, "America, Israel and the Arabs".
[6]Bell, "Expansion of Persian Gulf Policy".
[7]Thurber, "Political power and policy subsystem".
[8]Stork, "The Carter Doctrine and US Bases.

However, with the strategic value of Saudi Arabia as a bulwark against Soviet influence, the strategic value of Israel also emerged, as Secretary of State Henry Kissinger successfully positioned it as a surrogate fortress to prevent the Soviets from reaching the oil fields in case Arabs changed their loyalty. Saudi King Khaled had announced that the loyalty of Saudi Arabia was neither to the Eastern nor to the Western bloc, but to the Muslim people around the world.[9] Therefore, from the beginning of this strategic relationship, the US did not have full trust in its ally.

Nevertheless, under the premise of the strategic importance of oil, President Ronald Reagan was able to rally the American people in support of the Airborne Warning and Control System (AWACS) deal in 1981, in which the US sold advanced fighter jets to Saudi Arabia despite resistance from the pro-Israel lobby.[10]

In the eighties, Saudi Arabia, with its control over world oil prices, increased its strategic value for the West by maintaining low oil prices which deterred the Soviet Union from exporting its oil.[11] Of course it had its own rewards from this policy, including the fact that, being a theocracy, it saw the atheist Soviet Union as the ultimate enemy and therefore understood the importance of allying itself with the Soviets' enemy: the United States.[12]

Military cooperation

Though the US' interest in the Arab Gulf started with the discovery of oil, relations developed over the years to include other dimensions, such as military and security cooperation. Several events occurred at the end of the 1970s and early 1980s that put the Arab Gulf states under direct threat and led the US to buttress Saudi defence capabilities: the Soviet invasion of Afghanistan, the fall of the Shah, the Iranian hostage crisis and the Iraq-Iran war. On the Afghanistan front, Saudi Arabia played an important role in supporting the *mujaheddin*. The main aim of the US, during the Reagan era, was to contain the Soviets. This is why the US national defence budget increased from USD 134 billion in 1980 to USD 253 billion in 1989. The US adopted a war by proxy with the Soviets, and Afghanistan was an important front.[13]

The abundance of wealth resulting from oil production also gave Saudi Arabia the financial capabilities to become a prime acquirer of US arms.[14] Sales to the Arab Gulf were driven by two factors: the first was strategic and had to do with the maintenance of the safety and stability of the Arab Gulf states, the second factor was economic. Arms sales to the Arab Gulf generated thousands of jobs and billions of dollars in revenue to American companies.[15] Additionally, military transfers were coupled with long-term contracts for servicing and training. This also deepened relations between Arab Gulf countries and the US.

Finally, the Arab Gulf states gained another strategic advantage when they became the US' allies in the war on terror. Post 9/11, the US saw that it needed a more comprehensive

---

[9]US Senate, *Proposed AWACS/F15 enhancement sale.*
[10]Godsell, "Reagan prestige, US influence".
[11]Hilton, "The collapse of the Soviet Union".
[12]Levins, *Arab Reach: The Secret War.*
[13]Pridham, *The Arab Gulf and the West.*
[14]Pierre, "Arms sales: The new diplomacy".
[15]Simpson, *The Prince.*

strategy and started strengthening its ties to the smaller Gulf states in order to bring them into its camp in the war on terror.[16]

Relations with the administration rather than grass roots support

Over the years, Arab Gulf states have mainly focused their relations on the White House and the administration. This is due to the fact that they have relied on their strategic value to push for their interests within the US. The administration is more sensitive and responsive to strategic considerations as it is appointed, except for the president who is elected. The administration is also concerned with the entire country and not merely a narrow constituency that has specific criteria and preferences.[17]

This is all the more important as Arab Gulf states have not worked on building up indigenous support in the US, unlike countries like Armenia or Israel, which spend a great deal of effort on creating a bond between the diaspora and the country of origin. The classic example are the Jewish youths who spend summers in an Israeli kibbutz. There is no similar effort by Arab Gulf governments to appeal to the young Arab Americans. Conscious of the strategic value of oil and strong relations with the administration, Arab Gulf states have not felt the need to establish strong ties with grassroots Arab American organizations.

Changes in the region

The Arab Spring and the rise of ISIS

The Arab Spring shook the confidence of Arab Gulf states in their long-term ally, the United States. It showed how quickly the US can let down its allies. The US dropped rulers who had been allies for decades, like Mubarak, overnight. The US' non-intervention in Syria created further tensions between the US and Arab Gulf countries, especially Saudi Arabia. Despite requests to do so, the US refrained from striking the Assad regime, even after it crossed the famous 'red line', that is, the use of chemical weapons on its civilian population.[18]

At the same time, the US endorsed the government of the Muslim Brotherhood in Egypt, an action that appalled many Arab Gulf states, namely the UAE, which has a very strong stance on the Brotherhood.[19]

The 2003 US-led invasion of Iraq and its disastrous repercusssions in the region had already shaken the faith of many in the United States. Following the invasion, turbulance spread in Iraq, but was soon stabilised by General Petraeus. Nevertheless, the success was shortlived. The withdrawal of US troops from 2007 onward, while President Nouri Al-Maliki enforced sectarian policies, led to the radicalisation of the disbanded Baath members. The Arab Spring and the chaos that resulted from it represented the right opportunity for the Islamic State of Iraq and Syria (ISIS) to spread across Syria and Iraq. But here too, the failure of the Iraqi army in the face of ISIS, despite all the funds spent on it by the US,[20] was a signal of US failure in the region. To add to it, the inability of the US to train moderate factions

---

[16]Smith, *Power Game.*
[17]Congress, for example, composed of 550 elected members, is more responsive to the different electorates' preferences. *Ibid.*
[18]Halper, "Kerry: Obama's failure to enforce".
[19]Cohen, "Working with the Muslim Brotherhood".
[20]Cockburn, *The Rise of the Islamic State.*

of the free Syrian army in Jordan after it had pledged half a billion dollars for this purpose also revealed to the Gulf states the US' failure and incapacity.[21]

Sinking oil prices

Low oil prices have had catastrophic repercussions on Saudi Arabia and the region. Oil prices started to increase following the invasion of Iraq in 2003. The resulting turbulence in that country coincided with the increase in demand from China and led to a surge in the price of oil. The average between 2011 and 2014 was USD 90 per barrel. But it plunged dramatically thereafter as the market was flooded, partly because of shale oil from the United States coming onto the market, and the average in 2015-16 stood at USD 36 per barrel.[22]

Initially, it was the increase in the price of oil that led to the development of shale oil. Shale oil production was only viable when oil cost more than USD 50 per barrel. However, once investment in the technology started, it evolved rapidly and today shale oil can be extracted from some reservoirs at the cost of USD 30 per barrel.[23] It has created a revolution in the US and rendered the US energy independent. Thus, the Carter premise that oil fields have strategic value for the United States and have to be protected, even by force, no longer holds.

Additionally, environmental factors have pushed technology to produce more environment-friendly fuel-efficient cars and machines. And finally, Saudi Arabia has intentionally kept the price of oil low as a political tool to dissuade rivals like Russia, which is venturing into the Middle East, and Iran, which had just made its re-entry onto the oil market as a result of the Joint Cooperation Plan of Action (JCPOA), from becoming too active. The policy was also intended more generally as a strategy: keeping the price low would drive some producers out of the market which would automatically reduce the supply and hence raise the price.[24]

The low oil price has had important effects on the Arab Gulf countries, whose income is highly dependent on oil. The petroleum sector accounts for roughly 87 percent of budget revenues, 42 percent of GDP, and 90 percent of export earnings.[25] Many generous subsidies given out by the late King Abdullah to seek the acquiescence of the opposition following the outbreak of the Arab Spring, were reversed when the new monarch, King Salman, came to power. This policy will have economic repercussions. The forecast is a slowdown between 2-3 percent in 2017-18. A decrease in consumer spending is already being noticed. More importantly, though, a decrease in the perks citizens are used to receiving from the government could result in resentment towards the government and the House of Saud.[26]

Finally, the decrease in income resulting from the low oil prices coincided with a jump in military spending due to the Yemen intervention.[27] This mix makes the internal situation in Arab Gulf states more fragile.[28] The lack of prosperity is a signal for more trouble, which makes the US even more reluctant to intervene.

---

[21]Tomlinson, "US scraps 500M programme".
[22]Thompson, "What happens when?".
[23]Johnston, "U.S. Shale Oil Production".
[24]El Gamal, "Facing new oil glut".
[25]"Saudi Arabia profile". *Forbes*, December 2016. http://www.forbes.com/places/saudi-arabia/.
[26]Carey and Deema, "Austerity Could Backfire".
[27]Nasser, "Can Saudi Arabia afford Yemen war?".
[28]Naylor, "Austerity could stoke civil unrest".

The changes in the US

Obama's strategic shift to Asia

The general dissatisfaction with the outcome of US efforts in Iraq as well as the US' independence in oil production encouraged the Obama administration to shift the focus of its foreign policy to Asia. The pivot was an expression of President Obama's desire to build relations with emerging powers like India and China.[29] The pivot was not accidental, however, it followed Obama and his predecessors' failure to bring any true solutions to the Middle Eastern region. Obama's inability to bring change started with his failure to stop settlements. Following his call on Israel to stop settlements, Israeli President Benjamin Netanyahu went to the US Congress and humiliated Obama, receiving a standing ovation from the members of Congress.[30] Similarly, Obama's (albeit reluctant) intervention in Libya resulted in chaos.[31]

The pivot to Asia came as a departure from previous President George W. Bush's policies that were focused on taking a greater role in the Middle East.[32] After the disastrous invasion of Iraq, Bush adopted a narrative of democratising the region which, in the wake of the Arab Spring, seemed more and more unrealistic.

The pivot is also a pivot in trade. The US is interested in opening up new markets such as Indonesia and the Philippines, countries also interested in having the US as a buffer against China's growing prowess.[33] In November 2012, President Obama, joined by the heads of state of Brunei and Indonesia, launched the US-Asia Pacific Comprehensive Partnership for a Sustainable Energy Future, an energy cooperation framework for the Asia-Pacific region.[34] The extent of the pivot and how much it will affect US-Arab Gulf relations also depends on the opportunities East Asia presents to the US.[35]

The general mood is isolationist

Today, the US is in an isolationist mood. This isolationism was already evident in the reaction of Congress and public opinion to Obama's call for an intervention in Syria, even after Assad's use of chemical weapons.[36] The failure in Iraq and the repercussions that resulted in extremism and terrorism have created a sense of defeatism among the American public which is expressing itself in this isolationistic mood.

In addition the average American does not trust regimes in the region. The general perception is that American support for autocratic repressive regimes led to extremism and turmoil,[37] and this to some extent has increased the US' appetite to look for new sources

[29]Dyer, "Obama declares Asia 'top priority'". Li, "Assessing U.S.-China relations".
[30]Landler, "Score on Obama vs. Netanyahu".
[31]Jones and Beltyukova, "Libya's chaos, explained".
[32]Woodward, *The War Within*.
[33]Indonesia had a GDP of USD 861.93 billion in 2015 (*Trading economics*, http://www.tradingeconomics.com/indonesia/gdp), while the Philipines had a GDP of USD 292 billion and a growth rate of 6.3% in 2015 ("Philippines Economic Outlook", *FocusEconomics*, 21 February 2017, http://www.focus-economics.com/countries/philippines); Kagan, "The Obama administration pivot to Asia".
[34]US-Asia Pacific Comprehensive Energy Partnership, https://www.state.gov/e/enr/c56576.htm
[35]Campbell and Andrews, *Explaining the US "Pivot" to Asia*.
[36]Engel, "Obama reportedly declined".
[37]Koppman, "Endless Support for Dictators Powers Islamic State".

of energy and gain independence from Middle Eastern oil. This has been noticeable in the election campaigns of US presidential candidates since 11 September 2001. The various candidates have all adopted the narrative that energy independence is a national interest issue to be pursued.[38]

In addition, it is difficult today to convince the average American of the necessity of intervening in the region. In the early eighties, Reagan convinced the American public that selling AWACS to Saudi Arabia fell within the bounds of the US' strategic interest. Protecting Saudi Arabia was perceived as part of the Soviet containment strategy.[39] Today, there is no concrete enemy comparable to the Soviets of the eighties. Similarly, following the Iraqi invasion of Kuwait in the early nineties, President George Bush could address the American public and convince them of the need to protect the oil fields.[40] As explained, this is also no longer valid.

More generally, however, it is the national interest that is no longer a well-defined concept in the mind of the average American. During the Cold War, the national interest consisted of containing the Soviet threat; with the collapse of the Berlin Wall, the notion of national interest became fluid. Even fighting terrorism as promoted by George W. Bush does not represent an overarching national interest similar to the containment of communism.[41] Therefore, the US' national interests or strategic considerations are more complex and more difficult to gauge nowadays.

Changes in views of Gulf actors

In 1979, the Iranian revolution terminated the US' friendship with Iran. While Iran was the US' main ally at the time of the Shah, it became the Great Satan when Khomeini took over.[42] Conducting several attacks on American personnel and facilities as well as supporting several groups classified as terrorist, such as Hezbollah and Hamas, Iran was seen as the main source of terrorism. However, this view no longer prevails. With the current war in Syria, ISIS, with its videos of beheadings and the destruction of cultural heritage sites, has drawn the attention of the public. Described in Western media as the ideological by-product of Wahhabism, the official state-sponsored form of Sunni Islamism in Saudi Arabia, this has made the US public and political elite point a finger at Saudi Arabia.

However, the accusations against Saudi Arabia did not start with ISIS. They go back to September 11 as the hijackers of the planes that crashed into the twin towers in New York were Saudis. 9/11 led many to question the US-Saudi alliance at that time.[43] Bush later managed to present Saudi Arabia as his ally in the war on terror and developed relations with the smaller Gulf states. However, the rise of ISIS put the alliance into question a second time.

---

[38]Foster, "Energy Independence".
[39]Laham, *Selling AWACS to Saudi Arabia*.
[40]Bush, "Address on Iraq's Invasion of Kuwait".
[41]Paul and Paul, *Ethnic lobbies and US foreign policy*.
[42]Qasim, *Hizbullah: The Story from Within*.
[43]Al Faisal and Peterson, "United States and Saudi Arabia".

The public discourse shows a general trend that views Saudi Arabia as the main hub fuelling the extremist ideology that terrorist organisations like ISIS adopt,[44] despite the facts that the Wahhabism advocated by ISIS is different from the Wahhabism adopted by Saudi Arabia and that Saudi Arabia is part of the alliance fighting ISIS.[45]

JASTA, the Justice Against Sponsors of Terrorism Act is a US bill that allows parents of 9/11 victims to sue Saudi Arabia in federal courts, jeopardising Saudi assets in the US and damaging the Saudi Kingdom's image. The bill was passed unanimously in the Senate in May 2016, as it was in the House of Representatives in September 2016. Two days later, both houses of Congress passed the bill into law after overriding a veto from President Obama. It was the first time that Obama's veto was overridden.[46] JASTA demonstrates clearly how unpopular the US' relations with Saudi Arabia have become domestically. Iran is no longer seen as the hub of terrorism; on the contrary, it is seen as the nemesis of extremist groups that can pose a threat to the West.[47]

Additionally, Iran's growing influence over the region has compelled the US to acknowledge it as a force to reckon with. Seeing that international sanctions did not keep Iran from proceeding with its nuclear program, the US administration, at a time when the president was ending embargos around the world, and in an attempt to reduce risks in the Middle East, chose to negotiate with it. The JCPOA brought the US and Iran together at the negotiating table.

Iran is a major actor in Iraq and Syria. With its proxies, it has saved the Assad regime from total collapse. It has proved it has power on the ground, and hence has convinced the US that it can be a more reliable partner than its long-term ally, Saudi Arabia. After Saudi Arabia helped the US isolate Iran, Iran has now become a regional player recognised by the US.

Repercussions

US distancing from the Gulf

As a result of this isolationist mood, the loss of the strategic value of Gulf oil, and the US shift to Asia, the US is slowly distancing itself from the region and adopting the attitude of endorsing the winner instead of trying to take a proactive role in forging the course of events.

The US keeps stating that its alliances with Arab Gulf states still hold, but facts show differently.[48] Today the US is reluctant to take an active part in the Yemen war, even though Adel Al Jubeir, the Saudi foreign minister, has explained that Iran is in Saudi Arabia's backyard.[49] According to the *New York Times*, the UAE asked the US Special Forces stationed in Abu Dhabi for support in ground operations in Aden in July 2015. Fearing to be dragged into the conflict, the American military refused.[50] They also asked the Pentagon to support the assault in July 2015, but that request was also declined. The Emirates nevertheless conducted the planning for the operation themselves and succeeded.[51]

---

[44]Shane, "Saudis and Extremism".
[45]Hubbard, "ISIS Turns Saudis Against Kingdom".
[46]Smith, "Congress overrides Obama's veto".
[47]Di Giovanni, "Nemesis: The shadowy Iranian training".
[48]Carey and Sink, "Trump's Calls with Gulf Allies".
[49]Mazzetti and Schmitt, "Support for Saudis entangles U.S.".
[50]Maclean *et al.*, "Yemen counter-terrorism mission".
[51]Mazzetti and Schmitt, "Support for Saudis entangles U.S.".

GCC trying to act independently while seeking to garner US support

This American attitude has generated a sense of insecurity among Arab Gulf countries, but it is also, as just mentioned, encouraging them to work on their own. The Arab Gulf is acting more autonomously, creating new alliances and platforms independently of the US. Confronted with the threat of the Muslim Brotherhood in Egypt and the US' apathy, Saudi Arabia and the UAE acted without resorting to the US and helped Abdel Fattah Al-Sisi overthrow the government of Mohammed Morsi in Egypt.[52] Facing the take-over of the rebels in Yemen, Saudi Arabia has created a coalition to support the Hadi government and fight the Houthis.[53] At the same time, Arab Gulf states are trying to build relations with new players.

Despite their antagonistic attitude toward Russia regarding Syria, Arab Gulf states are warming up to the new rising power in the region. Following the cut in oil prices that hurt Russia, Saudi Arabia and Russia announced in September 2016, during the G20 Summit in the Chinese city of Hangzhou, that they will cooperate to keep the market stable.[54] Abu Dhabi's Crown Prince Sheikh Mohammed Bin Zayed has met Russian President Vladimir Putin seven times in the last five years. These meetings have increased the scope of cooperation between the two countries to include trade and defence.[55]

In addition to diversifying its alliances with global powers, Saudi Arabia is trying to forge a regional role for itself by placing itself at the epicentre of the Arab and Islamic world. On 15 December 2015, Saudi Arabia forged a coalition of Islamic countries against terrorism under the name of the Islamic Military Alliance to Fight Terrorism, without the participation of the United States.[56]

As events unfold, the Arab Gulf countries are increasingly realising the need for inter-GCC and inter-Arab cooperation and overcoming their 'security complex', that is the fear of their neighbours that used to govern inter-Arab Gulf relations.[57] Although Saudi Arabia was initially reluctant to endorse a joint military force, after seeing the difficulties in Yemen due to the lack of ground troops, Saudi King Salman visited Egypt to activate the joint Arab ground forces.[58] The force will be manned by troops donated by various Arab countries.

GCC efforts to engage the US

In parallel to acting autonomously and forging relations on their own, the Arab Gulf states are trying to improve their standing inside the US. Important lobbying firms have been hired by the UAE, Saudi Arabia, Qatar, Bahrain and Kuwait.[59] Arab Gulf states are also funding think tanks and academic programs in major universities, as well as investing in

---

[52]Hearst, "Why Saudi Arabia is taking risk".

[53]Maclean *et al.*, "Yemen counter-terrorism mission".

[54]Habriri, "New Page of Saudi-Russian Relations".

[55]Soldatkin *et al.*, "Putin, Abu Dhabi crown prince meet".

[56]"Oman joins Saudi-led Islamic alliance against terrorism", *Al Arabiya English*, 29 December 2016. http://english.alarabiya. net/en/News/gulf/2016/12/29/Oman-joins-Saudi-led-Islamic-alliance-against-terrorism.html.

[57]Gause, *International Relations of Persian Gulf*.

[58]"King Salman talks 'unity' at Egypt's parliament", *Al Arabiya English*, 10 April 2016, http://english.alarabiya.net/en/News/ middle-east/2016/04/10/Egypt-Saudi-Arabia-sign-new-deals-in-King-Salman-visit.html.

[59]In 2014, the United Arab Emirates spent more than USD 12 million on lobbying and public relations in the United States; Bahrain has spent USD 32 million on public relations and lobbying in the US since the start of the uprising in 2011(Ahmed, "Gulf States Shape Washington Game"). Recently, Saudi Arabia launched a pro-Saudi lobby in the United States: SAPRAC (Abbas, "Saudi lobby group SAPRAC launches").

media to keep the US engaged. The UAE sponsors a section in *Foreign Policy* magazine and has donated one million dollars to Harvard's John F. Kennedy School of Government, among many other initiatives.[60] The Brookings Institution has opened an office in Doha and the Atlantic Council has forged an alliance with the UAE-based Emirates Policy Centre.

Still, these efforts are not unified and each embassy works independently. The cohesion in military operations in the region is not yet reflected in diplomatic efforts and lobbying. With the exception of the Arab Gulf states' funding of a new think tank in Washington, the Arab Gulf Institute in Washington, there is no coordination to forge a common narrative to the general public. In addition, all these initiatives have to be registered under the Foreign Agents Registration Act (FARA), and lobbyists acting on behalf of foreign agents are regarded with suspicion by American citizens. The whole thing could backfire.[61]

In fact, Arab Gulf states suffer from a negative image. It is very difficult to lobby for an issue when that issue or the group sponsoring it carries a negative stigma.[62] That negative image has created a state of intimidation that prevents the Gulf states from being proactive in promoting their image as they are scared that such activities might be used against them. In addition, the way Saudis conduct their relations with the US makes it very hard to convince the average American that they are the US' trusted allies. This ties in to what Kissinger described as "opaque" when discussing Saudi relations with the US.[63]

At the same time, Saudi Arabia and the various Arab Gulf states try as much as possible to dissociate themselves from US policy at home. This is why, on a primary policy level, they take positions that might contradict American decisions, while on the secondary, practical level, which involves military, trade and technical partnerships, they cooperate. They keep the policy association low key while developing the secondary association because they do not want to look, domestically, like clients of the United States.[64] For example, while the Gulf states opposed the US war on Iraq, American troops used bases in these countries.[65] While Qatar opposed the Israeli strike on Lebanon in 2006, it reportedly helped the US deliver bombs to Israel.[66]

The Trump era and prospects for US- GCC relations

Trump started by sending mixed signals to the Arab Gulf during his election campaign, promising a harder approach towards the Gulf monarchies. He promised he would make Saudi Arabia pay for American protection through the years and would make Kuwait pay for the US' effort in the nineties in driving back Saddam Hussein.[67] However, since he took office, there has been a warming up between the US and the Arab Gulf, mainly because of Trump's strong stance on Iran: one of his campaign promises was to rip up the nuclear agreement with Iran.[68]

---

[60]Kilgore, "UAE to donate $1 million".
[61]Smith, *Power Game*.
[62]Baumgartner *et al.*, *Lobbying and policy change*.
[63]Kissinger, *Does America need a foreign policy?*
[64]Safran, *Saudi Arabia:The ceaseless quest*.
[65]Otterman, "Saudi Arabia: Withdrawal of US forces".
[66]Umrani, "US blocked missile deliveries to Hezbollah".
[67]Ibrahim, "Donald Trump's stance on Middle East".
[68]Daiss, "Trump Pledges to Rip Up Iran Deal".

The Arab Gulf countries supported Trump's decision to ban nationals of seven Muslim countries from entering the US. The UAE foreign minister said that the decision was not a Muslim ban and considered it part of the US' internal affairs.[69] Additionally, Trump reversed US policy towards Bahrain when his administration approved a weapons deal that had been denied by the Obama administration because of what it saw as repressive policies during the Shia uprising in the country.[70]

Therefore, many indicators signal a possible rapprochement between Trump and Arab Gulf countries in the coming years. The Gulf might once more take on the role it had during previous administrations, that is as an important ally in containing Iran. However, how relations develop will depend on many factors, including how Saudi Arabia performs in the war on terror as Trump's main aim is to go after ISIS.[71] But internal factors are also important and relations will depend on whether Saudi Arabia can enhance its image inside the US and get rid of the stigma of a country spreading extremist Wahhabi ideology. Finally, relations will also depend on Iran and whether or not it acquiesces to the US and international community and shows more cooperation in regional security.

References

Abbas, F. J. "Saudi lobby group SAPRAC launches in the USA". *Al Arabiya English*, 16 March 2016. http://english.alarabiya.net/en/perspective/features/2016/03/16/Saudi-lobby-group-SAPRAC-launches-in-the-US.html.

Ahmed, A. S. "How Wealthy Arab Gulf States Shape the Washington Influence Game. *HuffPost Politics*, 2 September 2015. http://www.huffingtonpost.com/entry/arab-gulf-states-washington_us_55e62be5e4b0b7a9633ac659

Al Faisal, S., and P. G. Peterson. "The United States and Saudi Arabia: A Relationship Threatened By Misconceptions". *Council on Foreign Relations*, 27 April 2004. http://www.cfr.org/saudi-arabia/united-states-saudi-arabia-relationship-threatened-misconceptions/p6982

Baumgartner, F.R., J.M. Berry, M. Hojnacki, D.C. Kimball, and B.L. Leech. *Lobbying and policy change: Who wins, who loses, and why*. Chicago: University of Chicago Press, 2009.

Bell, B. R. "Expansion of American Persian Gulf Policy by Three Presidents". *Globalsecurity.org*, 1990. http://www.globalsecurity.org/military/library/report/1990/BRB.htm

Bush, G. H. W. "Address on Iraq's Invasion of Kuwait". 8 August 1990. http://www.cfr.org/iraq/president-george hw bushs-address-iraqs-invasion-kuwait-1990/p24117

Campbell, K., and B. Andrews. *Explaining the US 'Pivot' to Asia*, Chatham House Programme Paper. London: Chatham House, 1 August 2013. https://www.chathamhouse.org/publications/papers/view/194019#

Carey, G., and A. Deema. "The soft pinch of austerity in Saudi Arabia could backfire". *Bloomberg*, 16 August 2016. https://www.bloomberg.com/news/articles/2016-08-16/as-saudi-austerity-starts-to-bite-a-testing-time-for-its-prince

---

[69] Abdullah bin Zayed: Trump's travel ban not Islamophobic, *Aljazeera*, Feb 2017, http://www.aljazeera.com/news/2017/02/abdullah-bin-zayed-trump-travel-ban-islamophobic-170201132819745.html

[70] Osborne, "Donald Trump 'to approve arms sales'".

[71] "Syria's Assad views Trump as 'promising' on Islamic State", *Reuters*, 7 February 2017, http://www.reuters.com/article/us-mideast-crisis-syria-assad-idUSKBN15M0HI

Carey, G., and J. Sink. "Trump's Calls with Gulf Allies Offer Insight on Mideast Policy". *Bloomberg*, 30 January 2017. https://www.bloomberg.com/politics/articles/2017-01-29/saudi-king-discusses-terror-business-ties-in-call-with-trump.

Cockburn, P. *The rise of the Islamic State: ISIS and the new Sunni revolution*. New York: Verso Books, 2015.

Cohen, R. "Working with the Muslim Brotherhood". *The New York Times*, 22 October 2012.

Daiss, T. "Trump Pledges to Rip Up Iran Deal; Israelis Say Not So Fast". *Forbes.com,* 22 November 2016. https://www.forbes.com/sites/timdaiss/2016/11/22/trumps-iran-deal-rhetoric-israelis-say-not-so-fast/#7119ef433d99

Di Giovanni, J. "Nemesis: The shadowy training Iranian Shia militias in Iraq". *Newsweek*, 27 November 2014, http://europe.newsweek.com/nemesis-shadowy-iranian-training-shia-militias-iraq-287610?rm=eu.

Dyer, G. "In Washington Obama declares Asia a 'top priority'". *Financial Times*, 18 November 2011.

El Gamal, R. "Facing new oil glut, Saudis avoid 1980s mistakes to halt price slide". *Reuters*, 14 October 2014. http://www.reuters.com/article/us-saudi-oil-policy-analysis-idUSKCN0I229320141014.

Engel, P. "Obama reportedly declined to enforce red line in Syria after Iran threatened to back out of nuclear deal". *Business Insider*, 23 August 2016. http://www.businessinsider.com/obama-red-line-syria-iran-2016-8.

Foster, M. "Energy Independence: An Impossible Campaign Promise". Duke University Nikolas School of Environment, 22 October 2012. http://sites.nicholas.duke.edu/loribennear/2012/10/22/energy-independence-an-impossible-campaign-promise/

Gause, F.G. *The International Relations of the Persian Gulf*. Cambridge: Cambridge University Press, 2009.

Godsell, G. "Reagan prestige, US influence ride on AWACS". *Christian Science Monitor*, 27 October 1981.

Habriri, N. "Deputy Crown Prince and Putin Open New Page of Saudi-Russian Relations". *Asharq Al-Awsat English*, 6 September 2016. http://english.aawsat.com/2016/09/article55357832/deputy-crown-prince-putin-open-new-page-saudi-russian-relations

Halper, D. "Kerry: Obama's failure to enforce red line in Syria came at a cost". *New York Post*, 5 December 2016. http://nypost.com/2016/12/05/kerry-obamas-failure-to-enforce-red-line-in-syria-came-at-a-cost/.

Hearst, D. "Why Saudi Arabia is taking a risk by backing the Egyptian coup". *The Guardian*, 20 August 2013. https://www.theguardian.com/commentisfree/2013/aug/20/saudi-arabia-coup-egypt

Hilton, R. "The collapse of the Soviet Union and Ronald Reagan", *WAIS*. http://wais.stanford.edu/History/history_ussrandreagan.htm

Hubbard, B. "ISIS Turns Saudis Against the Kingdom, and Families Against Their Own". *The New York Times*, 31 March 2016. https://www.nytimes.com/2016/04/01/world/middleeast/isis-saudi-arabia-wahhabism.html

Ibrahim, A. "In his own words: Donald Trump's stance on the Middle East". *Middle East Eye*, 9 Nov 2016. http://www.middleeasteye.net/news/what-will-middle-east-look-under-trump-298938440

Johnston, M. "U.S. Shale Oil Production: The Rise and Fall". *Investopedia*, 30 October 2015. http://www.investopedia.com/articles/investing/103015/us-shale-oil-production-rise-and-fall.asp

Jones, B., and A. Beltyukova. "Libya's chaos, explained in five graphics". *CNN*, 4 August 2016. http://edition.cnn.com/2016/08/04/africa/libya-chaos-in-graphics/

Kagan, R. "The Obama administration's pivot to Asia. A conversation with Assistant Secretary Kurt Campbell". *The Foreign Policy Initiative*, 13 December 2011. http://www.foreignpolicyi.org/content/obama-administrations-pivot-asia.

Kilgore, C. R. "UAE to Donate $1 Million to Harvard Kennedy School". *EdArabia*, October 2010. http://www.edarabia.com/10868/uae-to-donate-1-million-to-harvard-kennedy-school/.

Kissinger, H. *Does America need a foreign policy? Towards a new diplomacy for the 21st Century*. New York: Simon & Schuster, 2001.

Koppman, S. "Endless U.S. Support for Dictators Powers Islamic State". *The World Post*, 2015. http://www.huffingtonpost.com/steve-koppman/endless-us-support-for-di_b_6821136.html.

Laham, N. *Selling AWACS to Saudi Arabia*. Westport, Conn: Praeger, 2002.

Landler, M. and H. Cooper. "Keeping Score on Obama vs. Netanyahu". *The New York Times*, 20 May 2009. http://www.nytimes.com/2009/05/21/us/politics/21diplo.html

Lateef, A. "America, Israel and the Arabs". *Pakistan Horizon* 27, no. 1 (1974): 11–28.

Levins, H. *Arab Reach: The Secret War against Israel*. New York: Doubleday, 1983.

Li, C. "Assessing U.S.-China relations under the Obama administration". *Brookings op-ed*, 30 August 2016.

Maclean, W., N. Browning and Y. Bayoumy. "Yemen counter-terrorism mission shows UAE military ambition". *Reuters*, 28 September 2016. http://www.reuters.com/article/us-yemen-security-emirates-idUSKCN0ZE1EA

Mazzetti, M., and E. Schmitt. "Quiet Support for Saudis Entangles U.S. in Yemen". *The New York Times*, 13 March 2016. https://www.nytimes.com/2016/03/14/world/middleeast/yemen-saudi-us.html

Nasser, A. "How long can Saudi Arabia afford Yemen war?". *Al-monitor*, 21 January 2016. http://www.al-monitor.com/pulse/originals/2016/01/yemen-war-saudi-arabia-economic-repercussions.html#

Naylor, H. "Saudi pivot to austerity could stoke civil unrest". *Adn.com*, 24 June 2016. https://www.adn.com/nation-world/article/saudi-pivot-austerity-could-stoke-civil-unrest/2016/02/26/

Otterman, S. "Saudi Arabia: Withdrawal of U.S. Forces". *Council on Foreign Relations*, 2 May 2003. http://www.cfr.org/saudi-arabia/saudi-arabia-withdrawl-us-forces/p7739#.

Osborne, S. "Donald Trump 'to approve arms sales to Saudi Arabia and Bahrain' blocked by Barack Obama". *The Independent*, 8 February 2017. http://www.independent.co.uk/news/world/americas/donald-trump-arms-sales-saudi-arabia-bahrain-blocked-barack-obama-yemen-civil-war-middle-east-a7568911.html

Paul, D.M., and R.A. Paul. *Ethnic lobbies and US foreign policy*. Boulder: Lynne Rienner Publishers, 2009.

Pierre, A. J. "Arms sales: The new diplomacy". *Foreign Affairs* (Winter 1981/2).

Pridham, B.R. *The Arab Gulf and the West*. London: Croom Helm, 1985.

Qassem, N. *Hizbullah: The Story from Within*. London: Saqi, 2010.

Safran, N. *Saudi Arabia: the ceaseless quest for security*. New York: Cornell University Press, 1985.

Shane, S. "Saudis and Extremism: 'Both the Arsonists and the Firefighters'". *The New York Times*, 25 August 2016. https://www.nytimes.com/2016/08/26/world/middleeast/saudi-arabia-islam.html

Simpson, W. *The Prince: The Secret Story of the World's Most Intriguing Royal, Prince Bandar bin Sultan*. New York: Regan, 2006.

Smith, D. "Congress overrides Obama's veto of 9/11 bill letting families sue Saudi Arabia". *The Guardian*, 29 September 2016. https://www.theguardian.com/us-news/2016/sep/28/senate-obama-veto-september-11-bill-saudi-arabia

Smith, H. *The Power Game: How Washington Works*. New York: Ballantine Books, 1996.

Soldatkin, V., J. Stubbs and J. Lawrence. "Russia's Putin, Abu Dhabi crown prince meet to discuss Syria". *Reuters*, 11 October 2015. http://www.reuters.com/article/us-mideast-crisis-syria-russia-idUSKCN0S508820151011

Thompson, L. "What happens when America no longer needs Middle East oil?". *Forbes*, 3 December 2012. http://www.forbes.com/sites/lorenthompson/2012/12/03/what-happens-when-america-no-longer-needs-middle-east-oil/#73325fae64fa

Thurber, J "Political power and policy subsystem in America". In *Rivals for Power: Presidential-Congressional Relations*, edited by J. Thurber. Washington DC: Rowman & Littlefield, 2013.

Tomlinson, S. "US scraps its $500 million programme to train 'moderate' Syrian rebels after producing fewer than 80 soldiers, most of whom were either shot or ran away". *MailOnline*, 9 October 2015. http://www.dailymail.co.uk/news/article-3266509/US-scraps-500million-programme-train-moderate-Syrian-rebels-producing-fewer-80-soldiers-shot-ran-away.html

Umrani, M. "How U.S. Reportedly Blocked Missile Deliveries to Hezbollah". *The Diplomatic Times Review*, 18 August 2006. http://www.thediplomatictimes-review.com/2006/08/how-usreportedl.htm

US Senate, Committee on Foreign Relations. *The proposal AWACS/F-15 enhancement sale to Saudi Arabia*. Washington DC: US GPO, September1981. https://catalog.hathitrust.org/Record/002756952

Van Auken, B. "Terrorism is Largely US Imperialism's Own Creation". *Global research*, 6 December 2013. http://www.globalresearch.ca/terrorism-is-largely-us-imperialisms-own-creation/5360497.

Woodward, B. *The War Within: A Secret White House History (2006–2008)*. New York: Simon & Schuster, 2008.

Russia as a Gravity Pole of the GCC's New Foreign Policy Pragmatism

Alexander Shumilin and Inna Shumilina

ABSTRACT

Despite the obvious differences over the Syrian crisis and Iran, the GCC countries do not seem to be distancing themselves from Russia politically. To a large extent that is due to Russia's growing military role (in Syria) and military cooperation (with Iran), as well as the diminishing role of the United States under Obama. Having accepted the situation in Syria (after the fall of Aleppo) as a *fait accompli*, the GCC's elites seem to be looking at Russia as a powerful player able to reduce the scope of Iran's expansion in the region. Their approach involves a carefully established mechanism of economic interaction exploiting Russia's need for GCC finances and arms acquisitions.

Until recently, one could see a rather strange behaviour on the part of the Gulf Cooperation Council (GCC): despite the fundamental divergences with Russia over the developments of the Syrian crisis and the Iranian issue, GCC leaders and officials visited Moscow regularly and were received there at the highest level. In all cases, there was talk of cooperation, including in the military field. Only the Saudi princes seemingly insisted on some changes in Russia's approach to Syria as a precondition for broader cooperation and larger Saudi investments in Russia. Most of the other high-ranking GCC guests in Moscow overtly avoided mentioning such a precondition, apparently to favour a "strategy of attraction" aimed at creating areas of common interest (economic, security), while hinting at advantages for Russia in exchange for certain political and military steps in Syria and perhaps in other cases of conflict in the Gulf as well (such as Yemen and Iran). That was the way things stood regarding the bilateral relationship of the Gulf monarchies with Russia. But brought together in a meeting in Moscow on 25-26 May 2016, entitled "GCC-Russia strategic dialogue", the heads of the Ministries of Foreign Affairs of the "oil six" preferred to talk openly with their Russian counterpart Sergey Lavrov, putting the Syrian crisis and Russia's approach to it at the top of the agenda.[1] It was a manifestation of the Gulf monarchies' decision to try to pressure Moscow on the issue. Although Lavrov was surely prepared for such a *demarche*, his response sounded unconvincing to the Arabs chiefly for one reason: the situation was not ripe for a fundamental change in Russia's approach to the Syrian crisis.

---

[1] "Syria civil war tops Russia-Arab Gulf meeting agenda", *AJE News*, 26 May 2016, http://www.aljazeera.com/news/2016/05/syria-civil-war-tops-agenda-russia-gcc-meeting-160526085707690.html

The visits to Moscow of the leaders of the Gulf Cooperation Council are the most evident manifestation of foreign policy pragmatism, the basic principles of which are normally minimising the ideological or religious component of one's foreign policymaking and strengthening one's attractiveness. Another element of a pragmatic foreign policy is taking the constants and variables of the conceptual image of the potential partner into consideration. In some cases, a pragmatic approach is even designed to modify the relationship with a previously adverse country into a friendly one. In the case of the GCC's pragmatism with regard to Russia, there are, among others, some important points of basic convergence (related to the hydrocarbon market, arms trade, etc) amid a number of diverging issues related to Russia's activity in Syria, which have resulted in Russia's seemingly pro-Iranian (pro-Shia) deviation in its approach to the Gulf region as a whole. To understand this, the drivers of Russia's policy towards the Middle East will be discussed in this article.

Russia's evolving vision and perception of the Middle East

Unlike the Union of Soviet Socialist Republics (USSR), Russia's post-Soviet leadership does not aim to secure and expand its influence in the Middle East by binding "client" states to it through military-technical cooperation or economic aid. In other words, Moscow is not out to create a "sphere of influence" in the region.

It is worth remembering that during the Cold War, Moscow's cooperation with certain Arab countries in this region served the logic of opposing the West and the idea of "establishing socialism in the developing world". In essence, the countries of the region were divided into "pro-Western" and "pro-Soviet" camps. The USSR offered its clients favourable terms when supplying them with weapons and financing their infrastructure, mainly through loans. In many cases, it was clear that the loans would not be repaid – "first politics, then economics" was the logic. Today, Russia is trying to interact with all regional countries capable of paying (unlike the Soviet Union, which was denied access to certain markets) and on a strictly commercial basis.

In the 1990s, during the presidency of Boris Yeltsin, Russia saw the Middle East mostly in economic terms, as a market for its goods and a source of finance in the form of loans and credit.[2] To a great extent, this perception lives on to the present day. Indeed, after the West imposed sanctions on Russia in connection with the Ukraine crisis, Moscow tried to turn to the Arab monarchies of the Gulf for loans, but without success because of differences with these countries over the Syrian crisis.

Alongside this perception and as relations between Russia and the United States and the European Union have deteriorated, Moscow has increasingly begun to see the Middle East once more as a zone of confrontation between Russia and the West. A revival of the earlier Soviet way of seeing the region can be discerned then, but without the former alliances that Moscow enjoyed with its "traditional clients" from the Cold War era, such as Libya, Syria, Algeria, Egypt, Iraq and Yemen. Of these countries, links in the traditional sense survive

---

[2] Goods included weapons of different types to most Arab countries. The sovereign wealth funds of the UAE, Kuwait, Bahrain and Qatar have entered into partnership with the Russian Direct Investment Fund; Russia has received credit from a number of Gulf monarchies; efforts have been made to establish a cooperation mechanism between the Russian financial system and Islamic banking. For more detail, see "Rossiya zamenit zapadnye kredity islamskim financirovaniyem" ["Russia Replaces Western Credits with Islamic Financing"], *Rossiysko-Arabskiy Delovoy Sovet* [*Russian-Arab Business Council*], 29 June 2015, www.russarabbc.ru

only with Syria. Cooperation with all the others is on a commercial basis, with Arab countries feeling free to choose their partners in the military and economic spheres without considering their geopolitical affiliation.

Yet, the Russian approach of politics first, then economics can now also be seen in relation to Iran: as far as one can judge, Moscow is counting on forging a stronger partnership with Tehran by taking advantage of the formally anti-Western positions that dominate the Ayatollah's policy.[3] Iran is seen in the Russian Ministry of Foreign Affairs (MFA) as an important pole in the future "multipolar world".[4] The relationship is also about mutually beneficial economic cooperation and a certain amount of coordination in the military and political spheres. And all of this despite the fact that, now that sanctions have been lifted, Iran is returning to the energy markets. This will contribute to reducing global prices of Russia's most important exports (oil and gas), and will limit their volume, including those going to Europe. Such is the combination of motives and tools that Russia brings to its Middle Eastern policy.

Of note is that in the Russian socio-political realm, which is thoroughly dominated by pro-Kremlin TV channels, nostalgia is evoked both for the era of Soviet policy in the Middle East and for its leaders, "the USSR's reliable partners in the Arab world", like Saddam Hussein in Iraq, Muammar Qadhafi in Libya, the Assad family in Syria and so on. Their overthrow, usually attributed to the United States, is seen as the root cause of the appearance and growth of radical Islamism across the region. The TV audience is fed a simple message: democracy does not work in Arab countries and authoritarian rulers are therefore preferable to Islamists.

In practice, however, Moscow is pragmatic and ready to work with all the governing groups in these countries. Russia's relations with Egypt after the "Arab Spring" are instructive in this regard: in 2012-13, Russia successfully cooperated with the moderate Islamist Mohammed Morsi, despite the fact that the Muslim Brotherhood was formally banned in Russia. After Morsi was overthrown, Moscow worked even more fruitfully with the man who removed him, Field Marshal-President Abdel Fattah el-Sisi, who had initially positioned himself politically and ideologically as the polar opposite to the Islamist Morsi.[5]

Such pragmatism is characteristic of Vladimir Putin's presidency. When he took power in 2000, he picked partners in the Middle East in line with his foreign policy imperative, which was the fight against terrorism (this was the time of the Second Chechen war). It was precisely on the basis of their common front against terrorism that Russia's relations with Israel progressed so well, including in the period just after the terrorist attacks of 11 September 2001.[6]

If in 2004-05, the differences with the West expressed themselves in the rhetoric used by Russia's leaders and representatives, by January-February 2006, Moscow had taken its first practical steps. It acknowledged the victory of Hamas (the Islamic Resistance Movement) in

---

[3]Ivanov, "Iran, Russia and the West", 38.

[4]"Rossiyskiy ekspert: Iran I Rossiya — osnovnye polyusa mnogopolyarnogo mira" ["Russian Expert: Iran and Russia – the Main Poles of the Multipolar World"], *Iran.Ru*, 26 June 2015, www.iran.ru; Gordeev, "Vizit Putina v Iran" ["Putin's Visit to Iran"]

[5]"Putin supports Sisi's bid for Egypt presidency", *Al Arabiya News*, 13 February 2014, http://english.alarabiya.net/en/News/middle-east/2014/02/13/Egypt-s-Sisi-negotiates-arms-deal-in-Russia.html; "Egypt's Sisi Vows Muslim Brotherhood 'Will Not Exist'", *BBC*, 6 May 2014, http://www.bbc.com/news/world-middle-east-27285846

[6]Shumilin, *American policy in the Middle East*, 15.

the Palestinian elections, reneging on the international boycott of the Hamas government that had been provisionally agreed within the "Middle-Eastern quartet" (US, Russia, United Nations and EU), and refused to recognise it as a terrorist organisation. It even invited representatives of Hamas to visit the Russian capital in March 2006 (these visits later became a regular feature).[7] In other words, as in Soviet times, it was in the Middle Eastern arena that the differences between Moscow and the West began to take on a practical form. It was not long before Russia's partial return to the Soviet model of regarding the Middle East as a zone of conflict with the West received confirmation: in the rocket war (July-August 2006) between Hezbollah and Israel, Russia's position was interpreted both within the region and outside it as inclining more towards Hezbollah and Lebanon than Israel, which had suffered an unprovoked attack from its northern neighbour. One of the accusations levelled at Russia by Israel and the West was that Russian missiles supplied to Bashar al-Assad's government had found their way into the hands of Hezbollah and were now raining down on the Israelis. A year earlier, in an interview with the Israeli Channel-1, Vladimir Putin had said that he would continue supplying Syria with missile systems which, in his words, "merely complicate the work of the Israeli air force" but do not disrupt the balance of power in the region. "You (Israelis) can no longer fly over Bashar al-Assad's presidential palace", the Russian president stressed.[8]

A rather significant shift in Moscow's perception of the Arab Gulf countries came with the eruption of the Arab Spring in 2011, perceived and publicly interpreted by the ruling group in Moscow as a triumph of political Islam. Caused by a "conspiracy plotted in the US and the West at large", it was an "essentially anti-Russian" phenomenon hampering Russian policy in the region and threatening Russia's security needs in the foreseeable future.[9] Moscow, the theory went, will be the last country to join the Arab Spring and the series of "colour revolutions" orchestrated by the US to "destroy Russia's sovereignty", starting with the Georgian Rose Revolution in 2003 and followed by the Ukrainian Orange Revolution in 2004. The real anti-authoritarian nature of the Arab Spring is sometimes evoked (often with irony) on an official level (as a diplomatic gesture), but normally it is sharply criticised, especially on the popular television channels controlled by the authorities.[10]

The ruling group in Russia is openly concerned about the process of democratisation in any part of the world, fearing it might be an inspiring example to be followed by the democratic movement in Russia. The Kremlin's propagandists claim that the drive for freedom cannot spring from a country's population but is imposed by foreign countries and their agents. The main power responsible for "spreading such a virus of freedom" is, so Kremlin propaganda goes, the United States. This is an element of the broader anti-US angle of Russia's so-called state ideology defining the guidelines of its foreign policy. Those elements have grown in intensity since 2004.

What is the link with Russia's Middle East policy, one might ask? It is actually direct: in the context of the Arab Spring events, President Putin began to strengthen Russia's geopolitical

---

[7]Myers and Myre, "Hamas Delegation Visits Moscow".
[8]"Putin V: Rossiyskiye PZRK zashchityat Siriyu ot Izrailya" ["Putin V: Russian Man-portable Air Defence Systems Protect Syria against Israel"], *RBK*, 21 April 2005, www.rbc.ru.
[9]Shumilin, *American policy in the Middle East*, 23.
[10]*Ibidem*, 27.

positions against the US primarily in the Middle East region, given that the majority of conflicts in this part of the world are completely or at least partly viewed differently by Moscow and Washington. The divergence in Russian-American relations prevailed over convergence. The same started to happen in Moscow's relationship with the Gulf monarchies.

One should at the same time not underestimate the strong domestic motivation behind this move: to divert the attention of Putin's electoral base from domestic issues to the "outside threat", portrayed as being capable of undermining the Kremlin's efforts to stabilise the situation in Russia and its neighbourhood. For example, long before the Arab Spring, after the Beslan attack in 2004, Moscow had quickly pointed to "some circles in Saudi Arabia" as the key outside sponsors.[11] That was the first time Putin's team mentioned Saudis in negative terms, claiming Saudi Arabia was trying to gain influence over a part of Russia's territory.

The Syrian factor

The Syrian crisis contributed enormously to further increasing tensions in Moscow's relations with the Gulf Arabs and gave another push to Russia's policy shift toward the old "Soviet logic" mentioned earlier. One of the reasons for this was that Syria had largely been viewed in Moscow as its last stronghold in the Middle East. State propaganda has been trying to describe the events in Syria as being provoked by both the US and the Gulf monarchies, namely Saudi Arabia and Qatar (to a lesser extent the rest of the GCC countries).[12] In Kremlin propaganda, the last terrorist acts in Russia (in Moscow in 2010-11 and Volgograd in 2013), as well as a number of explosions in the Northern Caucasus were plotted and carried out with the financial and logistical assistance of "outside" Wahhabi centres funded by Saudis. This "outside feeding of terror in Russia" interpretation of the events served as the simplest explanation of what were actually miscalculations of the Russian counterterrorism services.[13] To maintain such a narrative (namely, Russia as the victim of terror inspired and plotted from the outside) in the eyes of Russian citizens, however, the Kremlin needed a convincing image of an "outside adversary/enemy". Saudi Arabia and Qatar appeared very suitable for this role – alongside the US, of course.

The situation changed slightly with the "chemical deal" reached by the US and Russia in September 2013. Moscow and Washington agreed upon total evacuation from Syria of Assad's chemical weapons arsenal in exchange for the US refusal to strike a number of military targets of the Damascus regime. The deal actually saved Assad from the defeat that would have resulted from an American and French intervention in Syria as punishment for his use of WMD. Ignoring their sharp criticism of the deal, Moscow seemed to be willing to sacrifice the prospect of its relationships with the Gulf monarchies for what it believed to be geopolitical benefits, namely, success in Syria, survival of the Assad regime and even Russia's partial international legitimisation. The deal was also regarded as an important

---

[11]For example, Russian Deputy Attorney General Nikolay Shepel called the Saudi-born terrorist Abu Dzeith, who was killed during the storming of the school in Beslan, "one of the main plotters" of the terrorist attack in Beslan. The General Prosecuter's Office of Russia insisted on conducting an investigation in Saudi Arabia, https://ria.ru/incidents/20050304/39484923.html. See also Schwartz, "Road from Riyadh to Beslan".

[12]Shumilin, *American policy in the Middle East*.

[13]For example, some terrorist explosions carried out by Chechen women in Moscow or Volgograd as revenge for their husbands or brothers killed during the local war in Chechnya were presented by the state media as "terrorist war instigated by Saudis and Qataris backed by the US". The same perception is widespread with regard to ISIS (Saudis and Qataris are behind it). See "Could Saudi Arabia or Qatar Be Behind the Crash of the Russian Airbus?", *Sputnik International*, 16 Nov 2015, https://sputniknews.com/analysis/201511161030197229-saudi-arabia-qatar-russian-airbus/

factor contributing to ensuring the internal stability of Russia in propaganda terms, by showing that "Putin's regime is strong and capable enough to rebuff any outside threat to Russia and its friends …".[14] Moscow's anti-Islamist line was soon to be rewarded by the change in the political situation in Egypt.[15]

All things considered, the Russian aerospace forces operation, which began at the end of September 2015 (and was officially reduced in scale on 14 March 2016) pursued more than its openly declared aims ("fighting terrorist groups" and "reinforcing Bashar al-Assad's position as a partner in the fight against terrorism"[16]). It was also meant to shift the balance of power on the battlefield in favour of the Syrian government and therefore bolster its position in the negotiations that would come, sooner or later.[17] Moscow also took advantage of the political vacuum (the breakdown of the "Geneva-2" negotiation process) and the military-strategic vacuum (the absence on Syrian territory of military infrastructure belonging to countries in the American-led international coalition, and of zones where Syrian and, therefore, Russian aircraft were not allowed to fly). After a Russian bomber was shot down by Turkish fighter jets in October 2015, Russian aerospace forces deployed surface-to-air missile systems around Latakia, which in effect closed the Western portion of Syrian airspace to aircraft from coalition countries. By doing so, Russia became the most important military factor in Syria.

As a result of the "chemical deal" and the air operation, Moscow seemed to have succeeded in compromising the stance of the US and its coalition politically and militarily. But since Russia became involved in the Syrian civil war on Assad's side, this success has had a cost in political terms: Russia is now regarded as an enemy by a large part of the Syrian population (suffice it to recall the civilian plane with Russian tourists which exploded in November 2015 over Sinai and the aforementioned Russian bomber downed by the Turks).

The Iranian factor

The so-called nuclear deal or Joint Comprehensive Plan of Action (JCPOA) Iran signed with the P5+1 group (five permanent members of the UN Security Council plus Germany) and the EU[18] is assessed as a positive step in Russia for several reasons. First, Moscow has always continued to perceive the Iranian regime in rather friendly terms, a stance that is in part explained by Iran's hostile attitude towards the West in general and the US in particular, as seen by the statements of the Supreme Leader Ayatollah Khamenei.[19] Second, the majority of Russians are convinced of the need to maintain access to Iran's promising market for

---

[14]*Ibid.*

[15]See the portraits of Putin beside al-Sisi in Cairo's streets, as well as al-Sisi's visit to Moscow in February 2014, http://raqeb. co/en/2015/02/meeting-minds-cairo-billion-dollar-arms-deal-table-putin-and-abdel-fattah-al-sisi-seek and http://www. bbc.com/news/world-africa-31310348, respectively.

[16]Phillips, *The Battle for Syria*, 211-3.

[17]The Russian leadership never intended to maintain its contingent for a long haul in Syria. The military involvement was basically designed to save president Bashar al-Assad and therefore to secure Russia's enforced position within the negotiation process over Syria – either Geneva-format talks or bilateral contacts with the US (Lavrov-Kerry). See "Political settlement in Syria can start only after stage of anti-terror struggle - Kremlin", *TASS*, http://tass.com/politics/830743

[18]In the agreement reached in Vienna on 14 July 2015, Iran agreed to eliminate its stockpile of medium-enriched uranium, cut its stockpile of low-enriched uranium by 98%, and reduce by about two-thirds the number of its gas centrifuges for 13 years. For the next 15 years, Iran will only enrich uranium up to 3.67%. Iran also agreed not to build any new heavy-water facilities for the same period of time. The agreement provides that in return for verifiably abiding by its commitments, Iran will receive relief from US, EU, and UNSC nuclear-related economic sanctions.

[19]See Gladstone, "Iran's Supreme Leader on America".

Russian companies, particularly in relation to arms exports.[20] Third, the notion that Tehran was pursuing a military program was highly disputed inside the Russian establishment: while some argued that development of an Iranian nuclear program would have negative consequences for Russia and should therefore be seen as a threat, others minimised the potential of such a threat and instead argued that cooperation with Iran might be important for Russia in economic and geopolitical terms.

With the JCPOA's implementation now underway, there is a growing concern in Russia that Iran, being dependent on the West to see sanctions lifted, might turn more in that direction with the hope of being embraced there, to the detriment of its relations with Russia. Iran has always been a lucrative market for many of Russia's manufactured goods. In the aftermath of the anti-Iranian sanctions easing (namely, from January to August 2016), Russian exports to Iran jumped by 91.5 percent (amounting to USD 697m), while Russian imports from Iran increased by 16 percent to USD 158 m. This surge involved supplies of machinery, ground vehicles and weapons exported to Iran versus chiefly agricultural products imported from Iran.[21]

For the time being, Russia seems to be the preferred economic partner of Tehran, while Iran is trying to open its market to the EU, US and Japan.[22] So, the competition of Russian companies with others appears to be unavoidable in the foreseeable future. Moreover, in some areas, Russia and Iran are doomed to rivalry. The most obvious example are their respective efforts to secure the greatest possible share of the European energy market.

More worrying, however, are the increasing divergences with Iran over the looming settlement in Syria: Russia seems to be betting on the Astana/Geneva talks (and political compromise there) in order to be able to reduce sharply its military presence in Syria, while Iran seems less inclined to compromise, seeking to perpetuate the military achievements in Syria – a country Tehran sees as a bastion ensuring its strategic leadership in the region. Syria is perceived as a "golden link" in the Iranian "chain of resistance" on the Western front, a bridge linking Iran to Hezbollah in Lebanon and Hamas in Palestine to confront Israel, as well as a strategic corridor to the Mediterranean coast for a future Iran-Iraq-Syria-Europe pipeline.

Moscow as an alternative to Washington?

Despite a clear and consistent Russian stance in favour of the Assad regime, most of the Gulf elites have been and still are turning toward Moscow. That is for one significant reason: after the abovementioned chemical deal, perceived by the Syrian moderate opposition and the GCC countries as a betrayal on the part of the Obama administration of the Sunni Arabs and evidence of a broader shift in American strategy (toward Iran), and the ensuing events, the Arab Gulf elites stopped concealing their disappointment with the US approach to Syria and started looking to Russia as a perhaps undesirable, but *de facto* only (by force of events) partner to deal with. In other words, angered by Obama's inaction in Syria, the

---

[20]"Russia may lose $13 bln to ban on arms exports to Iran", *Globalsecurity*, analyst//http://www.globalsecurity.org/wmd/library/news/russia/2010/russia-100803-rianovosti02.htm

[21]"Russia trade with Iran jumps more than 70 percent since January", *Intellinews*, 2016, http://www.intellinews.com/russia-trade-with-iran-jumps-more-than-70-sin

[22]"Iran will give Russia priority in any industry it wants to invest in – official", *TASS*, April 2016, http://tass.ru/en/economy/871740

Gulf Arabs started to manifest an inclination to find ways to come to an understanding with Putin, who was showing resolve and determination in managing the situation in Syria – albeit in accordance with his views.

One has to acknowledge that the Syrian crisis has, for years, become the symbol of the indecisiveness and inability of the Western coalition and Arab countries to deal with the problem (at both the humanitarian and military level). Thus the arrival of Russian aerospace forces gave Moscow the chance not only to demonstrate decisiveness (within its own conception of the nature of the crisis) and military power, but also to transform the crisis itself into an opportunity to reposition Russia in the world on new terms. It is logical to suppose that Moscow hoped that a side-effect of its growing involvement in the Syrian crisis would be a significant increase in the level of mutual understanding between the Kremlin and Western political elites, given their "common fight against terrorism".[23] At the very least, involvement in Syria would give Moscow the opportunity to overcome its political isolation on the world stage caused by the conflict in Ukraine.

It quickly became clear, however, that Russia's view of events in Syria and its actions on the battlefield were at odds with what the countries of the US-led anti-Islamic State (IS, ISIS, ISIL) coalition considered the right thing to do. From the very first days of Russian airstrikes, the leaders of Western countries and Arab states started to accuse Russia of hitting not IS and *Jabhat al-Nusra* positions, as was agreed at a meeting of the US and Russian presidents in New York in September 2015, but the positions of moderate Syrian rebel groups fighting against the Assad regime,[24] that is to say, the international coalition's allies, those who in the coalition's preferred future would replace the Assad regime as part of a negotiated political transition. Political circles in coalition countries began to think that Moscow's real strategy in Syria was to "weaken as much as possible or even destroy anti-Assad rebel groups on the field of battle".[25] Then, Moscow would supposedly present the international community with the same old black and white picture, according to which there are only two actors in the Syrian drama – Assad and IS terrorists.[26]

At a certain point, Russia found itself cornered between its political and strategic prerogatives in the region (backing the regime of Bashar al-Assad in Syria and maintaining special ties with Iran), on the one hand, and the urgent long-term need to improve its relations with GCC countries, particularly in the economic field, on the other. The Ukrainian crisis ended up dramatically strengthening this contradiction in Russian policy, as Moscow's ever increasing backing of Assad became regarded as a tool to be used in the broader standoff with the West, namely, something not to be abandoned without at least some clear steps by the West, in return, to ease sanctions on Russia. In short, any move on Syria should be viewed through the Ukrainian lens.

Nevertheless Moscow goes on presenting itself as an emerging centre of political gravity for the major regional actors, including the Arab Gulf countries, a role it manages to sustain despite its continued pro-Assad line. Russian strategists believe that such a view is

---

[23]Sengupta and MacFarquhar, "Russia Calls for Coalition".
[24]Shumilin, "US declines to cooperate"; "Russia says US declines to host Moscow delegation for Syria talks", *AFP*, 14 October 2015, https://guardian.ng/news/russia-says-us-declines-to-host-moscow-delegation-for-syria-talks/
[25]"Russia kills US-backed Syrian rebels in second day of air strikes as Iran prepares for ground offensive", *The Telegraph online*, 2 Oct 2015, https://goo.gl/M5jRr4;
[26]Aleji, "The world needs to know".

not unfounded: not only has Russia succeeded in underlining the US' and West's weakness and inconsistency with regard to the Syrian crisis, but as far as the nuclear deal with Iran is concerned, it shares some reservations with the Arab Gulf states. In particular, with the sanctions definitively lifted, Iranian oil and gas will certainly engulf the European and Asian markets causing the price of hydrocarbons to fall substantially. Since January 2016, there has been an only partial increase in Iran's presence on the European oil market, mainly due to the rather limited capacities of the Iranian petrol industry, direly in need of modernisation, as well as the lamentable state of Iran's financial ties with the outside world.[27] All in all, we can see a special, two-level model emerging with regard to the Russian-Arab Gulf relationship, that is a political model that reflects agreements and disagreements, and a business model whereby business deals prevail to some extent over politics. Amid the growing political and strategic divergences on the Syrian issue, both sides are tending to cooperate to sustain the oil and gas markets.

For the Russian leadership, the fact that a number of high-ranking Gulf officials have hurried to Moscow to discuss regional issues suggests a new weight. Furthermore, an impressive Russia-UAE business forum was held in Dubai in February 2014. But of even more importance is the special track to deal with Russia, the "Arab-Russian Forum" at the foreign minister level, established in 2013 under the auspices of the Arab League. It has become a yearly meeting with only one exception – 2015, obviously due to the deployment of the Russian air forces in Syria. Yet, if in its third session in February 2016, the GCC was represented by the foreign ministers of the UAE, Bahrain and Oman, one year later, at the fourth session in February 2017, Saudi Arabia and Qatar also attended. This means that the GCC views the mechanism as a means to influence Russia. For Russia, it is a way of overcoming its seeming tilt toward Iran, so as to be seen as positioned between Iran and the Sunni Arab community.

Russia's bilateral relations with the Gulf countries in the last three years can be depicted as Moscow moving between two extremes: namely rather cool ties with Qatar and Saudi Arabia (focusing to a large extent on the Syrian issue) and a trend towards warmer ties with Bahrain and the UAE. The latter apparently insist on a double-level approach as well: while keeping up their criticism of Russia for its actions in Syria, they prefer to have Russia as a useful partner for some of their regional manoeuvrings (with the aim, for example, of preventing Russia from betting totally on Iran in its regional policy in the Gulf).

Thus the patterns of GCC's interaction with Russia are diverse: even when political considerations dominate – as with the Saudis and Bahrainis – the outcomes of their approaches to Russia look quite opposite – the Saudis seem to be trying to curb bilateral interactions with Russia beyond the oil market issues (to punish Russia for Syria). In August and December 2013, as well as early 2014, the Head of Saudi intelligence, Prince Bandar bin Sultan, visited Moscow allegedly with the aim of striking a deal with Moscow over Syria based on the principle "economic benefits versus political shifts". At that time, Riyadh was reported to have offered to buy Russian arms for an estimated billion dollars in return for a substantial shift in Russia's approach to the Syrian crisis.[28] However, Prince Bandar bin Sultan's visits to Moscow did not succeed due in large part to the fact that Assad's army started to make

---

[27]"Iran's comeback to the European market won't be fast", *Vedomosti*, 19 January 2016, http://www.vedomosti.ru/business/articles/2016/01/19/624582-vozvraschenie-irana-nefti-ne-bistrim.
[28]Evans-Pritchard, "Saudis offer Russia secret oil".

advances on the battlefield at precisely the time that Bandar made his offer. Matters deteriorated even more in the aftermath of the deployment of the Russian air force in September 2015, but Riyadh has not stopped trying to pressure President Putin to abandon his support for President Bashar al-Assad. The only part of Saudi Arabia's political project that Moscow is willing to support is the creation of a weapons of mass destruction (WMD)-free zone in the Middle East and the Gulf. Moscow is further prepared to offer its services in the nuclear energy field as Saudi Arabia and other monarchies are contemplating the use of civilian nuclear power. Of course, there is also a constant Russian interest in exchanging data in relation to the issue of terrorism with the Saudi intelligence.

Bahrain, on the other hand, which hosts the US Navy's Fifth Fleet, has been seeking rapprochement with Russia since 2012, when the US imposed weapon sanctions following the crackdown on the mostly Shia-dominated uprising on the island.[29] Bahrainis seem to be inviting Russia to participate in various kinds of cooperation with the aim of easing Manama's dependency on the United States (or at least creating the appearance of Russia as a counterweight to the US in Bahrain), but also, probably, with the hope of seeing Moscow as an effective mediator in Bahraini-Iranian rifts and of overcoming Russia's allegedly pro-Iranian tendency in the region. Of note is that Bahrain remains one of the hottest points of the Sunni-Shia standoff in the Middle East, with the GCC viewing the conflict there as a result of Tehran's instigations of the Shiite majority to rise up against the Sunni minority governing the island.

Bahrain has also been looking at Russia because of its cooling relationship with the United States.[30] Indeed, Russia's relations with Bahrain have taken on a new quality. During 2014, both Crown Prince Salman bin Hamad bin Isa Al-Khalifa (April) and King Hamad bin Isa Al-Khalifa (October) visited Russia. Between those two visits, namely in July 2014, Bahraini authorities expelled the US Assistant Secretary of State for Democracy and Human Rights, Tom Malinovsky, from the country for his contacts with one of the leaders of an opposition group, *Wefaq*. The leading official newspaper, *Akhbar Al-Khaleej*, commented:

> During the 2011 events in Bahrain, the West's support of the opposition made it clear to the Gulf states that they had made a mistake in relying on cooperation with the West alone. Their foreign policy began moving toward other centers of power across the world, including Russia.[31]

The high-level visits were reciprocated by trips to Manama of two major Russian officials, the Minister of Industry and Trade, Denis Manturov, in December 2014, and the Commander-in-Chief of the Russian Air Force, Lt.-Gen. Viktor Bondarev, in January 2015. Manturov's visit was aimed at promoting economic cooperation and discussing certain business niches that were occupied by the West before it introduced rounds of "illegal" economic sanctions against Russia over the Ukrainian crisis.[32] The second visit was no less significant, given that Russia considers Bahrain a potential new window through which to introduce Russian weapons sales to the rest of the Gulf.

---

[29] "As U.S. shifts toward Iran, Bahrain turns to Russia for arms", *WorldTribune.com.*, 5 Nov. 2014, http://www.worldtribune.com/2014/11/05/bahrain-ready-russian-arms

[30] Cafiero, "Can Bahrain count on Moscow?".

[31] "Bahraini King's Visit to Moscow Sign of Persian Gulf's Russia Pivot", *Sputnik International*, 11 October 2014, http://sputniknews.com/analysis/20141011/193941224/Bahraini-Kings-Visit-to-Moscow-Sign-of-Persian-Gulfs-Russia.html#ixzz3R4W8WEM0

[32] "Russia Intends to Strengthen Commercial, Industrial Ties With Middle East", *Sputnik International*, 14 December 2014, http://www.russia-gcc.com/en/press-center/news/65-russia-intends-to-strenghten-commercial-industrial-ties-with-middle-east

In this context, it was not surprising that the Bahraini Minister of Foreign Affairs, Shaikh Khalid bin Ahmed bin Mohammed Al-Khalifa, assessed the growing cooperation of his country with Russia positively while taking part in the 4th session of the Arab-Russian Cooperation Forum in the UAE capital Abu Dhabi on 1 February 2017.[33] What was notable about Shaikh Khalifa's statements was his vision of the prospect of a Syrian settlement (later reproduced in the final communiqué of the Forum) which, in general terms, was not that different from the official Russian stance. He stressed the need to preserve the unity of Syria and its sovereignty, independence and territorial integrity, emphasising that the only possible solution to the Syrian crisis is the participation of all Syrian parties in an inclusive political process under the leadership of Syria, which meets the aspirations of the Syrian people according to UN Security Council Resolution 2254 (2015), and the final statement of the Conference of Geneva-1 dated 30 June 2012.

It should also be underlined that in the final declaration of the 2017 Forum, the Arabs did not mention Bashar al-Assad (his name was replaced by the term "leadership of Syria") and made mention of the Geneva-1communiqué, commonly interpreted as the road map for replacing Assad with a new governing body – without preconditioning the Geneva talks on the demand for Assad to leave first. The Russian side accepted this view. In return, the Arab participants took a further step towards Russia – they praised UNSC resolution 2336 of 2016 and the meeting between the Syrian government and Syrian armed opposition groups in Astana (Kazakhstan) in February 2017, which aimed to consolidate the ceasefire as part of the political process, without protesting openly against Iranian opposition to the Gulf Arabs' participation in the meeting.[34]

The UAE leadership is also pursuing an approach that is different from that of the Saudis. It might be described as "economics first – politics in mind" and explains the last two decades of fruitful cooperation between the two countries in the economic field – the most extensive in the region – especially in tourism (Russia is among the top 10 countries' for tourists visiting resorts in the UAE) and foreign investments (UAE investment in Russia stood at about USD 18 bn in 2015).[35] Some Emirati sources have gone so far as to define Russia as a "key economic partner for the UAE".[36] Recent estimates show that trade figures between Russia and the UAE stand at around USD 2 bn.[37]

Emirati officials have confirmed the UAE's willingness to enhance cooperation with Russia, especially in the field of peaceful nuclear energy. UAE Minister of the Economy Sultan bin Saeed Al Mansouri stressed that Russia is a major partner in supporting the UAE in the use of nuclear power for peaceful purposes. He further indicated that there are many

---

[33] He also commended the outcome of the "Russian Federation Days" held in Bahrain on 24-28 November 2016, which included an economic forum, business and trade meetings, and political seminars and cultural and art activities that reflect the deep-rooted Russian culture and civilisation. ("Foreign minister attends Arab-Russian forum", *Bahrain News Agency*, 1 Feb 2017, http://www.bna.bh/portal/en/news/768446).

[34] "Foreign minister attends Arab-Russian forum", *Bahrain News Agency*, 1 Feb 2017, http://www.bna.bh/portal/en/news/768446.

[35] "Impressive 131% growth rate in Dubai-Russia non-oil trade during 2010-14", *Emirates News Agency*, 27 January 2016, http://wam.ae/en/details/1395290789730. A drastic fall in the non-oil trade exchange between the two countries was registered in 2014 and 2015. In 2016, it was replaced by a slow growth of 16.6% . See "UAE Foreign Minister calls for closer trade ties with Russia", *The National*, 10 March 2016, http://www.thenational.ae/world/europe/uae-foreign-minister-calls-for-closer-trade-ties-with-russia.

[36] *Ibidem.*

[37] Russia exports diamonds, gold, steel, defence equipment and machines to the UAE, while it imports machines and food products. "Russia seeks UAE investments to boost its economy", *GulfNews.com*, 6 April 2015, http://gulfnews.com/business/economy/russia-seeks-uae-investments-to-boost-its-economy-1.1487197.

opportunities for Russia to help support knowledge transfer to the UAE, for example in such areas as light and heavy industries, telecommunications, petroleum and petrochemicals, clean energy, railways and construction projects, as well as space technology.[38]

There was no significant UAE direct investment in the Russian economy or infrastructure in 2015-16, however, even though this matter remains on the bilateral agenda. There are two major reasons for this: a political one related to the intervention of Russian airforces in Syria, and an economic one related mostly to the risk-calculation emanating from the Western sanctions imposed on Russia in the second half of 2014 due to the events in Ukraine.

A rather different approach to Russia was manifested by the Qatari leadership during the last months of 2016, early 2017. It decided to use finances as leverage in an attempt to impact Russian policy in the region. The evolution of the Qatari attitude toward Syria should not come as a surprise: given Moscow's intransigence toward abandoning Assad, Doha might be trying a different approach altogether: regarding Russia as a preferred actor to deal with with respect to Iran in the context of a settlement. Doha's main objective might be to bring Russia closer to the GCC so as to gradually push Iran out of Syria.[39]

Qatar is the only GCC country to have taken the risk to invest in Russia under current circumstances. In January 2017, the Qatar Investment Authority (QIA) made its biggest deal in Russia in conjunction with UK-based Glencore, finalising an investment of USD 11.3 bn in Russia's Rosneft for upstream projects, logistics and global trading in the energy sector. The deal, representing one-fifth of the Russian oil giant's privatisation portfolio,[40] was signed while Qatar's Emir, Sheikh Tamim bin Hamad al-Thani, was visiting Russia to address Middle Eastern geopolitics and energy issues.

Conclusion

From the foregoing, we can discern at least three different kinds of GCC approaches to Russia, all of which can be described as pragmatic. The first, manifested in the Saudi logic, can be summarised as follows: economic benefits versus political shifts. It implies striking a complex and simultaneous deal with Russia in which business agreements are conjunct with political ones (over Syria). The second is applied by the UAE and can be described as economics first – politics in mind. It aims at creating a complex economic infrastructure for the relationship with Russia (often based on joint ventures), laying the groundwork for friendly relations which make it possible to discuss contentious issues as they arise. The third is the one followed by the Qataris and involves creating financial leverage to impact politics in the future. In this case, the political side of the deal is not clearly formulated and not tied to any economic (business) agreement. It differs from the previous (Emirati) pattern in that the Qatari approach seems to be a kind of "one-sided aggressive investment" that does not seek to be balanced by Russian projects implemented in Qatar.

What do these three different kinds of Arab Gulf pragmatism have in common? The common points can be boiled down to their objectives to compel Russia to stop backing

---

[38]"Al Mansouri: UAE-Russian relations have been growing from strength to strength", *UAEinteract*, 23 May 2014, http://www. uaeinteract.com/docs/Al_Mansouri_UAERussian_relations_have_been_growing_from_strength_to_strength/61861.htm.

[39]"The Russian Intervention in Syria and the Position of Gulf", Fiker Center for Studies, http://www.fikercenter.com/en/p/ position_paper/view/566134810f551 //

[40]Karasik, "Why is Qatar Investing?".

Syrian President Bashar al-Assad and prevent it from furthering its rapprochement with Iran. Each one of the pragmatic approaches is motivated by the historic and geopolitical considerations of the respective country, which include the difference in priority attributed by the Gulf monarchies to the hot issues in the region (Yemen, Syria, Iran), as well as by the scope and intensity of their interaction with Russia, which define their respective perceptions of the role Russia should play.

Another driver behind the GCC's common pragmatism is the gap in GCC relations with the United States, especially after the so-called chemical deal (September 2013) perceived as a betrayal of Sunni Arabs and evidence of a broader shift in American strategy in the Gulf (toward Iran). Indeed, the GCC's new pragmatism is also explained by the need to respond to Russia's increasing presence in the region – mainly on the Shia (Iranian) side. In other words, it stems from the GCC's need to find a balance between the weakening US status in the region and the forcefully self-imposed Russian presence (through Syria).

On the other hand, Russia's Middle East policy has been shifting back over the last few years to the Soviet model, in which the region was seen primarily through the prism of strategic competition with the United States. Economic calculations are sidelined, namely perceived as secondary and subordinated to greater political goals. The basic logic of the Soviet model is to achieve geopolitical goals at any financial or economic price.[41]

One of the main reasons behind this shift is related to the phenomenon of the Arab Spring and the gains made by political Islam, which was widely seen and propagandised in Russia as a "conspiracy plotted in the US and the West". It was considered to be hampering Russian policy in the region and threatening Russia's security needs.

However, it was the GCC countries' disappointment with US policy in the region, especially President Obama's failure to act on his "red line" about the use of chemical weapons in Syria that triggered the GCC states' diplomatic outreach to Russia. But the implications of the Ukrainian crisis soon began to overshadow the Syrian crisis, at least from a global perspective. When the West imposed sanctions on Russia, the GCC countries backed off once again and reduced their interaction with Russia in the economic field in order to avoid potential risks, while leaving room for possible political deals. The monarchies are not in a hurry to offer the credits and investments that Moscow has been trying to obtain from them. That is seemingly out of fear of losing their money in case the economic recession in Russia worsens or a company or project with GCC investments in Russia is sanctioned by the West.

Iran seems to be emerging as Russia's preferred partner in the region. There are a number of reasons for this, including the geographic proximity to Russia, the common engagement in Caspian sea resources-sharing, Iran's capability to impact the Central Asian and Caucasus states in Russia's immediate neighbourhood, the common approach to the Syrian crisis, the shared anti-Western rhetoric, the growing understanding concerning gas supplies to Asia and perhaps, in the future, to Europe, etc. Therefore Moscow appears resolved to strengthen its relations with Tehran, while continuing to attempt to balance it by improving relations with the Sunni bloc in the Gulf.

The GCC's greater willingness to deal with Russia economically remains a very attractive prospect for Russia, but Moscow does not seem ready to sacrifice what it calls the

---

[41] The Soviet Middle East policy was conceived to confront the USA and its allies in the region without the USSR's direct involvement militarily. It involved propping up the Soviet allies by all means – economic assistance, financial aid, arms deliveries, etc. In this context, the idea of any economic or financial profits for the USSR was sacrificed in return for geopolitical advantages.

"military-political achievement" of its actions in Syria – namely, the strengthening of the Assad regime – for that. Russia is in need of some progress in the Geneva talks to be able to present its support for Assad as a "mission accomplished" before it can take a more balanced stance towards the Syrian civil war (in support of an inter-Syrian settlement which could include many armed opposition groups previously labelled as extremists or even terrorists). Such a shift in the Russian stance could be regarded by the GCC countries as a positive step towards activating economic deals with Russia.

In this context, it is hard to envisage any significant change in Russia's policy in the region in the near future, regardless of oil prices. This is due, above all, to Russia's increasing involvement in the standoff with the West in Europe. Normally, the Gulf region seems to be viewed by Moscow as a secondary element within its global confrontation with the West, unless an additional conflict breaks out there, which would help push oil prices up and shift the world's attention away from Ukraine.

For a long time to come, Russia's role in the region will be defined by the results of the Syrian settlement and Moscow's ability to strike a balance between Riyadh and Tehran (Sunni and Shia). But the foreign policy positions of the new US administration under Donald Trump also have to be taken into consideration. If the White House goes ahead with Obama's logic aimed at reducing the American presence in the Gulf, Russia's presence there is destined to grow for natural reasons – the vacuum has to be filled. Vice versa, should Trump resolve to work with the US' partners in the region (meaning that strategic understanding and cooperation between the GCC and the US in the political, economic and military fields are fully re-established), Russia's potential and prospects for expanding further in the region may be substantially reduced.

References

Aleji, W. "The world needs to know that the choice is not only Assad or Isis". *The Guardian*, 3 Oct 2015. https://www.theguardian.com/commentisfree/2015/oct/04/syria-russia-assad-isis-conflict

Cafiero, G. "Can Bahrain count on Moscow to fill Washington's shoes?". *Al-Monitor*, 8 July 2016. http://www.al-monitor.com/pulse/originals/2016/07/bahrain-russia-replace-washington-influence-iran.html#ixzz4bngvIp7o

Evans-Pritchard, A. "Saudis offer Russia secret oil deal if it drops Syria". *The Telegraph*, 27 Aug 2013. http://www.telegraph.co.uk/finance/newsbysector/energy/oilandgas/10266957/Saudis-offer-Russia-secret-oil-deal-if-it-drops-Syria.html

Gladstone, R. "Iran's Supreme Leader on America: Don't Trust, Don't Cooperate". *NYT*, 3 June 2016. https://www.nytimes.com/2016/06/04/world/asia/iran-supreme-leader-khamenei.html?_r=0

Gordeev, V. "Vizit Putina v Iran zavershilsya odobreniyem 35 sovmestnykh proektov" ["Putin's Visit to Iran Ended with 35 Common Projects Being Approved"]. *RBK*, 24 November 2015. www.rbc.ru.

Karasik, T. "Why is Qatar Investing so much in Russia?". *Middle East Institute*, 8 March 2017. http://www.mei.edu/content/article/why-qatar-investing-so-much-russia.

Ivanov, I. *Iran, Russia and the West //Russia-Iran partnership: an overview and prospects for the future.* Moscow: Russian International Affairs Council, 2016.

Myers, S., and G. Myre. "Hamas Delegation Visits Moscow for a Crash Course in Diplomacy". *The New York Times* 4 March 2006.

Phillips, C. *The Battle for Syria: International Rivalry in the New Middle East.* New Haven and London: Yale University Press, 2016.

Schwartz, S. "The Road from Riyadh to Beslan (How Islamists hijacked the Chechen separatist movement)". *The Weekly Standard*, 20 Sept 2004. http://www.weeklystandard.com/the-road-from-riyadh-to-beslan/article/5831

Seddon, M. "Qatar sovereign wealth fund plans another $2bn Russian investment". *Financial Times*, 25 January 2017. https://www.ft.com/content/86c658e8-401d-3582-815e-3e7dc4861c0d

Sengupta, S., and N. MacFarquhar. "Vladimir Putin of Russia Calls for Coalition to Fight ISIS". *nytimes.com*, 27 Sept. 2015. https://www.nytimes.com/2015/09/29/world/europe/russia-vladimir-putin-united-nations-general-assembly.html

Shumilin, A. *Syrian Crisis and Russia's Approach to the Gulf*, GRC Gulf Paper. Doha: Gulf Research Council: May 2014. https://www.files.ethz.ch/isn/180935/Gulf_Paper_-_Syrian_Crisis_15-05-14_5756.pdf

Shumilin, A. "Why the US declines to cooperate with Russia in Syria". *me-journal.ru*, 21 May 2016. http://me-journal.ru/357/64567/

Shumilin, A. *The American policy in the Middle East in the context of the Arab Spring.* Moscow: International Relations Publishing House, 2015.

Index

www.ingramcontent.com/pod-product-compliance
Ingram Content Group UK Ltd.
Pitfield, Milton Keynes, MK11 3LW, UK
UKHW010023280225
455677UK00024B/794